The Son that Elizabeth I Never Had

The Son that Elizabeth I Never Had

The Adventurous Life of Robert Dudley's Illegitimate Son

Julia A Hickey

PEN & SWORD HISTORY

First published in Great Britain in 2021 by
Pen & Sword History
An imprint of
Pen & Sword Books Ltd
Yorkshire – Philadelphia

ISBN 978 1 39909 112 1

A CIP catalogue record for this book is
available from the British Library.

Typeset by Mac Style
Printed and bound in the UK by CPI.

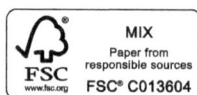

Pen & Sword Books Limited incorporates the imprints of Atlas,
Archaeology, Aviation, Discovery, Family History, Fiction, History,
Maritime, Military, Military Classics, Politics, Select, Transport,
True Crime, Air World, Frontline Publishing, Leo Cooper, Remember
When, Seaforth Publishing, The Praetorian Press, Wharncliffe
Local History, Wharncliffe Transport, Wharncliffe True Crime
and White Owl.

For a complete list of Pen & Sword titles please contact

PEN & SWORD BOOKS LIMITED
47 Church Street, Barnsley, South Yorkshire, S70 2AS, England
E-mail: enquiries@pen-and-sword.co.uk
Website: www.pen-and-sword.co.uk

Or

PEN AND SWORD BOOKS
1950 Lawrence Rd, Havertown, PA 19083, USA
E-mail: Uspen-and-sword@casematepublishers.com
Website: www.penandswordbooks.com

Contents

Part III

Acknowledgements

Writing this book during a pandemic has ensured focus but has meant that finding sources and references has not always been easy. I would like to thank the following people for their kindness and help during my research: the staff of Ashbourne Library, in particular Stefan Bobeszko and James Vaughan. I would also like to thank Karen Deakin of Derbyshire Libraries for her perseverance in locating texts. Given that Robin spent more than forty years in Tuscany I should also like to thank Enrico Andreoli for the help he provided with translating texts from Italian into English and Melanie V. Taylor for her encouragement and knowledge about art works associated with the Dudley family.

I am particularly grateful to the Revd. Kathy Lloyd-Roberts Master of the Foundation and Vicar of St Mary's Church for her permission to use the image of Lady Katherine Leveson, and to her PA Sharon Roche for her efficiency in finding the best image available, as I have come to greatly admire Robin's daughter during the course of my reading. I am similarly grateful to John Salmon for allowing me to use his photograph of Lady Frances Kniveton's monument.

Many thanks to everyone at Pen and Sword Books, particularly my commissioning editor Sarah-Beth Watkins and my editor Claire Hopkins for their patience, good humour and attention to detail. Thanks also to my family and friends who have encouraged me throughout, especially to my husband Kyle who is my own 'Eyes' and who proofread, questioned, discussed and generally put up with me being lost in Robin Dudley's exciting life and times.

Illustrations

Front Cover – *Sir Robert Dudley* (Watercolour on parchment, unknown date), Nicholas Hilliard.

1. *The Dudley family crest* carved by John Dudley, Earl of Warwick during his imprisonment in the Tower 1554 (engraving, Nineteenth Century) J Fry, after a drawing by F Nash
2. Title page, book six, *Dell'Arcano del Mare* (engraving, 1647) by Antonio Francesco Lucini
3. *Robert Dudley, 1st Earl of Leicester* (engraving, 1586) by Hendrick Goltzius
4. *Queen Elizabeth I 'The Ditchley Portrait'* (oil on canvas, circa 1592) by Marcus Gheeraerts the Younger
5. *Thomas Cavendish* (print, c.1595–1597) by Jodocus Hondius
6. Map for the North East coast of South America covering Guiana in *Dell'Arcano del Mare* (engraving, 1647) by Antonio Francesco Lucini
7. *Battle of Cadiz* (printed on paper, 1600–1601) by Bartholomeus Willemsz
8. *Astrolabe*, (brass c.1597) by Johannes Bos
9. *Diagram showing the use of an astrolabe*
10. *Ferdinando I de Medici, Grand Duke of Tuscany* (printed, circa 1589) by Agostino Carracci
11. *Restoring the Aqueduct in Pisa, from the Life of Ferdinand I de' Medici* (engraving, 1614–1620) by Jacques Callot
12. *Cosimo II de Medici, Grand Duke of Tuscany* (oil on canvas, 1597–1681) from the Workshop of Justus Sustermans
13. *Lady Frances Kniveton*, St-Giles-in-the-Fields (chest tomb in white marble, c.1663) by Joshua or Edward Marshall
14. *Lady Katherine Leveson*, (oil on canvas, 1625) by Cornelius Jansen
15. *Countess Teresa Dudley de Carpegna*, (oil on canvas, 1654), by Justus Sustermans

Author's Note

In order to avoid confusion between Sir Robert Dudley the Younger and his father Robert Dudley, Earl of Leicester, I shall refer to Sir Robert Dudley as Robin and to his father as either Robert or Leicester throughout. Contemporary records identify Robin, during his childhood, as Robin Sheffield and later as Robin Dudley. Leicester was raised to the peerage by Elizabeth I in September 1564 with the titles Earl of Leicester and Baron Denbigh, as part of Elizabeth's proposal that he should marry Mary, Queen of Scots, having initially denied him the title in 1561 when she created his elder brother Ambrose Dudley, Earl of Warwick.

Genealogical Tables

The Dudley Family
The Dudley claim to the Earldom of Warwick
The Howard Family

The Dudley Family

John Sutton
1st Baron Dudley
(c.1400-1487)
=
Elizabeth
de Berkeley

William
Bishop of Durham
(d.1483)

Oliver
(d.1469) = Katherine
Neville

Elizabeth

Edmund Sutton
(1425-c.1485)

John Dudley
Of Atherington
(d.1500)
=
Elizabeth
Bramshot

Edmund Dudley
(1472-1510)
=
1) Ann Windsor
(d. before 1502)
2) Elizabeth Grey
(c.1482-c.1525)

Elizabeth

Elizabeth
=
Thomas
Ashburnham

Ann

John

Robert Hall

Peter

1) Joyce Tiptoft 2) Matilda Clifford

Issue includes

Thomas
Dudley
(d.1530)

Edward
2nd Baron Dudley
(c1459-1532)
=
Grace Threlkeld
of Yanwath

Joyce

Cecilia Willoughby

William Stourton
7th Baron Stourton
(c.1505-1548)
=
Elizabeth

John Dudley
2nd Viscount Lisle,
2nd Earl of
Warwick
(1530-1554)

Andrew
(c.1507-1559)
=
Jane Guildford
(c.1508-1555)

Jerome

Bridget

Issue includes

Edward
John
Joyce

Thomas

1) John Dudley
Of
Stoke
Newington
(d.1580)

2) Thomas Sutton
(d.1611)
=
Elizabeth
Gardiner
(d.1602)

Thomas
Henry
(1525-1544)

Ambrose Dudley
3rd Viscount Lisle,
3rd Earl of Warwick
(1531-1590)
=
1) Anne
Whorwood
2) Elizabeth
Talbot
3) Anne Russell

Robert Dudley
Earl of Leicester
(1533-1588)
=
1) Amy Robsart
(1532-1560)
2) Contested marriage
Douglas Howard,
Lady Sheffield
(1542/43 -1608)
2 or 3)
Lettice Knollys
Countess of Essex
(1543-1634)

Guildford
(d.1553)

Henry
(d.1557)

Carolus

Mary Dudley
(c.1530-35 - 1586)
=
Sir Henry Sidney
(1529-1586)

Margaret

Temperentia

Catherine

Catherine
(d.1620)

Henry Hastings
Earl of
Huntingdon
(c.1535-1595)

John
3rd Baron
Dudley
(c1496-1553)
=
Cecily Grey

Anne

John
2nd Viscount Lisle,
2nd Earl of Warwick
(1530-1554)
=
Anne Seymour
(1538-1588)

Lady
Jane Grey
(1537-1554)

Margaret Audley
(1540-1564)

Sir Robert Dudley
(1574-1649)
"My base son"

Robert Dudley
Baron Denbigh
(1579-1584)

Issue includes

Robert Sidney
1st Earl of Leicester &
1st Viscount Lisle
(1563-1626)
=
Barbara Gamage
(1563-1621)

Philip Sidney
(1554-1586)
=
Frances
Walsingham
(1567-1633)

Francis Popham
(1573-1644)

Edward
4th Baron
Dudley
(c.1515-1586)
=
1) Katherine
Brydges
2) Jane
Stanley

Henry
(d. 1568/70)

John
(1569-c.1644)

Issue includes

Anne

Edward
5th Baron
Dudley
(1557-1643)
Issue

Francis Throckmorton
(1554-1584)

The Sidney earls of Leicester of
whom there were seven.
The line becoming extinct in 1743.

The Dudley claim to the Earldom of Warwick

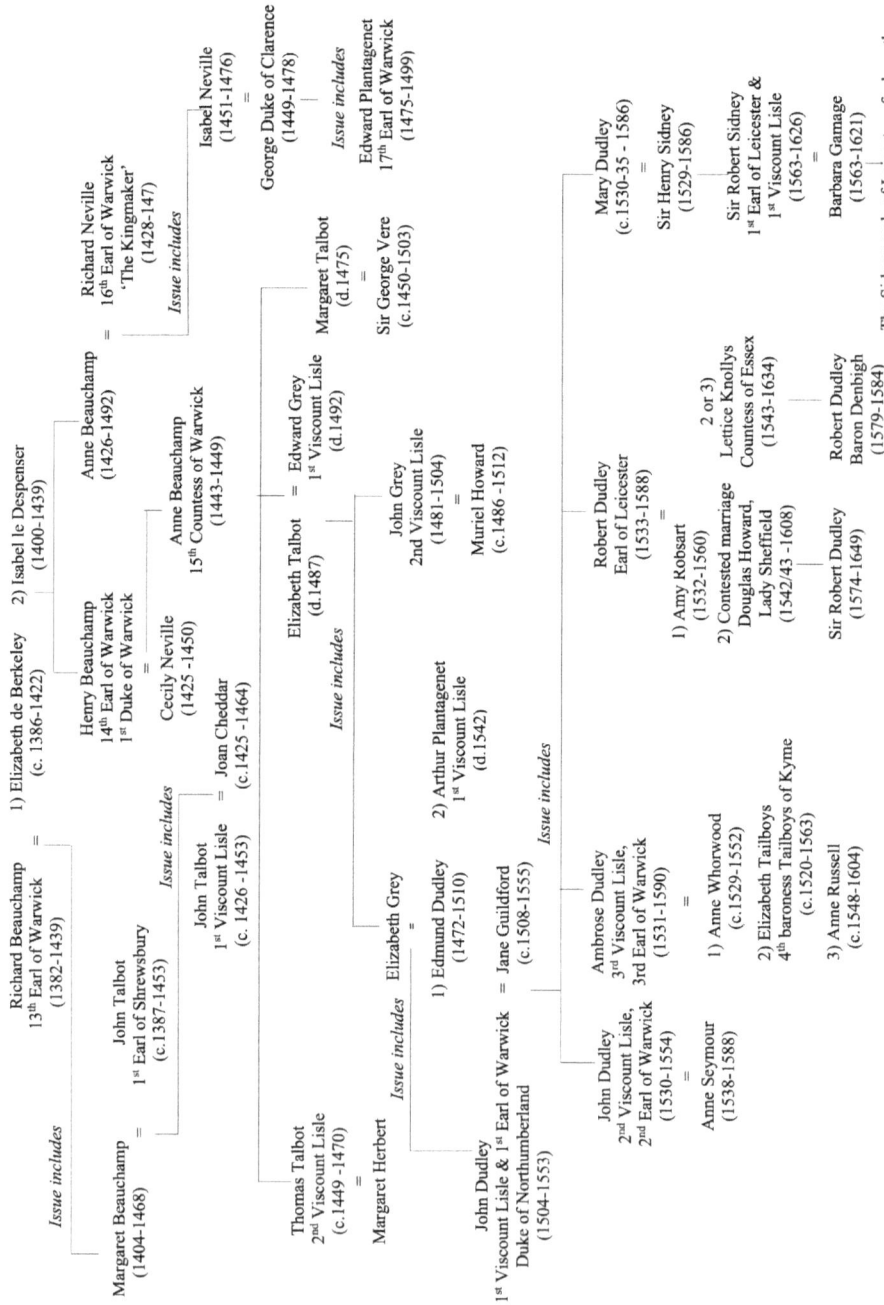

Richard Beauchamp
13th Earl of Warwick
(1382-1439)
=
1) Elizabeth de Berkeley
(c. 1386-1422)
2) Isabel le Despenser
(1400-1439)

Margaret Beauchamp
(1404-1468)
=
John Talbot
1st Earl of Shrewsbury
(c.1387-1453)

Issue includes

Henry Beauchamp
14th Earl of Warwick
1st Duke of Warwick
=
Cecily Neville
(1425 -1450)

Anne Beauchamp
(1426-1492)

Anne Beauchamp
15th Countess of Warwick
(1443-1449)
=
Richard Neville
16th Earl of Warwick
'The Kingmaker'
(1428-147)

Issue includes

Isabel Neville
(1451-1476)
=
George Duke of Clarence
(1449-1478)

Issue includes

Edward Plantagenet
17th Earl of Warwick
(1475-1499)

John Talbot
1st Viscount Lisle
(c. 1426 -1453)
=
Joan Cheddar
(c.1425 - 1464)

Issue includes

Thomas Talbot
2nd Viscount Lisle
(c.1449 -1470)

Elizabeth Talbot
(d.1487)
=
Edward Grey
1st Viscount Lisle
(d.1492)

Margaret Talbot
(d.1475)
=
Sir George Vere
(c.1450-1503)

Issue includes

Margaret Herbert
=
Elizabeth Grey

John Grey
2nd Viscount Lisle
(1481-1504)
=
Muriel Howard
(c.1486-1512)

Issue includes

1) Edmund Dudley
(1472-1510)
=
Elizabeth Grey
=
2) Arthur Plantagenet
1st Viscount Lisle
(d.1542)

John Dudley
1st Viscount Lisle & 1st Earl of Warwick
Duke of Northumberland
(1504-1553)
=
Jane Guildford
(c.1508-1555)

Issue includes

John Dudley
2nd Viscount Lisle,
2nd Earl of Warwick
(1530-1554)
=
Anne Seymour
(1538-1588)

Ambrose Dudley
3rd Viscount Lisle,
3rd Earl of Warwick
(1531-1590)
=
1) Anne Whorwood
(c.1529-1552)
2) Elizabeth Tailboys
4th baroness Tailboys of Kyme
(c.1520-1563)
3) Anne Russell
(c.1548-1604)

Robert Dudley
Earl of Leicester
(1533-1588)
=
1) Amy Robsart
(1532-1560)
2) Contested marriage
Douglas Howard,
Lady Sheffield
(1542/43 - 1608)
2 or 3)
Lettice Knollys
Countess of Essex
(1543-1634)

Mary Dudley
(c.1530-35 - 1586)
=
Sir Henry Sidney
(1529-1586)

Sir Robert Dudley
(1574-1649)

Robert Dudley
Baron Denbigh
(1579-1584)

Sir Robert Sidney
1st Earl of Leicester &
1st Viscount Lisle
(1563-1626)
=
Barbara Gamage
(1563-1621)

The Sidney earls of Leicester of whom there
were 7. The line becoming extinct in 1743.

The Howard Family

Catherine Moleyns (d.1465) = John Howard 1st Duke of Norfolk c.1425- 1485

Thomas Howard 2nd Duke of Norfolk (1443-1524)

1) Elizabeth Tilney (d.1497)

2) Agnes Tilney (1477-1545)

Issue includes

William Howard, 1st Baron Howard of Effingham (1510-1573) = Margaret Gamage (c.1515-1581)

Issue includes

Mary (d.1600) = Edward Sutton 4th Baron Dudley (1513-1586)

Frances (c.1554-1598) = Edward Seymour 1st Earl of Hertford (1539-1621)

Charles Howard, 1st Earl of Nottingham (1536-1624) = Catherine Carey Daughter of Henry Carey (1547-1603)

Douglas Lady Sheffield (1542/43 -1608) Alleged marriage Robert Dudley Earl of Leicester (1533-1588)

Issue includes

Elizabeth (1554-1646) = Robert Southwell (1563-1598)

Sir Robert Dudley (1574-1649)

Issue includes

Elizabeth Southwell (1584-1631)

Elizabeth (d.1538) = Thomas Boleyn 1st Earl of Wiltshire (c.1476-1539)

Issue includes

Anne Boleyn (c.1501- 1536) = Henry VIII (1491-1547)

Mary Boleyn (c.1499-1543) = William Carey (1500-1528)

Elizabeth I (1533-1603)

Henry Carey 1st Baron Hunsdon (1526-1596)

Catherine Carey (c.1526-1569) = Francis Knollys (c.1511-1596)

Issue includes

Lettice Knollys (1543-1634)

Edmund (c.1479-1539) = Joyce Culpeper (1480-1527)

Issue includes

Katherine Howard (c.1521-1542) = Henry VIII (1491-1547)

Issue includes

Thomas Howard 3rd Duke of Norfolk (1473-1554) = Elizabeth Stafford (1497-1558)

Issue includes

Henry Howard Earl of Surrey (1516/17 -1547) = Frances de Vere (c.1517-1577)

Issue includes

Thomas Howard 4th Duke of Norfolk (1537 -1572)

Henry Howard 1st Earl of Northampton (1540-1614)

Introduction

Robin Dudley was the offspring of two ambitious families whose abilities and political grasping gained them notoriety during the sixteenth century. On his mother's side, he was descended from the Howard family who provided Henry VIII with wives, mistresses and statesmen. His father's family remain synonymous with the Tudors. Robin's father, the Earl of Leicester entertained ambitions of marrying Elizabeth I despite being already wed to his first wife, Amy Robsart, who died in suspicious circumstances in 1560. The scandal meant that the queen could neither accept Leicester's suit nor have a son with him even if she did prefer him above all other men.

The Roman goddess Fortuna is pictured holding a wheel of fortune, or rather appropriately for Robin, a ship's rudder in one hand. She controls the destiny of those who believe in her with a turn of the wheel. Fate was an important part of the Elizabethan world view and it was one that Leicester and his family understood all too well. The son and grandson of a traitor, Leicester experienced his father's misfortune and then rose once more with Henry VIII's daughter Elizabeth. Throughout his life, the earl tried to determine his place on Fortune's wheel based on his devotion to the queen. The gift of Kenilworth Castle and its estate by Elizabeth to Leicester in 1563 reflects the favour in which the earl stood. His permanent courtship of the monarch meant that it was difficult for him to court, or marry, another woman without risking the loss of royal favour. Robin, described by his father as baseborn was part of the price Leicester paid for his continued position near the top of Fortune's wheel.

Part one of *The Son that Elizabeth I Never Had: The Adventurous Life of Robert Dudley's Illegitimate Son* explores Robin's family, the dealings it had with the Crown and the relationships that existed between Leicester and the women in his life. He continued to be an active suitor for Elizabeth's hand despite her rejection of him but he turned to other women. In 1573 he may have secretly married Robin's mother, Lady Sheffield. He eventually cast her aside and married clandestinely Lettice Knollys, widow of Walter Devereux 1st Earl of Essex, in 1578, who was pregnant at the time of the wedding. Camden later quipped that Leicester was 'given to wiving.'[1] The queen never forgave Lettice for marrying her own Sweet Robin. Fortune turned against the Dudley dynasty when the couple's only child, Lord Denbigh, died unexpectedly leaving the earl with only one living son who he himself rendered illegitimate.

Part two explores the childhood, friendships and maritime adventures of Robin Dudley, the son of Douglas, Lady Sheffield. Robin was acknowledged, loved and educated by his father. During Elizabeth I's lifetime he was able to capitalise on extended kinship networks and the protection of the queen. He became one of her seadogs voyaging to the West Indies, capturing Spanish prizes and searching for the fabled gold of El Dorado. The problem for Robin who had the talents of his forefathers as well as his own father's good looks, charm and arrogance was that what he most wanted was legitimacy and the titles of his father, uncle and grandfather which he believed to be rightfully his. He clung to the idea with increasing obduracy from 1604 onwards. Unfortunately for him, any evidence of a marriage between his parents was fragmentary at best. History's lens is darkened by suppression of evidence, contradictory information and flawed witness statements presented to Robin by an informer and sometimes governmental spy named Drury. In addition, Fortune's wheel turned against Robin with the death of Elizabeth. Without her protection, the political establishment led by the new Stuart dynasty closed ranks against Leicester's son.

The title page of the sixth book of Robin's *Dell'Arcano del Mare* contains an illustration of *Ursa Minor* or the Little Bear. The bear and ragged staff, the heraldic badge associated with the Earldom of Warwick were adopted by Robin's grandfather John Dudley and his sons who were all descended from Richard Beauchamp, 13th Earl of Warwick. Leicester decorated walls, chimneys, soft furnishings, book bindings and his suit of armour with the device. Robin's uncle John whiled away his time in the Tower in 1554 carving the family emblem. In later years Robin made a play on his father's chosen badge by naming his ships the *Bear* and the *Bear's Whelp*. In Tuscany, he constructed a pinnace which he named the *Ursa Minor*.

---

1. Camden, p.373.

With every vessel he launched, Robin proclaimed the birth right that he believed belonged to him. Even the boat he named *Benjamin* identified him in Biblical terms as the beloved son of his father's right hand.

Part three of *The Son that Elizabeth I Never Had* explores Robin's life after he left English shores amidst scandal. He made his home in Florence in the services of the Medici Grand Dukes of Tuscany. From Italy he negotiated for a return to England for almost forty years, ignoring the inconvenient truth that he deserted his wife and young family in England for the beautiful woman who went into exile with him dressed as a page. It was a decision that still tarnishes the reputation of a dashing and charismatic man.

Walpole, who believed Robin to be legitimate, considered how 'enterprising and dangerous a minister Dudley might have made, and what a variety of talents were called forth by his misfortunes.'[2] Fortune's wheel turned against him in England, his property was seized under the terms of the Fugitives Act of 1570 and he was declared traitor. But it was in exile that the full scope of his many talents was realised. Robin's greatest achievement was the *Dell'Arcano del Mare* or *Secrets of the Sea*, a unique maritime encyclopaedia in three folio volumes written after his retirement drawing on a lifetime of knowledge and passion for navigation. It was at the forefront of maritime technology using Mercator projections for all its maps as well as sounding depths, prevailing winds, ocean currents and observed compass variation. The atlas contains engravings by the Italian master Antonio Francesco Lucini, who claimed to have used 5,000 pounds of copper for the plates paid for by Robin as it was the finest quality paper that the printer used.[3] At the time of publication, Robin was seventy-three years old. He never lost his childhood passion for the sea. Jacopo Lucini who republished Robin's work twelve years after his death in 1649 provided Leicester's cub with a fitting epitaph. 'In this worthy enterprise, if one man is more signally eminent than others, it is the Duke of Northumberland ... (he) sacrificed full forty years of his life in unveiling, for the good of humanity at large, the mighty secrets of the sea.'[4] In a final twist of fate, at the time that Lucini wrote, Robin's coffin remained unburied by either his family or the Tuscan state.

---

2. Lee, p.71.
3. Sotheby's Catalogue, Wardington Sale, 2005.
4. Lee, p.228.

Part I

Chapter I

A Tangled Inheritance

Robin's great grandfather Edmund Dudley, one of the so-called new men associated with Henry VII's administration, was executed as a traitor on Tower Hill on 17 August 1510. Fortune's wheel threw him from a position of power to his death in a matter of months. By the time he went to the block, the story had spread that the old king's despised tax collector was the son of a carpenter. In an era where stability was associated with a well-ordered hierarchy the slur lingered. The truth, which few of the jeering crowd were interested in that summer morning, was that Edmund was part of the middle tier of society's landowning elite – the gentry. His father was Sir John Dudley of Atherington, the second son of John Sutton, 1st Baron Dudley.[1]

John Sutton, Baron Dudley of Dudley Castle in the West Midlands was at Agincourt. He carried the royal standard at Henry V's funeral in 1422 having accompanied the king's body home for burial. His brother-in-law was the Earl of Arundel, both men having married daughters of Sir John Berkeley of Beverston, a fact which gave the Dudley family a dash of illegitimate Plantagenet blood in their veins thanks to a line of descent from King John. Sutton was Lord Lieutenant of Ireland for two years and a councillor of Henry VI becoming something of a favourite with the Lancastrian monarch. Sutton turned his coat from Lancaster to York in 1460 following King Henry's capture at Northampton.[2] In due course, Henry VI's former favourite became the Constable of the Tower of London under Edward IV's regime. He held the office on the night of 21 May 1471 when King Henry VI, a prisoner of his York cousin, was murdered whilst at prayer. The baron went on to serve Richard III, but perhaps preferring to hedge his bets, did not attempt to stop Henry Tudor in August 1485 when he marched through Staffordshire with his army on

---

1. Collins, ODNB.
2. Ibid.

his way to Bosworth. Baron Dudley knew that good fortune required the favour of kings and he was well versed in a seamless change of master at an opportune moment.

Sutton fathered four sons; the eldest inherited his father's title, one died on the Lancastrian side at the Battle of Edgecote near Banbury in 1469, and a third became the Bishop of Durham. Robin's ancestor, the second son, named after his father, was required to make his own way in the world. He did this through marriage to Elizabeth Bramshot, a co-heiress, whose father owned lands in Hampshire and Sussex. John Sutton, calling himself Dudley after the castle in Staffordshire belonging to his father, settled in Sussex on his wife's estates where he took his place amongst the county's landowning gentry.

Edmund Dudley, a Tudor administrator and one of the chief instruments of Henry VII's financial policy, was John and Elizabeth's eldest son. Edmund's father and grandfather strove to provide him with an opportunity to become a more powerful player on both the local and national stage by drawing on the ties of patronage. One of the baron's connections was Sir Reginald Bray who served Lady Margaret Beaufort, the mother of Henry Tudor, as her Receiver-General since her marriage to Sir Henry Stafford in 1458. Bray, as well as managing Margaret Beaufort's estates and legal affairs, was a key player in the preparations for Henry Tudor's invasion of England in 1485. He went on to become one of the king's most trusted ministers, holding strategic administrative and financial positions devoted to securing and establishing the Tudor dynasty. Bray set about overhauling the financial machinery of the kingdom. He recruited 'the ablest men to be found'[3] to exploit yields from Crown Estates, arranged for forced loans to be implemented and efficiently collected the revenues from traditional parliamentary grants like tunnage and poundage which were customarily granted by parliament for life to each monarch. Tunnage was a fixed subsidy payable on each cask of wine imported whilst poundage was a tax on all imports and exports. Many of Bray's administrators, like Edmund, were from the gentry. They owed their position to the Tudors rather than a claim to rule which lay solely in their ancestry. King Henry VII, ever mindful of the power of landed magnates not to mention the fragility of the Tudor claim to the

---

3. Bacon, Francis, p.217.

throne, tightened his grip on his kingdom by using men of this ilk. Elite county families provided county officers, members of parliament and vied for power with one another. In order to rise within the hierarchy at local levels, county levels and a national level, connections were required. Edmund, patronised by Bray, as well as being knowledgeable in the law, began working for the Crown in Sussex[4] alongside his father before returning to London and the heart of Tudor financial administration as a member of the Council Learned in the Law, another of Bray's creations.

The administrative processes of the council enabled Bray to bypass other offices of state and even the law on occasion. The tribunal collected feudal debts owing to the king and took down payments from men that the Court of the Star Chamber deemed to owe money to the Crown. Over time Edmund became identified with the group of men led by Sir Richard Empson who sifted through old law books to find ways of keeping England's nobility leashed by the system of bonds and recognizances preventing them from retaining private armies or building up a power base that could threaten Henry's security. A bond was a contract that required someone to carry out a specified action e.g. not rebel against the king. Should the signatory break the contract to which they had agreed then they would be fined by the amount specified within the bond. A recognizance was a formal recognition of a pre-existing debt or a feudal obligation, with sureties and penalties for enforcement. It was held against the day when it might be needed. Both these strategies helped to ensure aristocratic compliance with the Tudor regime and to fill Henry VII's treasury. Edmund Dudley and his colleagues seem to have excelled at their task. In 1493 Henry's income from bonds and recognizances was £3,000. By 1505 it was somewhere in the region of £35,000.[5]

Edmund's importance as a bureaucrat within the cogs that formed the Tudor financial machine is amply demonstrated by his second, extremely advantageous, marriage into the Grey family following the death, before 1502, of his first wife Anne Windsor.[6] Elizabeth Grey's uncle was Sir John Grey of Groby and the first husband of Elizabeth Woodville. She was also the great-great-granddaughter of the last Beauchamp Earl of

---

4. Wilson, p.12.
5. 'Henry VII and Extraordinary Revenue.' History Learning Site, 16 March 2015, www.historylearningsite.co.uk/tudor-england/henry-vii-and-extraordinary-revenue/
6. Wilson, p.12.

Warwick from which future generations of the Dudley family, including Robin, would be proud to take the insignia of the bear and ragged staff. Eventually, the marriage would bring the barony of Lisle into the family. Fortune smiled upon Edmund thanks to his efficient understanding of increasingly archaic feudal laws. He was appointed justice of the peace for Hampshire in 1501. He also became a commissioner looking for concealed lands, using extensive powers to look for ways in which feudal laws had been broken in the past and imposing penalties. It was his job to look at property, inheritance, feudal dues and customary law. He needed to ascertain what belonged to the king, what royal rights had been eroded over time and to claw them back. He could arrest men suspected of breaking Henry VII's laws without indictment and on the word of an informer rather than backed by any substantiated evidence if he so chose. In 1504, when Sir Reginald Bray died, Edmund Dudley, nurtured and recommended to the king by Bray, became a privy councillor and continued to work on maximising revenue from Henry VII's indirect taxation as well as using a range of financial stratagems to coerce the nobility into compliance. Their methods may have been legal but most commentators agree that they were hardly just. It did not make either man popular with the nobility or London's wealthier merchants.

Edmund Dudley, by now president of the council, was arrested by Henry VIII's men as soon as the death of the old king became public on 23 April 1509, along with his colleague Richard Empson. Dudley's home in Candlewick Street was stripped of its valuables as its master was taken away in chains. Both Empson and Dudley were initially accused of profiteering. It was normal practise that Henry VII's agents received a percentage of any income generated by a successful prosecution. In July he and Empson were tried for treason, rather than profiteering or extortion, at the Guildhall. Empson argued that no one could condemn them for carrying out the laws of Henry VII. Taxation was part of the king's strategy for governing his realm. The charge sheet against Edmund included plotting to bring an army to London, seizing the new king and setting up a regency council.[7] Edmund's cousin, the 2nd Baron Dudley was a named correspondent. The baron had a choice between being arrested on the same charges as Edmund or testifying against him. On 18

---

7. Ibid, p.41.

May 1510, having made his decision the baron was awarded the Order of the Garter. Edmund was convicted on 18 July and executed the following month as a traitor to the Crown.[8] The verdict was a foregone conclusion. At a stroke, the new king distanced himself from his father's regime and won popular acclaim for himself.

When Francis Bacon wrote his history of Henry VII during 1621, the legend of Empson and Dudley included stories of false indictments, bribery and blackmail, jury manipulation and false imprisonment. His view is supported by the accounts of packed juries and perjuries committed detailed by the Great Chronicles of London. Polydore Vergil, a contemporary of Empson and Dudley, described them as a 'wicked pair'.[9] He could hardly have accused Henry VIII's father of tyranny. It was better to blame Empson and Dudley. Chronicler Edward Hall whilst not friendly towards them was not so gleeful. He recognised that Empson and Dudley had been scapegoated, 'by malice of them that with their authority in the late King's days were offended, or else to shift the noise of the straight execution of penal statutes in the late King's days'.[10]

Robin's grandfather John Dudley was only seven when Edmund was found guilty of treason. The attainder should have ended the influence of the family as it not only confiscated Dudley property but effectively declared Edmund's descendants to be of corrupted blood. However, within months the attainder was lifted and John's marriage planned. Having rid himself of the representatives of his late father's avarice and repressive regime, the youthful King Henry VIII was happy to let bygones be bygones. Edmund's widow, Elizabeth, married the king's own uncle, Arthur Plantagenet, by whom she had three daughters. Arthur was the illegitimate son of Edward IV. In April 1509 he became part of Henry VIII's household where he was one of the king's intimate associates. Elizabeth's wedding to Arthur was a stepping stone for her son but her new husband did not receive John Dudley's wardship.

Sir Edward Guildford who at the start of Henry VIII's reign was at the heart of the royal court, petitioned for guardianship of the boy. He was a childhood friend of Henry VIII. He was another of the young men who took part in the celebrations that marked Henry's accession to the throne

8. Ibid, p.42.
9. Vergil, p.153 and Hutchinson:2011, p.105.
10. Hall, p.505.

in 1509 followed by his marriage to Katherine of Aragon. Guildford and his half-brother played two of the merry men whilst Henry VIII assumed the role of Robin Hood during one of the entertainments that year. Edward did the job so well that he found himself responsible for planning many of Henry VIII's revels across the next decade. It was a time of merriment, feasting and tournaments. So great was Edward's favour that he was even pardoned a debt to the Crown arising from his late father's estate. By 1518, Cardinal Wolsey who controlled the Privy Council feared that the power of Henry's companions was too great. The following spring Wolsey declared that Henry's honour and dignity suffered because of the young men that surrounded him. Fortuna tilted her wheel and the courtiers with their poor manners and excessive gambling were banished. Edward was one of the men that the cardinal temporarily sent away from court because of their bad influence. Fortuna's caprice was brief on this occasion. By the autumn of 1519, most of the young men were returned to their old ways, amongst them Sir Edward Guildford. This intimate acquaintance with Henry VIII saw Guildford procure the office of Sheriff of Lincoln as well as land belonging to Edmund Dudley and the governance of John Dudley. In February 1512, Sir Edward petitioned parliament for the reversal of the attainder which hung as a taint on the Dudley name and to permit the marriage, in due course, of John to Edward's own daughter Jane.[11] Fortune's wheel was spinning upwards once again. John, the son of a traitor, became a man with prospects at the stroke of a pen. The act which restored John allowed him to inherit his father's property as well as to enter public life with his honour repaired.

John's guardian provided the boy with excellent military training in addition to introducing him to life as a courtier. Guildford, like Edmund Dudley, was a 'new man' rather than a magnate. His admission to the Tudor court was because his own father, Sir Richard Guildford, shared Henry Tudor's exile for two years. Sir Richard was part of the Kent gentry and another one of Sir Reginald Bray's many contacts. He and his father joined with Buckingham's ill-fated rebellion against King Richard III in October 1483, was attainted of treason and fled to Brittany when the rebellion collapsed. Tudor knighted Richard Guildford at Milford Haven in 1485 when he began his campaign to take the crown for himself. Sir

---

11. Wilson, p.63.

Richard fought at Bosworth, became a chamberlain of the exchequer and Master of Ordinance and Armoury in the Tower of London in the years that followed. His work encompassed shipbuilding and the construction of forts including a tower in 1512 at Camber in Sussex which guarded the estuary access to the Cinque Port of Rye. He drained nearby marshes, still known as the Guildford Level today, by building a sea wall. He even built a church at East Guideford on the land that he reclaimed. The same range of skills and practical application distinguished Robin's own career in the services of the grand dukes of Tuscany.

Sir Richard, a prominent figure in the exchequer during the first eighteen months of Henry VII's reign, did not acquire the notoriety of his colleague Edmund Dudley having been replaced in that post by Giles, Lord Daubeney in 1487. Nor did he acquire the wealth that Dudley garnered for himself. In 1505, Sir Richard was arrested for debt. Financial irregularities in the ordinance and armoury accounts saw him in the Fleet Prison for a time. Insolvency led to him being removed from office. In all likelihood, Guildford would have found himself on trial if he had remained in England. He chose instead to go on a pilgrimage. Sir Richard died in 1506 and was buried in Jerusalem.[12]

In 1523, John Dudley, coming of age, joined the Duke of Suffolk in a campaign in France along with his guardian Sir Edward Guildford. The boy distinguished himself and was knighted by the duke in November for courage in crossing the Somme. The English Army's march towards Paris was hindered by bad weather. John retreated with the rest of the army and returned to court where, for the time being, he developed tournament skills under the tutelage of his guardian. His reputation for jousting was an undoubted route to royal approval. Tournaments were not so much about practising for war as an expression of chivalric bravery and an opportunity for the pageantry in which Henry VIII loved to indulge.

Sir John Dudley married Guildford's daughter Jane as planned in 1525 when she was in her sixteenth year. When his father-in-law died in 1534 without leaving a will it was John rather than Guildford's nephew who inherited not only Guildford's wealth but his seat in parliament. Throughout the 1530s, John demonstrated his loyalty to the king as a soldier and as a presence at court. He served as cup-bearer for Archbishop

---

12. Cunningham, ODNB.

Cranmer after the coronation of Anne Boleyn, having kept his head down and his opinions on God and the King's Great Matter to himself. Continuing fortune was in the hands of King Henry but it would soon become impossible to avoid taking a side in the religious argument that polarised the Privy Council between Catholic and Protestant.

Blessed by Fortune with a career at court, a happy marriage and prosperous business engaging in land sales, John began to rise. In 1536, he was appointed vice-admiral with the task of protecting merchant shipping from French and Flemish pirates. In one encounter he captured the Admiral of Sluys. By 1542, he was created Viscount Lisle; following a successful campaign in Scotland was elected to the Order of the Garter and became a privy councillor. Henry now planned an invasion of France. John Dudley became Henry's lord admiral. At that time knowledge of the sea and ships was not an essential quality for naval commanders John, a permanent official rather than a wartime officer, was unusual in that he had a working knowledge of seamanship and artillery. He helped to shape the Council of Marine Causes, modelling it on the Ordinance Office. Thanks to Henry's bellicosity, John also distinguished himself by military service both on land and at sea in wars against Scotland and France. In 1539, concerned that the French might be contemplating invasion, he put together a fleet of 160 ships with enough men to crew them. It was the largest royal fleet that England had seen.

By 1547, Dudley was a figure of importance in Henry VIII's Privy Council as was Sir Edward Seymour, the brother of Henry's lamented third wife Jane Seymour and uncle to Prince Edward. Chapuys, the Imperial Ambassador, wrote that if the king was to die 'it is probable that these two men (John Dudley and Edward Seymour) will have the management of affairs'[13] It helped that the Earl of Surrey's dynastic ambitions had wrecked the political power of the Howard family for the time being at least. Surrey had little time for new men like Dudley and did not bother to hide his dislike of them. He was descended from the Plantagenets on both sides of his family tree but did not realise that as Henry VIII grew more paranoid about the succession that his own prideful arrogance placed him and his family at risk. The king became convinced that Surrey was planning to usurp the Crown and when he

---

13. Wilson, p.137.

quartered his arms with those of Edward the Confessor, the earl found himself under arrest along with his father. The Duke of Norfolk, Surrey's father, was saved from execution only because the king died the day before he was due to be executed. Seymour gained the upper hand on the regency council but elevated Dudley to the earldom of Warwick as he re-titled himself Lord Protector and Duke of Somerset. Fortune's wheel was still on the upwards trajectory as John became one of the most important and richest men in the kingdom.

In 1549, there were a series of revolts in the West Country and in Norfolk against the regency council. The former arose because of the way that services in English had been imposed on churches across the country and the latter, better known as Kett's Rebellion, was mainly to do with the enclosure of common land. Somerset was held to be partly responsible for the social unrest by his peers, disgraced and forced out of office. John Dudley, the son of an attainted traitor became the most powerful man in England but sought to demonstrate his continued friendship with Somerset with a marriage between his eldest surviving son, also named John, and Somerset's daughter Anne. The accord could not last. Somerset plotted against the council and was executed on constructed charges of felony rather than treason. Edward VI was not sympathetic to his uncle's plight, noting in his journal that Seymour was guilty of helping himself to treasury funds.

Ever mindful that power came from the monarch, Dudley swiftly elevated from the earldom of Warwick to the dukedom of Northumberland and was careful to involve the young king in the Privy Council's discussions which was a change for Edward who had been treated as a child by his Seymour uncle. Nonetheless, Northumberland filled the council with men loyal to him and on occasion visited Edward in his private chamber to coach him on the following day's meeting. Northumberland's time in power saw the Act of Uniformity strip Catholicism from churches and official forms of worship. In 1553, Cranmer's 42 Articles became law. England was a Protestant country in fact as well as name. The period also saw reforms of the coinage and the building of the naval dockyard in Chatham.

Recognising that the boy king's health was failing in the spring of 1553, Northumberland took steps to secure the throne for Lady Jane Grey through Edward's 'Devise for the Succession,' signed on 21 June, bypassing both Mary and Elizabeth Tudor in the process. Edward's wishes were not made law by parliamentary statute unlike Henry VIII's arrangements for the succession. Dudley had arranged for Lady Jane Grey to marry his son Guildford Dudley in May. It was a dynastic marriage as were others that took place at the same time. Jane's sister Lady Katherine Grey married Henry, Lord Herbert the son of William Herbert, 1st Earl of Pembroke. A third marriage saw Northumberland's daughter Katherine marry the Earl of Huntingdon's heir Henry Hastings. Each marriage sealed long-term political alliances. The House of Tudor looked as though it would soon be the House of Dudley even if Lady Jane Grey was quite insistent that her unwanted husband would not have the crown matrimonial.

Fortune turned against Northumberland as Edward's health failed more rapidly than expected. His mistake lay in how much support he thought he had for his actions in the days immediately after Edward's death. He relied on the backing he had when he displaced the Duke of Somerset. William Howard, 1st Baron Howard of Effingham, for instance, was originally an ally of Northumberland and had supported him in 1549. Howard benefitted from his allegiance with the appointment as Lord Deputy and Governor of Calais in 1552. But now, like many other powerful men, Howard more politically astute than Northumberland, watched how events unfolded and held the port for Mary Tudor rather than Lady Jane Grey.

Northumberland ran into further difficulties when Edward's sisters saw through the duke's subterfuges and refused to travel to Greenwich. Elizabeth claimed illness and took to her bed. Mary, having heard rumours that her brother was on his deathbed, left her home in Hertfordshire and sought safety at her castle in Framlingham. Despite Northumberland keeping Edward's death secret for three days, Mary was proclaimed queen and large numbers of people rallied to her cause. It was reported that she gathered an army of some 15,000 men which grew with each passing day.[14]

The duke dispatched vessels to patrol the coast in case the Spanish came to Mary's aid. After some delay, on 14 July 1553, he set off with a force from London to take Mary prisoner. It was a mistake leaving the Privy Council to its own devices but he had no other choice. Jane refused

---

14. Tallis, p.176.

to allow her father, the Duke of Suffolk, to lead an army, besides which he did not have Northumberland's experience. The duke's supporters in the capital immediately began to desert him. By 18 July, the Privy Council decided that Edward's device was insufficient to set Mary aside and the following day Queen Jane was queen no longer. Even royal vessels, stationed at Yarmouth, abandoned Northumberland and defected to the heir identified by the 1543 Third Act of Succession and reiterated in Henry VIII's will of December 1546.

Increasingly isolated, Northumberland recognised that the coup had failed and declared Mary queen at the market cross in Cambridge before surrendering to the authorities. He was arrested by the Earl of Arundel and returned to London to face trial. By 26 July, all his sons were in the Tower of London alongside him. John, Ambrose, Robert and Henry were imprisoned in the Beauchamp Tower where they carved the walls with their names and heraldic devices, the bear and ragged staff and a double-tailed lion, to pass the time. Guildford etched his wife's name into the stonework suggesting that the marriage was not completely without affection on his part at least. Their graffiti can still be seen today.

To a certain extent history now repeated itself with an act of deadly political theatre. Whilst it was true that Northumberland sought to override the Act of Succession it is also true that he did not do it by himself. The duke became a scapegoat. He was held responsible for the plot to put Jane Grey on the throne and for Edward VI's heresy. It was certainly in the best interests of Lady Jane Grey's mother, Frances Brandon, Duchess of Suffolk, to persuade her cousin Queen Mary that it was all Northumberland's fault. The marriage of her second daughter Katherine to Henry Herbert was hastily dissolved and eighteen months later, Queen Mary who had always been friends with Frances, granted Katherine, now fourteen years of age, a place in the privy chamber as lady-in-waiting.

On 18 August 1553, Northumberland was found guilty of treason and condemned to die on 21 August at 8.00 am. In between times, he recanted his Protestantism. On the morning of his death, he confessed his sins, confirmed his Catholicism and told the spectators awaiting his execution to be loyal to Queen Mary. It is likely that in embracing the new queen's faith he was hoping to protect his children, in particular his sons. His failure to hold fast to his beliefs is often cited as a lack of religious conviction and evidence that he was only ever motivated by ambition. In later times Leicester would become associated with the Puritan cause despite his scandalous affairs and patronage of the theatre. Northumberland's grandson Robin perhaps understood better the need for pragmatism in the face of adversity when he fled Protestant England for Catholic Italy in 1604. And certainly, Elizabeth I and her principal adviser William Cecil comprehended the need to adapt to the religious beliefs of the person sitting on the throne. Northumberland was not alone in his discovery that he had been Catholic all along. Not everyone could afford, or had the freedom, to remain true to their Protestant ideals.

Northumberland's sons remained in the Tower. His eldest son, John, was with Northumberland in Cambridge when the Earl of Arundel arrived to take him a prisoner. Like his father, John was tried for his part in the attempted coup. He passed his time by carving a rose for his brother Ambrose, oak leaves for Leicester, from the Latin *robur* meaning oak, honeysuckle for Henry and gillyflowers for Guildford onto the walls of his prison. Meanwhile, their mother Jane busied herself trying to secure her sons' release. Their future looked increasingly grim. On 13 November 1553, Ambrose, Henry and Guildford were arraigned in the Guildhall. Leicester was not with his siblings. He carried out his father's orders in Norfolk, declaring Jane Grey queen in King's Lynn. A commission of oyer and terminer (an assize court which literally means to hear and determine) was held in Norwich in January 1554. The report from the commission was sent to Thomas White, Lord Mayor of London after which another court met in the Guildhall.[15] Leicester, led from the Tower, was arraigned as plain Robert Dudley because Northumberland was already an attainted traitor and the family's titles were gone. Judgement was passed on 22 January. All of the Dudley brothers now waited under sentence of death for treason, the sons and grandsons of traitors.

In February 1554, as a direct consequence of Wyatt's Rebellion which had planned to depose Catholic Mary and replace her with Protestant Elizabeth, Guildford Dudley, his wife Lady Jane Grey and her father the Duke of Suffolk were all executed. Suffolk was implicated in Wyatt's rebellion and his involvement cost his daughter her life. The executions continued. Wyatt was hanged, drawn and quartered in April. The

---

15. Wilson, p.239.

London crowd transferred its affections to Princess Elizabeth. On 18 March, she made her famous arrival by barge at the Tower to join its prisoners from whence, due to a lack of evidence, she was eventually moved to Woodstock.

Jane Dudley, the former countess of Northumberland, was not welcome at court to plead for the lives of her sons as the drama played out around them but her son-in-law Sir Henry Sidney, married to Mary Dudley, came to her aid. Matters improved for the family after Sir Henry found favour with Queen Mary's new husband Philip II of Spain and Jane gained the friendship of the Duchess of Alva. As the summer progressed John became ill with prison fever, blamed on dank prison air; at the time it was actually spread by fleas and lice. The fever started with aching muscles, a head ache and flu-like symptoms. Ambrose, Robert and Henry would have heard John's dry cough and felt increasingly afraid. A week after the fever first started a tell-tale rash would have spread across John's body as he became delirious and doubled up by stomach cramps. When it became clear that he was dying, Mary who was not vindictive, sent him to Sir Henry Sidney's home at Penshurst in Kent. He died there on 21 October 1554. Jane became unwell in her turn and died on 22 January 1555 having written a last letter pleading for the lives of her remaining sons and her brother-in-law. A warrant for their release was signed on the day of her death. They remained attainted traitors.

Robert took part in the tournaments that were put on between the English and the Spanish as a way of coming to Philip II's attention. Like Northumberland before him, he excelled at tilting. Having demonstrated his prowess in the tiltyard Robert managed to raise the cash to fund his military campaign by selling a portion of his wife's marriage settlement and taking out a loan on his mother's estate at Halesowen in order to raise a small contingent of men. He and his two brothers left England for the Netherlands in July 1556 under the command of the Earl of Pembroke to join Philip II's army in the hope that they might eventually regain their father's estates and wealth. They took part in the Battle of St Quentin where Henry was killed in front of Robert by a cannon ball. The attainders on Ambrose and Robert were reversed but it cost one brother his life and the other two a significant amount of their remaining fortunes. It did not seem likely that Fortune's wheel would ever lift them back to the heights of 1550 even if Leicester's share of the loot from the capture of

St Quentin meant that he could afford to live quietly in Norfolk with his wife Amy Robsart for the remainder of Mary's reign.

William Howard, Northumberland's one-time ally, on the other hand, having declared for Queen Mary at Calais rather than Lady Jane Grey, continued in his loyalty to the Crown. He was rewarded with a place on Mary's Privy Council and was one of the group of men who met with the Spanish to negotiate Mary's marriage. He raised a militia to defend London from Sir Thomas Wyatt's rebels and effectively held Ludgate against them resulting in their surrender a short while later. On 11 March 1554, in recognition of his services to the Crown, he was created Baron Howard of Effingham and the same month made lord admiral. Loyalty to Mary had its rewards but without a Catholic heir, they were likely to be transitory. William Howard consistently supported the rights of succession of Princess Elizabeth, his own great-niece. His arguments eventually cost him his admiralship but were rewarded with several important posts in 1558 when Elizabeth became queen.

Howard of Effingham was Robin's maternal grandfather. His great-grandfather was Thomas Howard, 2nd Duke of Norfolk. Exploration of his Howard family tree shows that Robin was related to Elizabeth I several times over. Anne's mother, Elizabeth Boleyn, Countess of Wiltshire was the eldest daughter of the Duke of Norfolk and his first wife Elizabeth Tilney who died in 1497. Later that same year the duke married Agnes Tilney. A papal dispensation was required as Elizabeth and Agnes were cousins. Robin's maternal grandfather, William Howard, 1st Baron Howard of Effingham was the eldest child of the second marriage. Anne Boleyn, Elizabeth I's mother, was Robin's first cousin once removed as was Katherine Howard. Effingham's wife, Robin's great grandmother, Margaret Gamage was part of the St John family. Her forefather John St John was the eldest son of Margaret Beauchamp's by her first marriage to Sir Oliver St John who died in 1437. Margaret, a descendent of King Edward I, married for a second time to John Beaufort, 1st Duke of Somerset. The couple had only one child – Lady Margaret Beaufort, Elizabeth I's grandmother. Whether by chance or judgement Robin's family on both his mother and father's side owed both the upwards and downwards turns of Fortune's wheel to their connections with the Tudors.

Chapter II

Elizabeth's 'Eyes'

Sir Robert Dudley, the son of a traitor and the grandson of a traitor came within inches of the same fate as his father and grandfather during the reign of Mary Tudor but managed to avoid death. Men like William Cecil, whose papers Camden used as the basis of his history of Elizabeth's reign, considered Leicester to be greedy for power but recognised that he was skilled in 'fitting himself to the times'.[1] It was not a compliment. Nor could Camden understand how Leicester could be so favoured by the queen. In the end, he concluded that it was either because they had both shared imprisonment in the Tower under threat of execution during the reign of Mary or else, in an era that believed in the impact of the planets upon men's lives, 'the hidden consent of the Stars at the hour of their Birth'.[2] Of course, Camden had not considered that Robert was tall and handsome. In addition to which he dressed well, spent a fortune on rose water, loved dancing and had a wit to match Elizabeth's own.

Fortunately, so far as the Privy Council was concerned, Robert was already married when Elizabeth became queen and began to shower favours on her 'Sweet Robin' who was described by a contemporary as 'the goodliest male personage in England'.[3] He married Sir John Robsart's daughter Amy on 4 June 1550. It's likely that the couple met in the aftermath of Kett's Rebellion the previous year. The Dudleys stayed with the Robsarts in Norfolk during the campaign to quell the rebels. King Edward VI was present at the wedding and recorded it in his diary describing the entertainments which involved shooting at a live goose. Robert Dudley, was about eighteen years old as was his bride. The national average age for marriage during the Tudor period

---

1. Gristwood:2008, p.23.
2. Bacon, p.45.
3. Gristwood:2008, p.71.

was somewhere between twenty-four and thirty years of age for men. It was thought that until a man reached maturity there was a wildness about him and a lack of experience that would make him a poor husband. Couples were also expected to be able to maintain a household and family. Robert's marriage contract stated that Amy would inherit her father's estate after her parents' death. This would eventually make him a landholder in East Anglia but for the time being at least, it left him financially dependent on his father and father-in-law. William Cecil, an employee of Northumberland's, who was also a guest at the wedding, noted with disapproval that it was a 'carnal marriage, begun for pleasure'.[4] Certainly, John Dudley at that time still Earl of Warwick, arguably now the most important man in England, might have made a better marriage for his son. He married his other surviving children to men and women of greater rank. Though in the normal course of proceedings it would have been considered a good match for Robert, a third son, to have the opportunity of becoming an established part of the Norfolk gentry by marriage to an heiress. It was perhaps as much as Robert might reasonably have expected had not Fortune's wheel spun in his favour thanks to his close relationship with Elizabeth.

By the summer of 1558, Robert rehabilitated from his incarceration in the Tower on charges of treason, began to look for a more suitable Norfolk residence for himself and his wife than Amy's family home at Syderstone. From his point of view, it lacked both pasture and woodland. However, the attainder against his family followed by a military campaign as part of Philip II's army had left Robert in some financial difficulty despite his gains at St Quentin. He had extravagant tastes, was fond of gambling at cards and sold his possessions to fund Elizabeth Tudor.

In November that year, Mary Tudor died and her half-sister Elizabeth ascended to the throne. Fortune's wheel carried the Dudley family upwards again. One of the first things that Elizabeth did was to name Robert as her Master of Horse. The hunt for an appropriate family residence in East Anglia was no longer a matter of importance when there were so many opportunities at court. His appointment put him in constant attendance on the monarch. The rewards for his devotion included a house at Kew which was a New Year's gift from Elizabeth in January 1559. It was the

---

4. Skidmore, p.9.

first of several grants of property and land. Meanwhile, Robert organised the elaborate pageants that surrounded Elizabeth's coronation. During the procession through London to Westminster from the Tower, he and his brother Ambrose took the positions closest to the royal litter. By spring it was apparent to everyone that Elizabeth was passionately in love with her handsome horse keeper. He was required not only for the care and acquisition of her stables but also to arrange hunting parities, pageants and Elizabeth's famous progresses around her kingdom. It was a role that kept Robert near to the queen and far from his wife who never came to court which suited Elizabeth very well.

Amy, an heiress, maintained her own household of ten servants and received the income from her inheritance into her own hands rather than Leicester administering the funds. Robert's accounts reveal that Amy was not totally forgotten despite the evidence of their prolonged separation. She received a New Year's gift from her husband in 1559 which included six gold buttons. Behind his back it was said that should Amy, who was ill with a 'malady in her breast',[5] die that Elizabeth would marry him. The Venetians reported that Amy was 'ailing' and that 'My Lord Robert Dudley is in great favour and very intimate with Her Majesty'.[6] The nobility resented Leicester's relationship with the queen and was quick to remind themselves and others that the Dudleys were a family of traitors.

Written information about Elizabeth's relationship with Leicester before she became queen on 17 November 1558 is scarce but it had its roots in childhood friendship and shared dangers during Mary's reign. Robert once told the French ambassador that he had known Elizabeth from childhood. It is possible that he was a part of Edward VI's household after Northumberland was raised to the peerage in 1542 so came into contact with Elizabeth at that time. In addition to which, Leicester's mother, who attended Henry VIII's last wedding, was a friend of Katherine Parr's. Elizabeth gave her own explanation for her relationship with Leicester to the Duke of Saxony's ambassador in 1562. She said that Leicester remained loyal to her when she was deserted by everyone else, 'not only did he never lessen any degree his kindness and humble attention to her, but he even sold his possessions that he might assist

5. Gristwood:2008, p.124.
6. Ibid.

her with money'.[7] Despite the bickering and arguments that punctuated their relationship, lifelong faithfulness and loyalty on both sides lay at the heart of the matter.

During his conversation with the French ambassador, Leicester added that Elizabeth had always stated that she would never marry. It did not stop Leicester, both before and after Amy's death, from attempting to progress his personal ambition to make Elizabeth his wife. The queen's devotion to Leicester was the scandal of the time. They rode together, danced together and Elizabeth, it seemed, did not want to let him out of her sight. She even neglected state business to spend time with her favourite. De Quadra, the Spanish Ambassador, reported to the Bishop of Arras on 9 April 1560 that the queen failed to attend an important meeting citing an indisposition. In fact, she went to watch Leicester play tennis. For whatever reason, it was evident to all who saw them together that Elizabeth was deeply attracted to Leicester. Feria, the Spanish ambassador, sent the English gossip back to his master, 'It is even said that her Majesty visits him in his chamber day and night'.[8] There were persistent whispers that she was with child by him. Old Mother Dowe of Brentwood was sent to prison for telling her neighbours that Leicester had taken the queen's virginity. Elsewhere it was stated that Elizabeth's annual summer progresses were an opportunity for her to give birth to Leicester's children in secret. De Quadra's letters became more scandal filled with the passage of time. There was a rumour that Leicester sought Amy's death:

> A certain person who is accustomed to give me veracious news that Lord Robert has sent to poison his wife. Certainly all the Queen has done with us and with the Swede, and will do with the rest in the matter of her marriage, is only keeping Lord Robert's enemies and the country engaged with words until this wicked deed of killing his wife is consummated. The same person told me some extraordinary things about this intimacy, which I would never have believed.[9]

Amy, still without a home of her own and with her husband at court in London, lived with different friends and family in the East of England

---

7. Skidmore, p.11.
8. CSP Simancas, vol. I, p.57 cited in Skidmore, p.23.
9. CSP Simancas, vol. I, p. 112.

and later Compton Verney in Warwickshire. In the Spring of 1560, she moved to Cumnor Place near Abingdon in Oxfordshire. It was home to Sir Anthony Forster and his wife. Like Amy's earlier hosts, Forster was a friend and servant of the Dudley family. Robert visited her on occasion and sent gifts including russet taffeta to make a gown. His last documented visit to his wife was Easter 1559 at Throcking, the home of William Hyde. She came to London in the summer of the same year to seek a medical opinion about the illness which troubled her. It was undoubtedly difficult for Leicester to see his wife. Elizabeth refused to let him leave her side and he could not afford to risk her jealousy. Cecil, unusually critical of his royal mistress, told the Spanish ambassador, de Quadra, at the beginning of September 1560 that the realm would be ruined because of the relationship.

On the morning of Sunday 8 September Amy instructed her household to attend a fair in Abingdon. She remained at home in an upper storey chamber. It was situated in the eastern range of Cumnor Place which was built around a courtyard. She dined with Mrs Owen, a relation of Forster's. Later that afternoon Mrs Odingsells, another female dependent of Forster's, having refused to go to the fair on a Sunday because it was 'no day for a gentlewoman'[10] played cards with Mrs Owens in a different part of the house. That evening, servants and family members returned from the fair to discover Amy's body lying at the bottom of a short flight of stairs. Her neck was broken and there were two deep gouges in her head although according to *Leicester's Commonwealth* published in 1584, her headdress was barely out of place. She was twenty-eight years old.

News of his bereavement reached Leicester the following day at Windsor. He immediately ordered a thorough investigation of Amy's death, not it seems because his wife was dead but because he was concerned for his reputation. In addition to his own man Thomas Blount, a distant kinsman, he also arranged for Amy's half-brother John Appleyard to go to Cumnor. A verdict of 'mischance' was returned by the coroner's court. The coroner's report, rediscovered in 2008, records Amy's injuries as consistent with an accidental fall.[11] There was no post-mortem and there are no definitive answers just different interpretations

10. Skidmore, p.220.
11. Ibid, pp. 228–231.

of the available evidence. Whatever the truth, the rumours that Leicester was a murderer never went away. The scandal echoed across the throne rooms and courts of Europe. Elizabeth hastily distanced herself from her favourite. Leicester, banished to Kew, wore black silk whilst Elizabeth ordered the entire court into mourning for a month. Following Amy's lavish funeral in Oxford on 22 September 1560 and his own return to court six months later, Robert might have hoped that Elizabeth was now free to marry him. Cecil was so horrified by the idea that he considered resignation. De Quadra, the Spanish ambassador, believed that Elizabeth would lose her throne if she married her Master of Horse. In France, Sir Nicholas Throckmorton, the English ambassador who believed Robert to be innocent, put pen to paper warning the queen about the rumours that she would marry a man who murdered his own wife. In Scotland, Mary Queen of Scots made a joke to similar effect. A conversation between Robert and his brother-in-law Sir Henry Sidney, afterwards reported by Sidney to de Quadra, recognised the difficulty that Robert would have in continuing his suit to the queen. Elizabeth understood the realities of the situation much better than Sir Nicholas Throckmorton or even Cecil believed. She refused to give her favourite his earldom saying that she wanted no more treacherous Dudleys in the House of Lords. The queen made it plain that marriage to Robert was an impossibility for her if she wished to keep her throne whilst it was widely thought that he had arranged Amy's tumble. In reality, Robert's greatest crime was probably neglecting his wife to pursue his own ambitions.

Marriage would undoubtedly cause complications for Elizabeth, especially if she married a subject. Robert remained her favourite but she could not risk marriage to him even if his chamber was close to hers and she visited him there often. Her continued reliance upon the earl meant that he became one of the most important patrons of the period. He was essential to her and it meant that his influence was unmatched. In addition to applications from men in search of preferment, funding or artistic recognition he was even called upon to persuade the queen to reason in more personal matters. In August 1561, the court was on its annual summer progress. One of Elizabeth's ladies-in-waiting having married secretly the previous year found it increasingly difficult to disguise her pregnancy as the summer passed. Unable to find anyone willing to intercede on her behalf, she confided in Robert. The lady, Elizabeth's own cousin and heir, Katherine Grey was immediately sent to the Tower despite Robert's intercession on her behalf, whilst her husband the Earl of Hertford was recalled from Europe and arrested when his ship docked in Dover. By the following year, Katherine's marriage was declared invalid and her child made illegitimate.

In 1562, when she thought that she was dying from smallpox Elizabeth swore that 'although she loved and had always loved Lord Robert dearly, as God was her witness, nothing improper ever passed between them'.[12] She named him the Lord Protector of the Realm in the event of her death with an income of £20,000 per year and left his servant Tamworth, who slept in his chamber, a huge annual pension of £500.[13] She could not marry Robert but her testimony reflects the fact that he held her heart. Her privy councillors agreed to her wishes though whether they would have carried them out in the event of her death is another matter entirely. After Elizabeth's recovery, Robert became one of their number. In more normal times when the queen was in good health, his peers resented Dudley for his wealth, power and the scale of his personal ambitions. The Duke of Norfolk and Earl of Sussex were united in their opposition to him from the start of Elizabeth's reign. Norfolk went so far as to hint that Robert Dudley 'might not die in his bed'[14] if he continued in his pursuit of Elizabeth.

Elizabeth's illness compounded her Privy Council's resolve that she needed to marry and have children in order to settle the succession. If she died without issue the question arose of who would be crowned in her place. Cecil drew up a memorandum comparing her suitors with one another. The queen's favourite was without much in the way of credit as a prospective husband to Cecil's orderly mind. In April 1562 though, the Duke of Norfolk, better known as Leicester's opponent, petitioned that Elizabeth should marry Lord Robert Dudley. Everyone on the Privy Council agreed aside from the Marquess of Northampton and the Earl of Arundel who regarded himself as a suitable husband. Meanwhile, Elizabeth deployed marriage negotiations as part of her foreign policy to delay or defuse threats against England. Leicester opposed her suitors because of their Catholicism. He was blamed in some quarters for the

---

12. Stedale, p.210 and Wilson, p.278.
13. Wilson, p.278.
14. Skidmore, p.150.

queen's failure to marry Archduke Charles of Austria both at the start of her reign and during the more protracted negotiations of 1564–1568. Philip II of Spain advised his ambassador that the goodwill of the earl was an essential component for all his transactions with the English. There was still international uncertainty as to whether Elizabeth would marry her Master of Horse but it was evident that the queen, who could often be found closeted with Robert, could be swayed by her favourite even if there were times when his advice produced uncertain results or ran counter to that offered by Cecil.

At home, Elizabeth recognising that a single favourite resulted in resentment, turned her attention to Sir Christopher Hatton, whose skills as a dancer are said to have attracted her, and like Robert, he began to reap the rewards of Elizabeth's favour. Another man she showed affection to at about this time was Thomas Heneage. In the late autumn of 1565, Leicester, on the advice of Sir Nicholas Throckmorton, flirted with Elizabeth's pregnant cousin, Lettice Devereux née Knollys, to test the queen's feelings towards him. The result was to excite her anger. Matters did not improve when Leicester quarrelled with Heneage. Elizabeth may have needed Leicester at her side but as she told him on another occasion, 'my favour is not so locked up for you that other shall not participate thereof'.[15] Leicester did what he often did when the queen was angry with him, he retired to his apartment. Cecil and the Earl of Sussex found themselves unexpectedly in the role of mediators and Heneage was sent away. Lettice was also sent from court. Peace was restored. That Christmas Leicester perhaps thinking that Heneage's banishment was a good omen made an outright proposal to Elizabeth. She avoided answering him saying that he would have to wait until February for a decision. Candlemas came and went without an answer. But when Leicester left Court, he was made to return and ordered never to leave her again.

The price of Leicester's power was to be tied to the queen's side by bonds of faithfulness and loyalty without her being his wife. He could not marry another woman without risking his own 'utter overthrow'.[16] Elizabeth once raged at Leicester, 'I would have thought that if all the

---

15. Ibid, p.227.
16. Read:1936, p.24.

world abandoned me, yet you would remain loyal'.[17] But, no matter how much Elizabeth needed Leicester the one thing she could not do was to marry him. Even so, he did not entirely give up hope. There were times when Leicester's familiarity with the queen extended far beyond what was appropriate. He wagered his own future relationships on Elizabeth succumbing to her personal desire for the man she called her Gypsy or Eyes. He was not alone in supposing that he was her first choice for a spouse. De Feria and later de Quadra, Elizabeth's Spanish ambassadors, both thought that she was attracted to Leicester above all other men. But the queen, versed in the difficulties, intrigues and factions of the Tudor Court since infancy, knew she could not afford to take Leicester as a husband. There would be no Dudley prince to inherit the crown despite what the gossips might have thought.

---

17. Wilson, p.289.

Chapter III

The Virgin Queen

In February 1559, when members of Elizabeth's Privy Council and Parliament led by the Speaker of the House of Commons presented her with a petition asking her to take a husband, she told them that she was married to her kingdom. It became a matter of even more urgency after her illness in 1562. Most people believed that Elizabeth's marriage was a necessity for her physical and moral wellbeing as a woman. As queen, it was her duty to the nation to produce heirs. Without marriage, Elizabeth could have no natural heir. William Cecil, the queen's principal adviser, was of the opinion that marriage was the 'only known and likely surety'.[1] It seemed unthinkable that a young woman would not wish to have a husband and family whatever she might say.

Besides which, without a Protestant successor, England could find itself back in the hands of the Catholic Church. Parliament did not countenance Mary Queen of Scots who had a strong claim to the throne through her descent from Henry VII's daughter Margaret but who was Catholic. The Privy Council were torn whether Elizabeth's successor was to be Lady Katherine Grey, sent to the Tower in 1561 for marrying Edward Seymour without royal consent or Henry Hastings, 3rd Earl of Huntingdon, married to Leicester's own sister Katherine. Hastings' ancestry passed along a Plantagenet line to Edward III. The advantage of Hastings who lacked any Tudor pedigree was the fact that he was stoutly Protestant in his beliefs and that he was an adult male. Under the terms of Henry VIII's will and the Act of Succession, Katherine Grey was Elizabeth's heir. Cecil favoured Katherine because she was Protestant, the mother of a healthy son and because Hastings was associated with Puritanism. Cecil's own religious beliefs were Anglican rather than the more extreme Protestant principles of the Puritans. Elizabeth was reticent about naming any of her cousins as her heir. She had too much experience

---
1. Gristwood: 2008, p.112.

of the plots that coiled, like shrouds, around those waiting for power in the wings to name someone who would become the focus for men who were discontented with her rule. In 1561, the Scottish Ambassador pressed Elizabeth to identify Mary Queen of Scots as her heir, to which Elizabeth replied:

> Think you that I could love my winding-sheet? Princes cannot like their own children, those that should succeed unto them ... I know the inconstancy of the people of England, how they ever mislike the present government and have their eyes fixed upon that person that is next to succeed. More men love the rising sun than the one that sets.[2]

Given the mid-Tudor succession crisis, her reticence is understandable but her ministers had every reason to fear that she would die without naming a successor, plunging the country into civil conflict.

The reasons behind Elizabeth's virgin status are often discussed including her alleged incapacity to bear children but she did not have to look far outside her own family for reasons to avoid a husband. By the summer of 1536, Henry VIII's second marriage was dissolved and a second Act of Succession was passed by Parliament bastardising Elizabeth who was not yet three years old. Her mother Anne Boleyn was dead – beheaded with a sword on charges of adultery and incest. Elizabeth joined her elder half-sister Mary in the purgatory of being daughters of the king but illegitimate. By her twelfth year, not only had her own mother been executed but a stepmother had died as a consequence of childbirth and another was divorced and put to one side. Katherine Howard, a cousin as well as Elizabeth's third stepmother had gone to the block for her lack of chastity having been dragged screaming for her husband from the gallery at Hampton Court. It was not a record that recommended marriage.

At fifteen-years-old Elizabeth learned to be even more suspicious of personal entanglements as well as the need for self-possession in a hostile world. Whilst living in the household of her stepmother the Dowager Queen Katherine Parr, Elizabeth was at the centre of a scandal involving Katherine's new husband Thomas Seymour, the Lord High Admiral

---

2. Pollen, pp.38–45.

of England, uncle to Edward VI. Seymour's ambition saw him propose marriage to Mary Tudor, to thirteen-year-old Elizabeth by letter and finally to Katherine who accepted him. From June 1547, Seymour took to visiting Elizabeth in her bedchamber early in the morning before she was dressed. Kat Ashley, Elizabeth's governess, reported that he arrived earlier each day in order to find Elizabeth in her nightwear and would often indulge in horseplay including slapping the princess's buttocks. On one occasion he climbed into bed with her. At another time he was accompanied by Katherine Parr who joined with Seymour in tickling Elizabeth whilst she was still in bed. In another incident, Seymour cut Elizabeth's gown to pieces whilst Katherine held her down. Seymour's behaviour eventually aroused Katherine's jealousy when she caught her husband and step-daughter alone together in a room, 'he having her in his arms'.[3] To modern eyes, Seymour's behaviour is inappropriate at best and abusive at worst. In January 1549, Seymour was arrested for plotting to kidnap the king. One of the charges was that he tried to marry Elizabeth without the consent of the Privy Council. Elizabeth was closely questioned by Sir Robert Tyrwhitt on Somerset's orders. Her governess and treasurer were imprisoned in the Tower for a time and she was forced to deny rumours of a pregnancy. On 5 March, Seymour was attainted of treason and executed with two blows of the headsman's axe a fortnight later.

Aside from the traumas of her family life Elizabeth also understood that the closer a woman stood to the Crown the more likely she was to become a pawn on the political chessboard. She did not have far to look for an example. Lady Jane Grey, Elizabeth's cousin, was married against her own wishes to Northumberland's son Guildford Dudley placing the duke's family a step nearer to the throne. King Edward VI decided to change the order of succession identified in Henry VIII's will and ratified by parliamentary statute. Initially Edward's 'devise' not only sidestepped both his half-sisters but also bypassed Lady Jane Grey in favour of any sons that she might have. When it became clear to Edward's physicians that there would not be time for Lady Jane Grey to produce any sons the will was amended to read 'the Lady Jane and her heirs male'. The king's wishes did not have the force of law behind them as there was

---

3. Ashley, Katherine, The Robert Tyrwhitt Commission of Enquiry (February 1549) cited in Norton, p.134.

no accompanying statute. In the space of a few months not only was Jane required to take a husband she did not want but her father-in-law ensured that she was elevated from third in line to the throne to being Edward VI's successor. Jane's reaction to this was recounted by the papal envoy Commendone. It includes her impassioned exclamation, 'The crown is not my right and it pleases me not'.[4] It is generally thought that Northumberland intended to govern for Jane and her young husband. Power, in the duke's mind, would have eventually passed to a Dudley king – the House of Tudor replaced by the House of Dudley.

Cries of 'Long live the Queen,' were mercurial as Elizabeth knew. Commendone noticed that Londoners did not cheer Lady Jane Grey. Mary Tudor was initially acclaimed by Protestants and Catholics alike who saw her as Edward's rightful successor. Despite early popular support she faced rebellion less than a year later. The reasons lay in her intention to marry King Philip II of Spain and to restore England to Catholicism. Plotters intended uprisings in Leicestershire, Hertfordshire, the West Country and Kent with the aim of replacing Mary with Elizabeth. In January 1554, after the marriage treaty had been signed, Wyatt's Rebellion in Kent raised an army of 2,000 to 3,000. Wyatt was executed along with ninety other men. Victims included the Duke of Suffolk, his daughter Lady Jane Grey and her husband Guildford Dudley. Even after Mary's marriage unrest continued. One of Northumberland's cousins, Henry Dudley, fled to France where he plotted Mary's overthrow. In 1557, Thomas Stafford, a Plantagenet descendent of Edward III, seized Scarborough Castle as part of his own plot to take power from Mary. Like Wyatt, he faced the executioner's block. As for Elizabeth, she learnt that where there were heirs, there were plots and where there were husbands, there were both personal and political dangers. In later years Leicester would claim that a foreign marriage brought greater prestige to the husband than to the wife. He also noted the risk of civil conflict arising from religious differences as well as the likelihood of national income draining away to pay for foreign wars that were not in English interests. Leicester had his own agenda but Elizabeth was undoubtedly aware of the truth of his words – had not Mary's marriage to Philip II demonstrated the case?

4. Tallis, p.152.

Mary Queen of Scots, Elizabeth's cousin, became Queen of Scotland when she was six-days-old. A year after her birth the Treaty of Greenwich between England and Scotland agreed the marriage of Mary to Henry VIII's son, Edward. It was followed almost immediately after by the conflict between England and Scotland known as the Rough Wooing. The confrontation helped to strengthen the links between Scotland and France. The ties between these two counties were further strengthened by the marriage of the little Scottish queen to the heir to the throne of France. Francis died from a brain tumour in 1560 having ruled France for fewer than two years. Mary returned to Scotland. Like Elizabeth, she was a much sought-after prize but unlike her English cousin, she recognised the need to marry and provide an heir for her kingdom. Time would prove that her choice of husband was a costly mistake.

In March 1563, Elizabeth offered Leicester to Mary Stuart as a potential husband. She enumerated her favourite's qualities for the benefit of William Maitland of Lethington. She noted that 'if she wished to marry herself, she would prefer him to all the princes in the world'.[5] By the autumn of that year, the conversation had turned into an official negotiation for a marriage between Mary and Leicester. Elizabeth elevated Leicester to the peerage giving him the title Earl of Leicester to make him a more attractive proposition. She took the opportunity to advance her favourite across the political board giving him the Lieutenancy of the Castle of Windsor and its forest amongst several other appointments as well as several large land grants. By the end of his life, Leicester's estates extended from the Midlands into Essex, Yorkshire and Wales. There are almost as many theories about the marriage proposal and its seriousness as there are books about Elizabeth and Mary. At one point Elizabeth suggested that if Mary married Leicester that she should allow the Earl of Moray to govern Scotland whilst she and Leicester lived with Elizabeth because she could not bear for Leicester to be absent from her own side.[6] But Mary had a condition of her own before she would countenance the arrangement, namely that she should be identified as Elizabeth's heir.

Ultimately the discussion was concluded by Mary's marriage to Henry Stuart, Lord Darnley in July 1565. Darnley could trace his ancestry back

---

5. Gristwood:2008, p.206.
6. Ibid, p.207.

to James II as well as Margaret Tudor, which gave him a claim to the English throne. The Scots queen was attracted to Darnley's dynastic rights as well as his good looks which initially disguised his weakness and arrogance. Mary, seeking to please the handsome youth, restored Darnley's father, the Earl of Lennox, to the estates and titles that he forfeited for his support of the English during the so-called Rough Wooing as a preamble to Darnley's own arrival in Scotland. She made the decision without conferring with her council, a parcel of faction-ridden rebellious nobles, which weakened her own position with them. Darnley's ambition was to become King of Scotland and thought that once he married Mary that he would have sovereign rights. To make matters worse the Earl of Moray, Mary's half-brother, was against the match as he wanted to maintain his own influence. The nuptials cost Mary most of her political support in Scotland.

Mary married Darnley but although he ruled alongside his wife as King Consort, she refused to allow him to become King of Scots. The tensions within her council escalated as Darnley's behaviour deteriorated into drunkenness and debauchery. The resulting power struggle culminated in March 1566 when Darnley took part in a coup against his wife. The Earl of Morton killed her French secretary, David Riccio, in front of her and took Mary, who was pregnant, hostage. Darnley planned to rule whilst Mary was held in captivity but she managed to persuade her spouse that he was in as much danger as her. He helped Mary to escape to Dunbar Castle where she was offered help by James Hepburn, 4th Earl of Bothwell.

Darnley was assassinated on 10 February 1567 at the Kirk O'Field where he was recuperating from an illness which was probably syphilis. The air reverberated with the explosion that destroyed the house. The semi-naked bodies of Darnley and his servant were discovered in a nearby orchard. Their deaths were caused by strangulation rather than the force of the blast. Suspicion fell upon Mary and the Earl of Bothwell. Hepburn was tried and acquitted of the murder in April 1567. Popular opinion found the Scottish queen guilty of murder. She faced abduction and a forced marriage at Bothwell's hands less than three months after the death of Darnley. Mary became a pawn, just as she had been as an infant, in a dangerous struggle for power. All three of her marriages resulted in a Scottish rebellion against her rule but this time she was deposed. Mary was captured, escaped, faced defeat on the battlefield and was forced to flee to England in 1568, a queen without a kingdom. It was another example of the consequences associated with taking a husband so far as her royal English cousin was concerned.

A foreign groom might be of equal rank and birth, thus improving her status but where in Europe was a Protestant prince that Elizabeth might marry? She received an offer from Eric of Sweden which was given serious consideration by her Privy Council because of his Protestantism. However, there were no other benefits to be gained from the union. William Cecil, Lord Burghley, advocated a match with Charles, Archduke of Austria, a son of Ferdinand I, the Holy Roman Emperor during the 1560s. Elizabeth, taking a note from her father's experience of marrying someone he had never met, said that she would not wed someone she had not seen. There was also the matter of religion. Elizabeth refused to have Mass celebrated at court which meant that a Catholic husband would not be able to worship as he wished. In 1564, she declined Charles IX of France who was in his fifteenth year at the time but did accept the courtship of Charles' brother Henri, Duke of Anjou. The question of religion arose once again, stalling negotiations.

Francis, Duke of Alençon, was the third of Catherine de Medici's sons to ask for Elizabeth's hand in marriage in 1579. He courted the queen in person along with his agent Simier who was responsible for conducting Alençon's wooing. Francis was twenty-three years old. Elizabeth was forty-five years old. Despite this difference, he came to England not once but twice. When Francis's brother Henri became King of France following the death of Charles IX from tuberculosis, Francis became Duke of Anjou in his turn, although Elizabeth preferred to call him her 'Frog'. Elizabeth announced that she would marry him. It would have been a useful alliance and it was perhaps the last chance for Elizabeth to answer the succession question with an heir of her own. Some historians believe that her desire for the match was real, others think it was another courtship that Elizabeth allowed to develop to further her own political agenda. Her privy councillors and courtiers, notably Leicester and Sir Francis Walsingham, were less enthusiastic about an Anglo-French alliance. Anjou departed from England in 1581 when Elizabeth called a halt to the marriage negotiations but gave him money to support the French in the Low Countries against the Spanish without sending her own troops. Elizabeth knew that any husband might reasonably expect that as well as reigning as her consort that they should be the one to rule. James Melville, the Scottish Ambassador, perhaps had it right in 1564 when he noted that Elizabeth was unwed because she wanted to be both king and queen.

Throughout most of her reign ambassadors speculated as to her relationship with Leicester, whether she was married to him or whether they shared a bed. Henry IV of France joked in the 1590s that one of the three big European questions was whether 'Queen Elizabeth was a maid or no'.[7] The Swedish Ambassador writing in the 1560s saw no sign of immodesty in the English monarch. Despite this, there were reports throughout her life that she had borne at least one child to Robert Dudley, Earl of Leicester. In 1575, there were rumours that Leicester was looking for a husband for his illegitimate daughter by the queen. In 1587, a young man calling himself Arthur Dudley, captured by the Spanish off San Sebastian, told the story of being raised by a servant of Kat Ashley. Eventually, he was told by the man he believed to be his father that he was in fact the illegitimate son of Elizabeth and Leicester. The Spanish believed Arthur to be an English spy. He was questioned by Sir Francis Englefield, Philip II's English Secretary, in Madrid and told a tale of adventure including service in the Low Countries under the protection of Leicester, conversion to Catholicism and shipwreck. Arthur told Englefield that he was in fear of his life. He asked if the Spanish would protect him. The story found its way to Venice through diplomatic channels and through more clandestine routes back to Walsingham. The Spanish took the precaution of housing Arthur Dudley and giving him a pension. There is no proof to confirm his story other than the circumstantial evidence that at the time when Elizabeth would have been pregnant with Arthur in 1561 she was ill with dropsy and her body swollen and that Arthur bore a passing resemblance to Leicester. Englefield concluded that Arthur's story was probably true, but that he was being used as a spy by the English to scotch both James VI of Scotland's aspirations for the English throne as well as those of his own master, Philip II. He resolved that Elizabeth wished to keep Arthur, 'in his low and obscure policy, and also that her personal immorality might

---

7. Ibid, p.166.

not be known'.[8] It was more likely that Elizabeth and her councillors used the rumour-mill as a method of infiltrating the Spanish court.

It is impossible for any historian to know whether the queen was a virgin or not. What history does know is that she presented herself as a chaste woman. The cult of Elizabeth which evolved with the passage of time constructed an image of a virtuous monarch and court. The idea of Elizabeth as the Virgin Queen came into being during the 1580s once it became evident that there would be no more marriage proposals and that it was too late for her to give birth to an heir of her own. The queen's attire was layered with symbolism associated with chastity and her ladies were required to dress in either white or black – representing virginity and constancy. Elizabeth having made herself unobtainable also required her courtiers to present the world with a picture of virtue.

8. Ibid, pp. 452–467.

Chapter IV

Douglas, Lady Sheffield

Wooing of the kind associated with chivalric values and the tradition of courtly love were an essential part of Elizabethan Court mechanics. The queen required the undivided attention of her favourites. However, obligatory adulation of an unattainable woman, for political purposes, turned real courtship and marriage into a difficult maze for her ladies-in-waiting. Elizabeth claimed that it was only the unsuitable matches she became angry about. On a political level, illicit affairs challenged the queen's authority as well as her personal reputation. As an unmarried woman, she learned early in life that she could afford little scandal even if she did move Robert's chamber closer to his own. More than one couple found themselves banished from court or sent to the Tower for their indiscretions as well as for marrying. Both the Earl of Oxford and Sir Walter Raleigh were imprisoned at the Crown's 'pleasure' although they had broken no laws. The Earl of Southampton married one of Elizabeth's maids, Elizabeth Vernon, in secret when she became pregnant in 1598 and spent time in the Fleet Prison as a consequence. Whilst the men were allowed back to court very often the women were not. The queen was also 'liberal both with blows and evil words'.[1] When it was discovered that Mary Shelton secretly married John Scudamore without royal consent in 1574, Elizabeth broke the girl's finger with a hairbrush so great was her rage. Elizabeth was angry not only because the marriage was an unequal one but because Mary was one of her favourite companions. Illicit sex, illegitimate children and secret marriages produced from the queen a torrent of bad language, projectiles, imprisonment, banishment and the curtailment of royal favour that might pass like a spring shower as in the case of Mary and John Scudamore or could rage for months or even years.

---

1. Tallis, p.167.

For Robert, a master of the art of courtly love, this presented a range of difficulties. His hopes of persuading Elizabeth to marry him went beyond the language of courtly love. Whilst the death of Amy Robsart in 1560 had set him free to make a second marriage he was trapped by the queen's expectations that he would be content with courtly rituals. If Robert deceived Elizabeth, the betrayal would be a personal one because of his oft-expressed love and devotion. In addition, he owed his wealth and status to the queen. In 1558, he and his siblings were living on the income generated from land belonging to their various spouses as a result of Northumberland's treason. Although Queen Mary lifted the attainder from both Robert and Ambrose Dudley, their father's estates were not restored. Both of them were reliant upon the generosity of Elizabeth for the lands which she granted them – for instance, she gave Robert the manor at Balsall which had been originally been acquired by the Dudley family in 1553 when it passed from Somerset to Northumberland. She granted him Kenilworth Castle on 20 June 1563. Leicester's wealth, power, influence, titles and honours came from a permanent courtship of Elizabeth. She had no option but to accept the existence of Amy Robsart who helped Robert by being absent from court. Another contender for Leicester's affections was not something to be countenanced lightly.

The earl was faced with a difficult choice. He needed an heir to inherit his estates and titles. Of his twelve siblings only Mary, Katherine and Ambrose survived. Ambrose, married three times, had no children to inherit either his titles or Leicester's. Katherine married to Henry Hastings was also childless and, of Mary's seven children with Sir Henry Sidney, only Leicester's godson Robert and his niece Mary survived into the reign of King James I. If Leicester made a secret marriage and it was discovered, he ran the risk of incurring Elizabeth's wrath followed by imprisonment. Nor could he guarantee that she would forgive him. Sir Walter Raleigh remained out of favour for five years after he married Bess Throckmorton in 1591 and even after he returned to court, the financial benefits of earlier days were not so readily forthcoming. One of the reasons that the Earl of Southampton joined in Essex's rebellion in 1601 was that he had never been able to regain his place as a royal favourite following the scandal of his marriage. Katherine Grey so enraged Elizabeth with a politically dangerous marriage to Edward Seymour in December 1560 that her illicit union was annulled, her children declared were illegitimate, and the rest of her short life was spent under house arrest separated from her husband and her children. Seymour was only permitted to return to court after Katherine's death in 1568.

Leicester knew from experience that flirtation with other women was sufficient to bring the queen's wrath down on his head. Elizabeth made it abundantly clear that she came first if Leicester wished to maintain his position at court. The queen would not marry him but she did not like it when he was away from her side. Her dependency upon the earl fluctuated as the band of favourites at court grew. It was during this phase of Elizabeth's relationship with Leicester that his attention strayed. Lady Douglas Sheffield, named after her godmother, Margaret Douglas, Countess of Lennox was a widow with two children. There is little evidence of the affair's progress in the records. And whilst he was attracted to her, Robert had no intention, he wrote in an undated letter, of marrying Lady Sheffield. 'If I should marry, I am sure never to have favour of them (the Queen) that I had rather yet have a wife than lose them.'[2] Douglas seems to have accepted his suit on the terms he proposed and it was only later in the relationship that she began to press for marriage.

Douglas's life had been conventional until she met Leicester. She would have been at court during the time that Europe speculated about Elizabeth's relationship with her Master of Horse given that she had become one of Elizabeth's maids-of-honour prior to the coronation. In about 1560, Douglas, daughter of William Howard 1st Baron Howard of Effingham married John, second Baron Sheffield. On 27 October 1560, the Groom of the Robes and Walter Fish, the queen's tailor, received eight yards of purple velvet and satin 'to make a French kirtle and sleeves for Douglas Howard one of our Maids of Honour against her marriage. And two yards of black cloth of silver...to make a forepart to another kirtle for her'.[3] The marriage was one of which Elizabeth approved and in due course, she became godmother to Douglas's first child, Edmund, born circa 1564. After her wedding, Douglas left royal service demonstrating that she was not as close to the queen as some members of her extended family. Lady Catherine Knollys, one of Elizabeth's Boleyn cousins,

2. Read, p.24.
3. BL Add MS 5751 Am f.59 cited in 'The Elizabethan Court Day by Day', 1560, Folgerpedia.

combined the role of Chief Lady of the Bedchamber with marriage and motherhood until her death in 1569.

History does not record exactly when, or indeed where, Leicester encountered Douglas again after she left the queen's service upon marriage to Lord Sheffield. Gervaise Holles, the seventeenth century antiquarian, believed that Leicester met her in 1568 at Belvoir Castle during one of Elizabeth I's annual summer progresses around her kingdom. Douglas was something of a beauty,[4] she was said to look like her cousin Katherine Howard. Leicester was smitten and sought to 'debauch hir'.[5] Holles pauses long enough to note that Douglas put up little resistance to Leicester's advances. 'He found hir an easy purchase (a fraylty the women of hir family have beene generally but over prone to)'.[6] The antiquarian progressed from telling the story of a court affair to something much darker. Leicester, Holles suggests, wrote Douglas a letter plotting the murder of her husband. This highly incriminating piece of evidence was then lost by Douglas when she took a handkerchief from her pocket. The letter, according to Holles, was discovered by Sheffield's sister who immediately warned her brother of imminent peril. Meanwhile, Douglas realised that her lover's letter was missing and questioned her ladies before seeking her sister-in-law in a state of distress to assure her that no harm would come to Lord Sheffield. This raises two questions. Firstly, why would Leicester who was afraid of losing Elizabeth's favour put himself in a position where he might be required to marry the woman of his desires when she was already safely married to someone else? And secondly, how did Douglas know that her sister-in-law found the letter? In this version of events Lord Sheffield, having taken steps to prevent the lovers from meeting, sought an honourable and just revenge upon Leicester for turning him into a cuckold. Leicester took the opportunity to bribe an Italian physician whom Sheffield trusted to poison him. Holles concludes by turning the colourful account into a fable with Douglas getting her just deserts for betraying her husband. Leicester ultimately rejects her and marries

---

4. Vaughan, p.54 includes an image of a portrait that he believed to be a likeness but did not identify his source.
5. Holles, p.8.
6. Ibid, p. 81.

someone else because it is, the antiquarian thinks, 'the nature of all men who think basely of their prostitutes'.[7]

The problem with this version of Douglas's relationship with Leicester is that Holles recorded a story for which there is very little, if any, evidence other than the tale which was told in *Leicester's Commonwealth* published in 1584. Even Holles described it as a 'satyricall book written against the Earle of Leicester'.[8] It is possible that one of the potential writers of the tract, Charles Arundell, a cousin of Douglas's, surmised some things about his cousin's relationship with Leicester from Sir Edward Stafford, the English Ambassador and Douglas's husband, who he visited several times in Paris. Arundell fled England in 1583 and was in receipt of a Spanish pension. He was made welcome by Stafford not because of his Howard kinship but because of his intelligence links to both Spain and the Guise family. There are a number of flaws in the narrative. The most obvious being that Elizabeth I is not recorded as having visited Belvoir Castle on any of her progresses.

Elizabeth's summer progresses were an opportunity for the relaxation of rigid court rules so it is not unreasonable to think that Leicester may have had more occasion for courtship but equally, Elizabeth was also freer from the constraints of court life. Leicester was responsible for organising horses, transport and entertainment. Elizabeth loved to ride and hunt. She visited Kenilworth for the first time in 1566 and then again in 1568, the year Holles puts forward as the start of Leicester's affair with Douglas. Leicester was there by himself in 1567, 1568 and 1569 when he went north to help put down the Northern Rebellion led by Catholic supporters of Mary Queen of Scots. It is possible that he met Douglas on an occasion when the queen was not present. An alternate date for a potential first meeting between Leicester and Douglas is 1566, the year following the earl's flirtation with Lettice Knollys and an outright proposal of marriage to the queen which she side-stepped at Christmas. De Silva writing to Philip II in March noted that:

Since the Earl of Leicester came back they say that the queen does not treat him with so much favour as formerly. She has begun to

---

7. Ibid, p.82.
8. Ibid, p.81.

favour the Earl of Ormond, an Irishman, of good disposition, some thirty years of age. They tell me that Lord Robert is much annoyed thereat.[9]

Leicester's problems were compounded by the enmity of the Earl of Sussex. De Silva wrote in July that the queen applied pressure on Sussex to bring about a reconciliation. The ambassador surmised that the antagonism lay in Leicester's objection to Archduke Charles' courtship of Elizabeth which Sussex supported. A week after a tourney at which both Leicester and Ormond competed the queen began her summer progress which extended to Lincolnshire that year.[10] It included a visit to Oxford University which might have provided the backdrop for a meeting between the earl and Lady Sheffield.

On Monday 29 July 1566, Elizabeth was at Collyweston which was a Crown property that once belonged to Elizabeth's grandmother Lady Margaret Beaufort. From there she travelled to Stamford but did not stay at Burghley House because Cecil's daughter, Anne, was ill. By mid-August, the queen was in Coventry and the castle of Kenilworth belonging to Leicester before travelling on to Woodstock, another Crown property. Her next stop was Oxford. On 29 August, Leicester, who was the University's Chancellor, Sir Nicholas Throckmorton, Lord Burghley and more significantly Lord Sheffield, arrived in Oxford to see the preparations being made by the University for entertaining Elizabeth. The queen arrived on 31 August with a large company. Her visit was not altogether without incident as a wall fell upon spectators during a theatrical production in the common hall of Christ Church killing three people. Leicester lodged at Christchurch for the duration of the visit along with his brother the Earl of Warwick. Sheffield's lodging is not recorded. It is not unreasonable, although it cannot be certain, that Douglas would have been with her husband especially as he is not listed in bachelor lodgings. One of the challenges faced by household officers was finding accommodation for Elizabeth's retinue whilst she was on progress. There were hundreds of people to be housed and fed. If ministers and courtiers could not be lodged with the queen, they had to be found places to stay

9. CSP Simancas, vol. I, p. 517.
10. Details of Elizabeth's itineraries can be pieced together in Cole and in 'The Elizabethan Court Day by Day', Folgerpedia.

elsewhere in the neighbourhood. Sir Thomas Heneage was in charge of accommodation so it was to him that Sir Henry Lee, Robin's godfather, addressed his complaint about lack of rooms or stabling. It is perhaps not surprising that specific evidence of Lady Sheffield's attendance with her husband at Oxford is hard to locate given the chaos of moving Elizabeth and her possessions around the countryside.

After Lord Sheffield's death on 10 December 1569, Douglas returned to court to serve Elizabeth in the capacity of Gentlewoman Extraordinary of the Privy chamber. This role meant that she was only required when one of Elizabeth's salaried ladies was absent. She is not mentioned in her husband's will, written on 10 December 1568 and proved at the end of January the following year. At the time, if there was no other provision, Douglas was entitled to one-third of the income from the Sheffield estates as a dower. Sheffield's trustees were Thomas Howard, 4th Duke of Norfolk, William Cecil and Sir John Zouche. When Sheffield died his son, Edmund, was four years old. In order to escape the difficulties of the boy becoming a ward of court, Sheffield set up a form of trust before his death. Sheffield's estates were made over to Sheffield's nominated trustees with the understanding that they would be returned to Edmund when he came of age. An *inquisition post mortem* would have been held in order to discover what income was due to the Crown, what estates were held with feudal obligation and also to ensure that everyone with an interest, including Douglas, was allocated what was rightfully theirs.

Douglas's father died on 12 January 1573 at Hampton Court. He was buried, as his will instructed, at St Mary Magdalene Church, Reigate in the family vault. Douglas went into mourning. Her brother Charles now became Lord Howard of Effingham. Meanwhile, much of the court year was taken with the Duke of Alençon's courtship of Elizabeth. The queen graciously received loving letters from her suitor but maintained that she could not marry someone who she had not first seen. There was also the issue of Alençon's Catholicism. Sir Francis Walsingham wrote with some asperity that the general opinion was that 'her Majesty hath no intention to marry, a thing partly proceeding from her own disposition, and partly through the dissuasion of others'.[11] This was a reference to Leicester who set his face against all Elizabeth's potential foreign spouses. Meanwhile,

---

11. Gristwood:2008, p.196.

Alençon promised to come and kiss the queen's hands as soon as he had taken La Rochelle from the Huguenots.

Leicester was not alone in Elizabeth's favour at home. The gifts and grants that once might have been his now had to be shared with others. By 1573, Sir Christopher Hatton was the Captain of the Gentlemen Pensioners who provided a ceremonial guard for Elizabeth. Although he was often absent from court due to ill-health, he continued a literary attendance upon the queen in the form of passionate letters declaring his love and devotion. The Earl of Oxford also competed for Elizabeth's affections. The relationship between Leicester and the queen was evolving. In time Elizabeth would describe him as a brother and best friend. Leicester looked elsewhere for consolation.

The first written independent proof of Leicester's relationship with Douglas is found in a letter sent from Gilbert Talbot to his father the Earl of Shrewsbury in May 1573. In it, he recounts how Leicester can often be found in the queen's company and that two sisters were competing for Leicester's affections. The love affair was discreet but Elizabeth was aware of its existence thanks to the argument between the two sisters:

> …my lord of Leicester is very much with her Majesty, and she shows the same great affection to him that she was wont; of late he hath endeavoured to please her more than heretofore. There are two sisters now in the Court that are very far in love with him, as they have been long; my Lady Sheffield and Frances Howard; they are of like striving who shall love him are at great war together, and the Queen thinketh not well of them, and not the better of him; by this means there are spies over him.[12]

Frances Howard, also one of Elizabeth's maids-of-honour, would go on to have marital troubles of her own. Edward Seymour, Earl of Hertford, courted her for nine years following his rehabilitation at court after his secret marriage to Lady Katherine Grey, imprisonment and subsequent annulment of the union. Frances and Hertford eventually married in 1582. Although other people were aware of the union, Elizabeth did not give her consent until 1585 demonstrating, if nothing else, the difficulties

---

12. Wilson, p.309.

of placating a queen. Hertford made a third clandestine marriage after Frances' death in May 1598.

The undated letter from Leicester to Douglas, an initialled copy of which exists in the earl's own papers, places the start of their relationship after Sheffield's death in 1568. No one, at the time, suggested that Sheffield died from anything but natural causes. Leicester's letter, written before Douglas became pregnant with Robin, makes it clear that the terms of their relationship were limited but that at the time of writing Douglas began to press him for a more formal recognition of their union. Concubinage was not an appropriate stopping place for the daughter of Howard of Effingham. But Leicester still could not risk losing Elizabeth's favour. He says that Douglas should choose whether to continue as they are but that she must not depend on him. He recognised that in paying never-ending court to a queen who is jealous of his affections that he would miss the opportunity of a wife and legitimate heirs. There remained the hope that he might one day persuade the queen to marry him.

Later, after Elizabeth's death, Douglas would say that the Duke of Norfolk, her late husband's trustee and the titular head of her own family, insisted that Leicester was formally contracted to marry her. This took place, she said, in 1571 at a house in Cannon Row. Unfortunately, Norfolk, whose father, the Earl of Surrey, had been executed for treason by Henry VIII in 1547, was not able to ensure that Leicester legalised the union with Douglas. He was executed in June 1572 for his part in the Ridolfi Plot which involved a scheme for him to take Mary Queen of Scots as his fourth wife. Rumour states that Leicester went through with the betrothal because Douglas was pregnant. *Leicester's Commonwealth* alleges that Douglas kept her pregnancy secret and was sent by Leicester to stay with her younger sister Mary who was married to Leicester's own relative Edward Sutton, 4th Baron Dudley.[13] Douglas stayed at Dudley Castle in Staffordshire until her child was born and then returned to court, the infant having died shortly after birth. The writer of *Leicester's Commonwealth* insists that Leicester and Douglas had two children; Robin and a daughter 'born (as is known) at Dudley Castle'. The writer goes on to say that he was acquainted with the minister who was:

13. Ibid, p.309.

used at Dudley Castle for complement of some sacred ceremonies at the birth of my Lord of Leicester's daughter in that place, and the matter was so ordained by the wily wit of him that had sowed the seed that, for the better covering of the harvest and secret delivery of the Lady Sheffield, the goodwife of the castle.

also (whereby Leicester's appointed gossips might without other suspicion have access to the place) should feign herself to be with child, and after long and sore travail (God wot) to be delivered of a cushion.[14]

The *Commonwealth* continues with the story of an empty coffin but that the minister repented of his actions shortly before his death. The tale is not an unreasonable one given the number of accounts of women at Elizabeth's court who concealed various relationships and pregnancies. Douglas herself denied that she had more than one child by the earl.

Robin believed that his father and mother secretly married in the winter of 1573 at a house in Esher in Surrey. Leicester gave Douglas, so she said, a ring set with five pointed diamonds centred on a table diamond, which he had been given by the Earl of Pembroke on the condition that he would give it to no one other than the woman he married. Sir Edward Horsey acted as one of the witnesses as well as giving the bride away. Horsey was associated with Leicester's cousin Henry in the 1550s at a time when Henry Dudley was abroad plotting against Queen Mary. He also served in Europe under the command of Ambrose Dudley. Leicester became one of Horsey's patrons as a result of the information that Horsey sent from Europe about the French. His reward was an appointment as Captain of the Isle of Wight in 1565, a job which he retained until his death in 1583. In 1573, La Mothe, the French Ambassador, wrote to his employer Catherine de Medici saying of Horsey that 'he is entirely the Earl of Leicester's man'.[15] He was a credible choice of witness for a clandestine wedding.

Dr Julio, Leicester's doctor and supposed personal assassin, was also present. He was a risk. He became the queen's physician in September

---

14. Ibid, p.90.
15. Lodge, Edmund, ed., Illustrations of British History, 2nd ed. (1838), p.352 cited in 'The Elizabethan Court Day by Day,' 17 June, 1573, Folgerpedia.

1573. His wife Eleanor, or Mrs Julio, is amongst those listed giving New Year's gifts to Elizabeth, so she too must have been in the royal household. Other witnesses came from among Douglas's family and servants. They included Robert Sheffield and his wife. There are two men by the name of Robert Sheffield listed as beneficiaries under the terms of Lord Sheffield's will. One was his brother Robert who died in 1568 and the other Robert Sheffield of Epworth whose daughter was called Douglas. He may be the Robert Sheffield who witnessed the marriage. Also present were Douglas's gentleman usher Henry Frodsham and her gentlewoman Magdalen Frodsham. In total there were ten witnesses, the majority of them servants.

Part of the problem about whether Douglas and Leicester were married or not lay in the way in which marriages were permitted. By the Tudor period, most weddings took place under the auspices of a church ceremony but not every marriage took place in the public sphere. It has been suggested that as late as the eighteenth century up to a third of all marriages were irregular or clandestine. Marriages without a priest, taking place in private chambers, were increasingly deemed inadequate. In the simplest terms of the law, if a couple exchanged vows to marry one another in the present tense (I do take thee to be my wedded wife/ husband) in front of witnesses, they were regarded as being married in the eyes of the law assuming that there were no other impediments to the union. Equally, if a couple exchanged vows to get married in the future it also became binding when followed by sexual intercourse. This law was not changed until Lord Hardwicke's Marriage Act of 1753.

The Book of Common Prayer, 1549, stated, as did later editions, that the Anglican Church required the posting of marriage banns and the holding of license to marry. Weddings were supposed to take place during canonical hours, that is in daylight. This stipulation was designed to ensure that secret marriages did not occur. A public marriage was a safeguard against deception, bigamy and the taint of illegitimacy. Leicester had every reason to avoid a public wedding. His fortune lay in his favour with Elizabeth. If he took a new wife, he might forfeit the source of his power and wealth. Various authors across the centuries have considered the problem. Some have concluded that Leicester did marry Douglas, others think not. Much of Robin's grief arose from the fact that his parents' marriage may well have been made but that it was undocumented at the time, and therefore unsupported by the Church when Leicester tired of Douglas and became enamoured of Lettice Knollys, allowing Leicester to repudiate the union and effectively bastardise his son.

As an adult, Robin would browbeat his mother into a description of her marriage to Leicester in an attempt to prove his own legitimacy. He held fast to the belief that a ceremony took place for the rest of his life. The wedding, if it happened as Douglas said, took place with a degree of formality. There were witnesses. There was a priest. It did not necessarily matter that she could not remember the name of the cleric who conducted the wedding service, that there had been no banns or licenses or that the event was not recorded in a parish register. Without those things in place, there was no safeguard against deception or proof that Robin was legitimate. The State could unmake such marriages as though they never happened. Katherine Grey's marriage to the Earl of Hertford was declared invalid. Her son Edward had a strong theoretical claim as Elizabeth I's heir in the event of her having no children of her own but by declaring him illegitimate, this claim was nullified. Later Edward's son William would succeed his grandfather as Earl of Hertford during the reign of James I despite the problem of legitimacy. Much of Robin's difficulties in proving his legitimacy after Elizabeth I's death lay in the fact that King James did not favour him.

Court gossip knew that Douglas was in love with Leicester. Gilbert Talbot's letter to his father revealed that Elizabeth was unamused by the whole situation but tolerated the affair coming as it did after Leicester's flirtation with Lettice in 1565. Douglas did not present the same threat to the queen's vanity that Lettice did, even if the two women were the same age and both acclaimed beauties. No one was sent to the Tower or banished from court. Marriage was different. If it happened, it remained a secret from everyone. Leicester and Douglas carried on with their separate lives. On Tuesday 24 November Leicester paid 12d to St Clement Danes for ringing their bells when the queen visited Leicester House on the Strand in order to avoid a potential outbreak of the plague at court. Elizabeth departed Leicester's home for Somerset House and from there to Hampton Court where she intended to keep Christmas. Leicester's secret, whether it was an affair or a secret marriage, was safe for the time being at least.

During the summer of 1574, Mary Shelton's marriage to John Scudamore caused an uproar in the Privy Chamber but by the autumn, Mary was forgiven. The question of Elizabeth's marriage to Alençon continued in the background. At the end of May, King Charles IX died and was succeeded by his brother Henri, Duke of Anjou, who been a potential royal suitor in the past. His former title now passed to Alençon who as well as becoming the Duke of Anjou, became heir to the French throne in his turn. Leicester continued to campaign against the suit based on Anjou's Catholicism.

At the start of summer 1574, the Court prepared to go on its annual progress. Leicester was with Elizabeth. She and her companions left Windsor for Sunninghill on the 12 July before arriving on the 15 July at Binfield. Lady Sheffield remained at her home in Richmond. She was preparing for her laying-in and the birth of a child that the queen was not supposed to know about. The progress that year included parts of Berkshire, Oxfordshire, Gloucestershire, Somerset, Wiltshire, Hampshire and Surrey. On Monday 2 August, Elizabeth was at Langley. Her host, Sir Edward Unton, was married to Anne Seymour the widow of Leicester's brother John. It was almost ten years, at the time of the royal visit, since Anne had been diagnosed a lunatic. By the 4 August, Elizabeth was at Sudeley Castle where Katherine Parr died in 1548 due to complications after childbirth. Did Leicester think of Douglas in Richmond in her warm laying-in chamber with childbed linen at hand, the swaddling clothes and the cradle prepared for a child that he could not openly acknowledge? On 6 August, the city of Gloucester having made its preparations for the queen's arrival, which included the construction of unicorns and a dragon, greeted her with church bells and a gold cup. She left on the 10 August. Leicester was still part of her retinue. The progress journeyed on to Churcham and Berkeley Castle before arriving in Bristol on 14 August where a trade treaty was signed with Spain.

On 7 August 1574, whilst Leicester was with Elizabeth in Gloucester, Douglas gave birth to a son at Sheen House in Richmond, Surrey.[16] A member of Douglas's household, William Clewer, was sent to find Leicester with the news that he was a father. The earl did not keep his son's birth a secret from a trusted network of kin, friends and servants. He

---

16. Warner, p.iii.

sent a letter, it is said, to Douglas giving thanks for the birth of their son. He concluded, 'Your loving husband'.[17] Clewer returned in time to act as Sir Henry Lee's proxy godparent at Robin's baptism. Sir Henry Lee, the Queen's Master of Arms and self-appointed champion, was Leicester's long-time friend. Robin's second god-parent, also by proxy, was Leicester's brother Ambrose Dudley, Earl of Warwick. Mrs Avice Erisa who had been with Douglas during her laying-in became Robin's godmother as did Ann Fiennes, Lady Dacre of the South, by proxy. She was another of Elizabeth I's cousins as well as a lady of the bedchamber. There was also a family connection with Leicester. Lord Dacre's grandmother, Jane, was one of the 2nd Baron Dudley's daughters. When Ann died in 1595, she left Lady Sheffield a pointed diamond, a £100 and voided a debt which Douglas owed to her.

Later in the month Douglas's companion, Mrs Erisa, travelled home. During her journey, she encountered the Earl of Leicester who asked 'How doth my Lady and my boy?'[18] Douglas behaved in private as though she was the Countess of Leicester and was addressed as such in the privacy of her own rooms. The earl put a stop to it for fear that the queen should hear. Douglas, aware that Leicester needed Elizabeth's favour acquiesced. Leicester and Douglas continued as they had done before Robin's birth, meeting when they could, hoping that Elizabeth would not ask too many difficult questions. Glimpses of Lady Sheffield can be caught in various records of the period from New Year gifts to the queen which were often embroidered items of clothing or to taking part in court entertainments.

By the end of 1574, Leicester found himself interceding with the queen over another illicit marriage involving royal blood. Margaret, Countess of Lennox and Leicester's friend Elizabeth, Countess of Shrewsbury (better known as Bess of Hardwick) met at Rufford Abbey in mid-October. With them were Bess's eighteen-year-old daughter Margaret Cavendish and the Countess of Lennox's younger son, Charles Stuart, brother of the murdered Darnley. The countess became ill and retired to her bed. Bess nursed her for a week, during which time the young couple fell in love, betrothed themselves to one another and married within days in Rufford's chapel. Countess Margaret wrote to Leicester explaining that

---

17. Adlard, p.279.
18. Lee, p.24.

Charles 'entangled himself, so that he could have none other'.[19] Elizabeth was furious. She ordered Margaret, her son and new daughter-in-law to return to London immediately. Historians tend to think that the countess's illness was contrived as both she and Bess wished for the match but knew that a marriage with Charles, who was in line to the throne by right of his descent from Margaret Tudor, would be frowned upon by the queen. In addition to facing Elizabeth's wrath, it caused friction in Bess's marriage to the Earl of Shrewsbury who was fast to distance himself from the Rufford nuptials. Charles' mother also sent a letter to Cecil bemoaning the heavy burden of Elizabeth's anger. It was a feeling that Leicester, in a secret relationship with Douglas and the father of a young son, perhaps understood better than Margaret could have known.

By 27 December, the Countess of Lennox was in the Tower where she remained for the next three months for encouraging a marriage that might produce a child who could one day sit upon England's throne. The following autumn Charles and his wife became parents to a little girl – Lady Arbella Stuart. She would have her own part to play in Robin's story. In the meantime, Leicester was reminded that marrying without the queen's consent was a rash undertaking.

---

19. Gristwood:2004 p.34.

Chapter V

A Stepmother and a Stepfather

As Robin approached his first birthday, Elizabeth travelled to Warwickshire on her summer progress. She left Greenwich on the 24 May, arriving at Kenilworth on 9 July. The entertainments provided by Leicester over the next nineteen days were the most splendid to date. It was described by George Gascoigne in *The Princely Pleasures at the Court at Kenilworth*. There was a floating island, nymphs, mermaids, Triton emerging from the lake, fountains of wine, picnics, trees that sang, masques, hunting, tilting, jugglers and fireworks as well as music, scenes from the story of Robin Hood and Maid Marian, performances by Leicester's players and bear-baiting. The recurring motif behind the pageantry was that of marriage. There was even a scene depicting a country wedding. Leicester's suit to the queen was in its twentieth year. A 'wild man' of the wood was overcome by Elizabeth's beauty and observed upon the number of gifts given to her out of love by Leicester.[1] The inference being that she ought to accept the earl. For many, Leicester's entertainments, known as the Princely Pleasures, during the summer heat of August 1575, were a last proposal of marriage to Elizabeth from himself at a time when a match with the French seemed like a possibility. If he was married to Douglas, it did not stop him any more than it had when his acknowledged wife Amy was still alive.

There is no record of Douglas's presence at Kenilworth that year but another of Elizabeth's ladies, Lettice, the Countess of Essex, was in attendance. Court gossip whispered that Lettice was a little too much like her grandmother Mary Boleyn, Henry VIII's mistress, for comfort. A few of the countess's critics may have murmured very quietly behind their hands that all the Boleyn girls were the same when it came to flaunting their beauty and enticing lovers into their arms. Leicester first flirted with Lettice in 1565 to see if the queen might be jealous. At that

---

1. Wilson, pp.311–313.

time Lettice's husband Walter Devereux, the 1st Earl of Essex, was in Ireland. Lettice was the daughter of Elizabeth's cousin and close friend Catherine Knollys. Historians today consider that the relationship was, in all likelihood, a much closer one given that Catherine was the elder of Mary Boleyn's children and conceived at a time when she was Henry VIII's mistress. Lettice was part of Elizabeth's family so she was almost guaranteed a place at court though whether Elizabeth was ever close to the young cousin who was said to resemble her is another matter.

Lettice married Sir Walter Devereux in 1560. She was banished from court for a time in 1565 whilst he was in Ireland for flirting with Leicester. The Spanish Ambassador, De Silva, told his master that Sir Nicholas Throckmorton advised Leicester to 'to fall in love himself with one of the ladies in the palace and watch how the queen took it'.[2] Elizabeth did not take it well. She lost her temper and Leicester took to his rooms in a sulk until the queen sent for him and the matter was smoothed over.

During the summer progress of 1575, Lettice's presence caused an upset in Leicester's carefully planned entertainments. The High Sheriff of Warwickshire, Edward Arden, described Leicester as a 'whore-master' and refused to wear the earl's livery because of the whiff of scandal attached to Leicester's relationship with Lettice.[3] Arden, a cousin of Shakespeare's mother Mary, was also in dispute with the Dudley family over a land deal. In October 1583, Arden's son-in-law, John Somerville, left Warwickshire for London. He told at least five people of his plan to assassinate Elizabeth. Even Cecil thought that the man was insane. Nevertheless, when Somerville implicated his whole family, including Arden, they were all arrested and charged with treason. The family was Catholic. Arden maintained his innocence throughout. He was hanged, drawn and quartered at Smithfield on 28 December 1583. His parboiled head was dipped in pitch and impaled on a spike on the southern end of London Bridge as a warning to the rest of the queen's subjects. Leicester's detractors blamed the earl for Arden's death.

If rumours were to believed, Lettice and Leicester took the opportunity to develop their affair during the summer of 1575. It is possible that Arden's accusations were not unfounded. *Leicester's Commonwealth*

2. CSP Simancas, vol I, p.72 cited in Tallis p. 85.
3. Enis, pp.170–210.

claimed that Lettice became pregnant by Leicester shortly before Essex's return from Ireland and that she resorted to abortion. An affair could have begun during the later stages of Elizabeth's progress once Leicester realised that the Princely Pleasures had failed to have the desired effect upon the queen. The illicit nature of Leicester's relationships with both Douglas and Lettice is one of the reasons why there is very little physical evidence as to the course that either took. Meanwhile, Elizabeth continued on her progress to Dudley Castle where Mary Sidney played hostess and to Chartley on the 6 August where Lettice was once again in residence. The queen stayed with her cousin just one night. Chartley had little entertainment to offer in comparison to Kenilworth. It was, however, an indication that Elizabeth valued the Earl of Essex and his campaign in Ireland which was subject to much criticism because of its failure to colonise Ulster.

What is certain is that Essex returned from Ireland in the autumn of 1575. He came back to England in October and spent time with his family. It was more than two years since he had last seen them. Once the reunion was over Essex looked at his finances which were in a parlous state given the amount of money he spent on the Irish campaign. Camden claimed that Essex openly threatened Leicester because of the rumours that the queen's favourite had cuckolded him. There is no evidence of any threats although it is clear that there were tensions. Guerau de Espés, the Spanish ambassador, speculated as to the reason why there was animosity and concluded it was because Leicester was having an affair with Essex's wife. The hostility between the two men had not always been a factor. Leicester was godfather to Devereux's heir, named Robert in his honour. De Espés also shared the rumour that Lettice had two children by Leicester whilst her husband was in Ireland. *Leicester's Commonwealth* stated that Leicester began a relationship with Lettice by 1565 at the latest. There was also gossip that Lettice gave birth to Leicester's daughter who was handed over to be raised in secret by the Knollys family. Other rumours whispered that Sir Walter was not necessarily the father of all four of the children who bore his name. Camden speculated that it was Leicester who arranged for Essex to be returned to Ireland in September 1576 in the role of Earl Marshal of Ireland so that Leicester could continue his assignations with Lettice.

Sir Walter was joined in Dublin by Sir Henry Sidney, Leicester's brother-in-law. It was Sidney's job to publish the news that Elizabeth had appointed Essex Earl Marshal of Ireland. On the evening of 30 August, Essex ate his evening meal at home. That night he began to suffer from the flux (diarrhoea) which continued to bother him over the coming days and weeks. He grew weaker from its effects. He found time to write to his lawyer to say that a servant had also become ill and that he suspected poison in his drink. The servant recovered but the earl did not. Essex continued to deteriorate. By September he knew that he was dying. He petitioned Elizabeth requesting that she should care for his children. He also wrote to William Cecil, Lord Burghley asking that his son Robert should be received into Burghley's household. There was no final letter for Lettice. If one existed it is lost. Essex died in Dublin on 22 September. Today it is thought that he died from dysentery as did two other members of the garrison. It cannot have helped that with its onset the earl continued to eat as usual worsening the condition.

Gossip now added Essex to Leicester's tally of suspected poisonings caused, in this instance, by 'an Italian recipe'[4] belonging to a doctor in Leicester's employment described as 'newly come to my Lord from Italy'.[5] Dr Julio, the queen's physician was not mentioned on this occasion but he was suspected of being a poisoner. *Leicester's Commonw*ealth of 1584 described the Italian art of poisoning as practised by Leicester's best-known Italian doctor:

> Neither must you marvel though all these died in divers manners of outward diseases, for this is the excellency of the Italian art, for which this surgeon and Dr. Julio were entertained so carefully, who can make a man die in what manner or show of sickness you will.[6]

Sir Henry Sidney ordered a post-mortem to quell any slander against Leicester. He reported that there was 'no appearance or cause of suspicion'. Essex's secretary, Edward Waterhouse, backed Sidney in his own account of events. Even Camden concedes that it was unlikely that Essex was poisoned.

Whatever the truth of the matter Lettice, to all intents and purposes a grieving widow, was not named as an executrix of her husband's will

---

4. Peck, p. 82.
5. Ibid.
6. Ibid.

and was required to find a home other than Chartley. The Earl of Essex lived beyond his means as well as incurring liability for half the costs of the Irish Campaign. When he died, he owed Elizabeth more than £6,000 because she advanced him his share of the capital for the Irish enterprise. Had he been successful in capturing the northern counties of Ireland he would have been able to recoup his expenditure by selling parcels of land. Instead of becoming wealthy, the campaign forced him to sell off some of his estates to cover part of his debt before he died. One of the consequences of the failure of Walter's campaign and the size of his debts was that Lettice was assigned a smaller jointure than that which she thought was rightfully hers.

Her family was also to be broken up. The younger children were placed in the care of the Earl and Countess of Huntingdon. The countess, Leicester's sister, had no children of her own but together with her husband, a respected Puritan, she fostered many noble children. Dorothy, Penelope and Lettice's youngest son, Walter, went to live with their new guardians in York. Walter went north immediately but Lettice's daughters stayed with their mother until 1578. At the beginning of 1577 Lettice's thirteen-year-old son Robert, now 2nd Earl of Essex, was sent from Chartley to live with Burghley's family at Cecil House in London where he may have encountered William's son, Robert Cecil, for the first time. From there Essex would be sent to Trinity College, Cambridge. Lettice and her daughters returned to her father, Sir Francis Knollys, at Greys Court in Oxfordshire having delivered the queen's New Year gift on the way.

In February 1577, Lettice re-joined Elizabeth at Hampton Court where her troupe of actors presented a performance on the evening of Shrove Tuesday. It was a show of favour from her cousin but Lettice did not have a place in the royal household and soon found herself back at Greys Court. During the spring she travelled to the home of the Digby family. They were old friends. She was soon taking part in regular hunting parties to Kenilworth which was ten miles from the Digbys' home at Coleshill. Whilst she was there Leicester arrived with the news that he had arranged the lease of Wanstead Manor in Essex from Lord Rich. He purchased the property a year later. If Leicester and Lettice had been friends before, the relationship, wrapped in secrecy, deepened. Lettice had not yet been widowed a year when the couple began to talk of marriage.

At the end of May 1577, Leicester and his brother Warwick took the waters in Buxton. Douglas was forgotten but her son Robin had a part to play in Leicester's plans for the future. The earl met with his old friend Bess of Hardwick whose movements were somewhat hampered by her husband, the Earl of Shrewsbury's, role as goaler to Mary Queen of Scots. Bess and Leicester agreed that her granddaughter Arbella Stuart should be betrothed to Robin.[7] Arbella, the only child of Bess's daughter Margaret Cavendish and her husband Charles Stuart, was a potential candidate for the throne. It did not matter to Bess that there was a question mark over the legitimacy of Leicester's son. It was more important to her that her granddaughter should receive the support of someone as powerful as the Earl of Leicester. And he, it appeared, had not given up on the family hopes of becoming royalty. Unsurprisingly the betrothal was largely kept secret. Both Bess and Leicester knew how Queen Elizabeth would react to the news.

Leicester was also concerned about the way Elizabeth might respond if she discovered the extent of his involvement with Lettice. He may have hit upon a strategy for deflecting suspicion. At the end of the year, the queen arranged for Leicester to write to the Princess Cecilia of Sweden who had been recently widowed. Cecilia, the beautiful and scandalous half-sister of Eric of Sweden, visited England in 1565. The visit was part of an attempt to convince Elizabeth to marry Eric. Leicester now proposed to the widowed princess despite the fact that he may have been married to Douglas and was carrying on a liaison with Lettice. Cecelia declined his offer. Her memories of England included flight under cover of darkness from creditors. Equally, it is possible that the queen, having a better understanding of Leicester's tangled relationships than he realised, was testing the magnitude of his ambitions against the strength of his affections for Lettice

New Year came and went at Hampton Court. Leicester's gift to Elizabeth at the beginning of 1578 was more glittering than ever, being an enamelled gold chain garnished with diamonds, rubies, opals and pearls. Douglas's gift was an embroidered satin doublet with white cutwork. Lady Sheffield's gifts were often apparel as she knew that her cousin delighted in both fine embroidery and costly attire. Lettice's gift, which

---

7. Lee, pp.29–30.

she could ill afford, were lawn ruffs edged with seed pearls. Her claim for a third of Essex's estates as her dower right rather than a diminished jointure had been refused. She was forced to negotiate with Cecil for an extension to the allowance her husband allocated her.

When spring arrived Lettice's daughters travelled to York to begin their life as part of the Huntingdon household. The countess discovered that she was expecting a baby. As Douglas had done before her, Lettice hid her pregnancy and carried on with life as a widow. Meanwhile, Lettice's own sister Elizabeth married Thomas Leighton with the queen's blessing in May 1578. It was unlikely that Lettice and Leicester would be blessed with Elizabeth's approval in the event of their own marriage or be in receipt of a royal gift to celebrate their nuptials. Elizabeth Knollys, like her mother and Lettice before her marriage to the Earl of Essex, was a longstanding Gentlewoman of the Privy Chamber. She continued in her role at court even after her marriage to Leighton who was the governor of Jersey and Guernsey.

Elizabeth visited Wanstead in May where she was entertained by Leicester's nephew Philip Sidney because the earl was in Buxton taking the waters again. Before Leicester's return to court in July, his onetime rival Sir Christopher Hatton warned him that the queen had got wind of a marriage that displeased her. He also wrote that Elizabeth was bored without Leicester to entertain her. The earl re-joined the queen, who was on progress, at Audley End. Their host was Thomas Howard whose father the 4th Duke of Norfolk was executed in 1572 for his part in the Ridolfi Plot. The queen was at Kirtling where Roger, 2nd Baron North, was her host for three days when Leicester slipped away once more and hurried to Kenilworth where Lettice was waiting. The pair married in secret, in much the same manner that a ceremony of some description had taken place at Esher. In reality, Lettice's situation was no different to that which Douglas found herself in when she became pregnant with Robin four years earlier. Neither woman could be secure whilst there was no documentary evidence and the earl was unprepared to acknowledge one or the other of them as his wife.

Lettice's father, Sir Francis Knollys, now took matters into his own hands. He was one of Leicester's friends and an ally in the Privy Council but he also recognised that a secret marriage might be no marriage at all. Unlike Douglas, whose powerful Howard family does not seem to have involved itself with her relationship with Leicester, Sir Francis Knollys insisted on a second wedding surrounded by witnesses. Early on the morning of 21 September 1578, having supped with Sir Francis the night before, Leicester married Lettice Knollys, Elizabeth's first cousin once removed, at Wanstead in the presence of her father, his brother Ambrose and the Earl of Pembroke. The clergyman who officiated, Humphrey Tindall, was Leicester's own chaplain. He was later required by the bride's father to make a sworn deposition that he had legally married the couple. He was also obliged to provide evidence that he was an ordained minister. It may also have been Knollys who insisted that Leicester arrived at a proper settlement with Douglas. He did not want any loose ends to turn his unborn grandchild into a bastard should the earl decide to repudiate Lettice as he had Douglas. Two days later, Elizabeth I arrived at Wanstead at the end of her summer progress. There was no indication that her favourite was a newly married man. Remarkably, given the number of rivals who might have wished harm to Leicester, the illusion was maintained for the next year.

Leicester arranged to meet Douglas along with two of his friends, Sir John Hubard and George Digby,[8] in the grounds of Greenwich Palace soon after his marriage to Lettice at Wanstead. He offered her £700 a year if she would 'disavow marriage'.[9] He wanted to be free of complications but he wanted to keep his son even if his actions in marrying Lettice and rejecting Douglas made Robin illegitimate. Leicester proposed that he should have Robin in exchange for £1,000 and the knowledge that Douglas gave up any legal claim to her son. Leicester's idea was that Robin should go with Edward Horsey, a witness to his marriage with Douglas, to the Isle of Wight where he would be raised. Douglas refused. The information about her relationship with Leicester is fragmentary at best but it is clear that until that moment in their relationship she had done as Leicester asked, so much so that she is sometimes viewed as inconsequential. Now, for fear of losing her son and his place in the world she stood her ground – or so she later testified. The earl stormed that 'he would never come at her again'.[10] She claimed that Leicester told her that even if she thought she was married that she was wrong because the

---

8. Ibid, p. 30.
9. Wilson, p.314.
10. Ibid.

secret marriage had never been a legal one. Equally, when Douglas swore that she was Leicester's wife, the earl was safely dead and in no position to repudiate her statement. That he loved her sufficiently at one time to risk Elizabeth's anger is readily apparent. He must have gambled in 1578 that Lettice, a stronger character than Douglas, and already the mother of two boys would be able to provide him with heirs. Douglas continued to resist the pressure that the earl placed on her. In 1605, during the Star Chamber trial revolving around Robin's legitimacy, she would testify that she only agreed to Leicester's proposition when her hair began falling out and that her nails started to turn black. The stories contained in *Leicester's Commonwealth* about murder by poison may have offered her a way of saving face.

Leicester's marriage to Lettice was not such a well-kept secret as his liaison with Douglas. Servants talked. Nor was Lettice so compliant as Douglas. Even Mary Queen of Scots knew that Elizabeth's horse keeper had taken a bride. The only person who seemingly did not know was Elizabeth herself. As the complications of his domestic relationships became common knowledge Leicester remained brazen in his continued devotion to the queen. He continued to oppose her marriage to the Duke of Anjou. Elizabeth discovered the truth of Leicester's marriage to Lettice, according to Camden, on 17 July 1579 when Simier, Anjou's agent, an enemy of Leicester's, told the queen, believing that Leicester was behind an assignation attempt on his own life. He also believed that she would console herself with the duke whom she called her 'Frog'. It was not right he said, that Leicester should try and prevent Elizabeth from marrying when he himself had recently taken the queen's own cousin as a wife.[11]

The Court quaked under Elizabeth's fury. She was completely heartbroken one moment, the next denouncing Lettice as a she-wolf. Not only was Leicester married, but he had kept the truth from her – so much for loyalty and faithfulness. The truth was awful for Elizabeth. Her trusted 'Eyes' had married a beautiful woman ten years younger than her, the daughter of an old friend, who had served Elizabeth since she was a girl. She spoke of sending Leicester to the Tower but the Earl of Sussex, an opponent of Leicester's, persuaded her that the scandal would be too

---

11. Lee, p.32.

great.[12] Instead, she boxed Lettice's ears when she showed insufficient remorse and 'banished her from court'.[13] Leicester went to Wanstead. He was not permitted to say his farewells to Lettice before he went. He wrote to Burghley complaining, 'I have lost both youth and liberty and all my fortune reposed in her'.[14] He would have married Elizabeth but she always refused him. He wanted a family life and an heir to follow after him. In the meantime, Leicester's enemies at court looked on with glee. Lettice did not help matters by dressing magnificently and being seen in her carriage in Cheapside. The carriage was pulled by four horses and the livery of her expensively clad footmen incorporated the bear and ragged staff. Lettice was lucky to avoid the Tower even if she had broken no law but she did not care. She was married to Leicester and Elizabeth was not. Having made her point, Lettice retired to the countryside to wait for the queen to forgive her and her husband. Even she realised that she could not stay in London if Leicester was going to get his place at court back.

Elizabeth's next action demonstrates that she knew of Douglas's association with Leicester and that she turned a blind eye to the liaison because she knew that Lady Sheffield was not a threat to her own position. She ordered an enquiry. The Earl of Sussex was sent to question Douglas who was tearful. She said that 'she trusted the said Earl too much to have anything to shew to constrain him to marry her'.[15] Elizabeth did not like the answer. She was hoping for evidence that Leicester was already married, making his union with Lettice bigamous. If Douglas declared to Sussex that she was married to the earl he would have been ruined and Lettice humiliated. The queen, no doubt exasperated with Douglas, banished another cousin from court and placed Robin under her own protection.

Douglas, ostensibly a widow for more than ten years, married Sir Edward Stafford of Grafton in November 1579 in another secret ceremony at Blackfriars. It was later claimed that Leicester arranged the marriage for her. Her new husband was close to the Crown but not wealthy. Part of Douglas's appeal for her new husband was her dower income from Lord Sheffield's estate. Stafford's mother was Lady Dorothy Stafford.

---

12. Tallis, p.178.
13. Peck, p.26.
14. Tallis: 2008, p.182.
15. Lee, p.33.

Plantagenet blood ran in her veins. Her grandmother, Margaret Pole, the 8th Countess of Salisbury was executed in the Tower without trial for treason in 1541. Edward's parents were staunch Protestants. They had chosen to go into exile during the reign of Mary I. Once Elizabeth I ascended the throne in 1558, the family moved home. Dorothy, widowed, became a close companion of the queen and exercised her influence to promote her friends and family.

Elizabeth discovered the truth of Douglas's new marriage in February 1580. She even told the French Ambassador, Castelnau de Mauvissiere, that Stafford had secretly married one of her cousins. She summoned Sir Edward to court. The queen now claimed that she had evidence that Leicester married Douglas despite the fact that she refused to admit it when questioned. Douglas was pregnant with Stafford's child. One of her children must be illegitimate – Robin whom Leicester had already branded or her unborn child. Stafford was adamant that Douglas had not made a bigamous match. Elizabeth forgave Douglas for her marriage to Stafford as she would never forgive Lettice for her marriage to Leicester. The following March, Elizabeth became godparent to Douglas's new son, a demonstration that she accepted the match. The queen's gift was a silver gilt bowl. It was a similar gift to that which she gave to Douglas's son by Lord Sheffield when she became Edmund Sheffield's godmother. In 1582, in a further show of favour, Elizabeth visited Douglas at her home in Highgate. Her union with Stafford bought Lady Sheffield few financial advantages but it did give her a fresh start in life. In 1583, the same year that he was appointed English Ambassador in Paris, her husband admitted in a letter to Burghley that he was dependent upon her income from the Sheffield estate.

Douglas prepared to travel with Sir Edward to Paris where he was to be the English ambassador. Amongst the arrangements was the appointment of a new chaplain. Richard Hakluyt also acted as Stafford's secretary. It was Leicester, as Chancellor of the University of Oxford, who told Hakluyt of his appointment. The household arrived in Boulogne on 28 September 1583. Douglas's knowledge of court life and her ability to speak French made her a useful ambassadorial addition. Jacques de Thou, the French statesman and historiographer, described the fact that she became a confidante of Catherine de Medici which is confirmed by the warmth of Douglas's reception at the French court.[16] In 1585, when Henri III introduced a series of household ordinances designed to offer him greater privacy it was thanks to Douglas's understanding of Elizabeth's domestic arrangements.

Leicester may have ensured that Robin was rendered illegitimate but he did not wish to be parted from him. There may have been a number of reasons for this. It was only ten years since the St Bartholomew's Day Massacre in Paris. Leicester wished to keep the boy safe. The earl was also increasingly Protestant in outlook. Douglas's branch of the Howard family was conservative in its sympathies which inclined them to the Old Religion and Walsingham had his doubts about Robin's stepfather. Hume's edition of the Spanish State Papers pointed to the correspondence of the Spanish Ambassador in Paris as evidence that Stafford sold information to Philip II. Leicester would not have wished his son to be raised a Catholic or to be exposed to the dangers of an anti-Protestant Parisian mob. Douglas departed from Robin's life. She returned when he was fifteen years old.

16. CSP Foreign, Elizabeth, p.145.

Part II

Chapter VI

Childhood and Education

Robin spent the first four years of his life in his mother's care. There is little specific information about his infancy. As a very young baby, he would have been swaddled to help his bones to straighten, and to protect him from the cold. Infancy was a chancy business in Tudor times with up to a quarter of children dying before the age of ten. Although Douglas may have worried about the well-being of her small son, she is unlikely to have cared for him herself, especially as she returned to her role at court as soon as possible after the birth. Wealthy Tudor women usually employed wetnurses so that they would be able to get on with the business of providing a family with more children. A woman, having recently given birth to a child of her own, would have been employed to nurse Robin. Many of these nurses were family retainers or recommended by word of mouth. As the mother of two children prior to the birth of Robin, Douglas may have known someone she could trust or perhaps Leicester found a woman in the country to take Robin until he was weaned when he was about two years old. Nurses were selected based on their good nature and placidity. It was also recommended that the woman should have clear skin, look healthy and be respectable. It was thought that the baby took elements of the wetnurse's character along with her milk. Often nurses became part of the wealthy household into which the child was born. Alternatively, infants, probably including Robin, were sent to live with the wet nurse in the country away from the dangerous miasmas of the city. So far as Leicester was concerned the countryside offered more secrecy than an infant and its nurse causing speculation in one of Douglas's own residences.

From his mother he would have learned table manners and also how to conduct himself as the son of the Earl of Leicester. Later Robin would say that he 'acquired the etiquette and social graces which could only be learned in a noble household' during his time in his father's care, probably with John Dudley of Stoke Newington.[1] From either his mother, or John Dudley, he also acquired basic literacy skills from an ABC or horn book. The latter was described by Speaight as:

a primer framed by wood and covered with a thin plate of transparent horn. It included the alphabet in small letters and in capitals, with combinations of the five vowels with b, c, and d, and the Lord's Prayer in English. The first of these alphabets, which ended with the abbreviation for 'and,' began with the mark of the cross. Hence the alphabet was known as the 'Christ cross row'.[2]

By the time he was five years old, and in Leicester's care, Robin would have memorised the catechism and started to learn mathematics at which he must have excelled given his adult understanding of the subject. The Jacobean schoolmaster John Brinsley noted that formal education often began at seven years of age but as Richard Mulcaster wrote, 'ripeness is all'[3] and that children should begin to learn according to their talents and aptitudes. It is evident that he was tutored early in his life by the men Leicester patronised although it is unknown who Leicester sent to tutor his son or what books he was able to access from his father's library at Leicester House. More than one hundred writers, covering a multitude of topics, dedicated their work to the earl.

Leicester did not neglect Robin even if his hopes for the future of the Dudley family lay elsewhere for a time. Education was an important subject for Elizabethan writers. During the 1560s Roger Ascham published *The Scholemaster: a plain and perfite way of teaching children, to understand, write, and speak, the Latin tong, but specially purposed for the private bringing up of young gentlemen.* It was dedicated to the queen and to Cecil. Leicester realised the value of such an education. The growth of humanism during Leicester's childhood ensured that he and his siblings were well-schooled. He was tutored by Roger Ascham, as was Elizabeth, even if it was unlikely that they shared any lessons. John Dee, Elizabeth's court astronomer, taught Leicester mathematics and astronomy. The

---

1. Lee, p.34.
2. Speaight cited in Mabillard, Amanda. Shakespeare's Education and Childhood, Shakespeare Online. 12 Sept. 2000. www.shakespeare-online.com/biography/shakespeareeducation.
3. Mulcaster, pp.14–19 in Cressy:1975, p. 70.

Countess of Northumberland's Protestantism was an equally important factor determining the kind of education that Leicester received. His mother, like many other reformers, valued education and the ability to read the Bible because she believed that it was faith alone that saved an individual from damnation. Literacy was an essential building block to faith, conscious awareness of the need to repent and thus to salvation. Although history does not know exactly what programme of education Leicester himself followed, it will have included French, Latin, maths, the classics and cosmography – a mixture of geography and astronomy. In addition to book-based lessons, Leicester and his brothers would have also received tuition for dancing, music, shooting and tilting. Archery was a skill required of all boys aged between seven and seventeen-years-of-age. A law of Henry VIII's dating from 1512 stipulated that each boy should be provided with a bow and two arrows in preparation for war. The programme of study that Leicester experienced was probably not so different from that laid down for Robin during his childhood. Both father and son shared a love of navigation, hunting and tilting. It is not unreasonable to think that enjoyment of these pursuits grew from lessons in childhood.

After Robin was transferred into his father's custody he did not go to the Isle of Wight as originally proposed. Instead, he was placed in the care of Lord North. His mother was able to visit him whenever she chose. Roger, 2nd Baron North, was part of the East Anglian elite and a personal friend of Leicester's. He was a witness to the earl's marriage to Lettice. Robin also lived with John Dudley of Stoke Newington, a second cousin of Northumberland who hailed from Yanwath near Penrith. John and his wife Elizabeth had a daughter, Ann, a similar age to Robin. Both Douglas and Leicester visited him. Owen Jones, Robin's childhood servant, recalled at the Star Chamber trial of 1605 that Leicester desired his son to have 'good usage and education' and confirmed that the earl visited his son whilst he lodged at Newington Butts in Surrey and elsewhere until he left for the Low Countries in 1585.[4] There was no doubt that Leicester fully acknowledged his son but life for Robin was complicated by the question mark over his legitimacy. Once Leicester and

---

4. Lee, p.37.

Douglas married other people, bigamous or not, Robin's position, so far as the wider world was concerned, was that of bastard.

John Dudley became ill in 1580. A local doctor, Edward Atslowe, attended Robin's guardian and medicines were sent from the apothecary costing £5, but John Dudley died on 29 December 1580 and was buried on 13 January 1581 in Stoke Newington Church. An account of the funeral and the bequests made in John's will can be found in Leicester's papers. The accounts reveal that John left Leicester a cup worth £100 and the Countess of Warwick some tapestry hangings with the caveat that she should care for his widow Elizabeth and daughter. Elizabeth is thought to have let the manor house at Stoke Newington to Leicester but there is no evidence of either Leicester or Warwick owning or leasing property in Stoke Newington. There is only the circumstantial evidence of one of Lettice's servants being buried in the parish in 1582 to show a continued association. In March 1581, Elizabeth Dudley wrote to Leicester saying that she had been touched by John's death and Leicester's recent anger against her husband but that her comfort could now only come from Leicester's protection which she begged for both herself and her daughter. John's widow was remarried to Thomas Sutton who had strong connections to both Leicester and the Earl of Warwick. His name suggests that there may also be an extended kinship connection. Sutton became one of the wealthiest commoners in England prior to his death in 1611.

By May 1581, Robin was seven years old. His mother had gone to Paris with Sir Edward Stafford and he was part of a household in mourning for the man who took on his care. His stepmother, Lettice, who kept her husband's illegitimate son at a distance, was pregnant once again. To ensure there could be no doubt about the legitimacy of the coming child the witnesses at Lettice's wedding gave their testimonies proving without doubt that Leicester and she were married. There would be no shortage of documentation on this occasion. Lettice, in her thirty-eighth year, gave birth on 8 June in Leicester House on the Strand to a much longed-for son also named Robert. During the three years that she and Leicester had been married Lettice may have suffered at least one miscarriage as well as the child who died soon after birth. Leicester's undoubted heir was swiftly styled Baron Denbigh. Any marriage plans that Leicester may have entertained for Robin were now supplanted by plans for his new half-brother. Leicester called this Robert 'the Noble Imp'. There are two portraits of him in the list of Leicester's pictures as well as a third with his mother. Leicester had no intention of keeping this child a secret, unlike Robin of whom there are no known portraits as a child.[5]

Robin was sent to school in Offington near Worthing in Sussex in 1583 along with Owen Jones who was employed by Leicester to look after the boy. The boy's Sidney cousins attended grammar school before they went to university so the fact that Robin was sent to school rather than being tutored at home was not unusual. He would remain there for the next four years with sojourns in various of Leicester's residences accompanied by a tutor as well as time spent with both his godfathers. During his time at Offington, he was under the guardianship of the Earl of Warwick. His uncle who was also his godfather had a house near Worthing known during the nineteenth century as Warwick House. There is a picture of Warwick with an unknown page by his side held in the Longleat Collection. It is tempting to think that it might be Robin though unprovable. The boy was also welcome at the home of his godfather, Sir Henry Lee, at Ditchley in Oxfordshire. Being a welcome guest is not the same as having a home. Lettice who doted on her own son Robert Devereux, Earl of Essex, had nothing to do with Leicester's boy. Robin did not write a great deal about his childhood in his memoirs other than to say he 'had from his youth, a natural sympathy for the sea'.[6] Some of that fascination may have been as a result of spending time with Warwick, who like his father and his brother the Earl of Leicester was a patron of explorers. From both his uncle and his godfather he learned about tilting and the chivalric code.

The parish of Offington and Broadwater were closely associated. It was a landscape dotted with ancient tracks dropping from the Downs towards the sea. In 1581, the schoolmaster was recorded as living in the neighbouring parish of Broadwater. The school day started early for many pupils running from six in the morning until five at night. Discipline was strict. Much schooling involved memorization and recitation. As a scholar, Robin would have learned Latin which was the language of

5. There is an image of Ambrose Dudley, Earl of Warwick by an unknown artist that can be found in the Longleat Collection. He is standing with his hand on the shoulder of a young unidentified page.
6. Lee, p.37.

scholarship across Europe. Geographical discovery was considered of importance. It was part of Cosmography. French or sometimes Italian was also studied. There were opportunities for enjoyment as well as study, nearby Broadwater hosted two fairs; one on St Barnabus Day which fell on 11 June and a second larger three-day fair was held in October each year.

In 1583, Bess of Hardwick came to London. She stayed at Leicester House as a guest of the earl. Whilst Bess stayed in London, she and Leicester arrived at new terms for Arbella's marriage into the Dudley family. Instead of marrying Robin, Bess's granddaughter would now marry Leicester's undisputed legitimate heir. Arbella, who was eight years old, sent her portrait to Leicester's little son and received one back in return. The betrothal came to the attention of both the Spanish Ambassador, Mendoza and Mary Queen of Scots who wrote about the proposed match in a letter to the French Ambassador:

> ...nothing has ever alienated the Countess of Shrewsbury from me more than this imaginary hope, which she has conceived, of setting this crown on the head of Arbella her granddaughter, by means of marrying her to the son of the Earl of Leicester.[7]

For once Mary and Elizabeth would have been in agreement but it appears that Leicester was able to keep the engagement from the queen's notice. Besides, Elizabeth was angered by another scheme that came to her ear. Leicester proposed that Dorothy Devereux, his younger step-daughter, should marry James VI of Scotland. Elizabeth was not amused. She placed the blame squarely on Lettice's shoulders exclaiming she would, 'proclaim her all over Christendom as a whore, even now cuckolding her husband'.[8] Dorothy, wishing to avoid an arranged marriage of the kind endured by her sister Penelope to the radical Puritan Lord Rich, took matters into her own hands and eloped with Sir Thomas Perrot, marrying him at Broxbourne in July 1584 ensuring that Leicester's plan came to nothing. This marriage also angered the queen because her permission had not been sought and it would almost certainly have been refused. Thomas, whose own father claimed to be an illegitimate son of Henry

---

7. Gristwood:2003, p.40 and Lovell, p. 307.
8. Lee, p.35.

VIII, found himself in prison whilst Dorothy faced banishment from court. Elizabeth raged at Leicester's ambitions for the proposed Scottish match but as usual, forgave him.

Leicester's dynastic plotting was to no avail. Fortuna's wheel took a downward turn leaving Leicester devastated when Lord Denbigh died suddenly at Wanstead in July 1584 whilst Leicester was at Nonsuch Palace in Surrey with the queen. He was heartbroken. He described the 'loss of my only little son' in a letter to William Davidson, Elizabeth's secretary. The earl left court without asking for royal permission. It was Sir Christopher Hatton, one of the fraternity of royal favourites, who informed Elizabeth of Leicester's loss. She sent a personal messenger expressing her condolences but no formal letter. Burghley invited Leicester and Lettice to visit his house near Cheshunt so that they could grieve in peace before the funeral which took place on 1 August.[9] The couple drew closer to one another. Lettice became pregnant again but she miscarried. It seemed likely that Robin would be Leicester's only son but as one who had been declared illegitimate by his own father, in the eyes of the law he was *filius nullius*, or a son of no one. An illegitimate child had few legal rights and would certainly be unable to inherit his father's titles. Leicester's heir at this time was his nephew Sir Philip Sidney, not Robin.

Leicester's Disbursement Book for 1584 reveals that Robin was not always in Sussex. In the aftermath of Lord Denbigh's death, it seems that Leicester moved his remaining son to his manor at Witney in Oxfordshire. On the 24 October, £3 was given as a reward by Leicester to Robin's schoolmaster, Mr Canellae. Robin himself received 10s.[10] There is also evidence that Robin was resident for a while in the care of Dr Delabere in January 1585 as Leicester paid for horse hire and 'their meate for Mr Robert Dudley when he came from Oxford to Witney'.[11] John Delabere was the principal of Gloucester Hall, Oxford from 1581 to 1593. By October 1585, Robin and his tutor, who received £5 for his services, were at Leicester House on the Strand with his father who departed from there for Richmond at the beginning of November. On 26 November Leicester

9. Wilson, p.334.
10. Adams:1995, pp.188–189.
11. Ibid, p. 216.

ordered a repayment to Canellae for the purchase of a hat[12] for Robin which suggests that Canellae took care of all aspects of Robin's life.

Leicester's Commonwealth was published in Antwerp the same year. One theory is that the tract was written by Jesuits, a second view places authorship in the pens of a group of lay Catholic exiles based in Paris including Douglas's cousin Charles Arundell. It was written whilst Lord Denbigh still lived but its claim that the Noble Imp had falling sickness or epilepsy as a consequence of parental sin must have been a hurtful jibe. A copy of the damaging book was handed to the Lord Mayor of London on 29 September. Walsingham described it as 'the most maliciously written thing that ever was penned since the beginning of the world'.[13] It was part of a smear campaign then raging between Catholics and Protestants. The anonymous author raked up every scandal he could find about Leicester who had become a leading supporter of Puritanism – despite his unconventional private life. The book dredged up the story that the Dudley family was low born, that Leicester had murdered Amy Robsart, Lord Sheffield and the Earl of Essex. It also claimed that he poisoned the Countess of Lennox, Arbella Stuart's grandmother, who died the day after she dined with him. It asserted that the earl conspired to murder Simier in order to prevent Elizabeth from marrying Anjou. Within a year *Leicester's Commonwealth* was widely available in Europe. Douglas's husband Sir Edward Stafford wrote a letter to Sir Francis Walsingham explaining that Douglas was 'prostrate with melancholy and near to losing her mind'[14] as a result of the treatise's publication. He continued:

> I am in a peck of troubles what to do ... if by a device I could have it suppressed I would do it ... I shall not stir in it, but by making no account of it, make it thought a jest, as the Queen Mother has done in all things set out against her, which has made them die the sooner.[15]

Robin was ten years of age when the book arrived on English shores. Although the authorities were quick to limit its circulation it broadcast

---

12. Ibid, p.337.
13. Cotton MSS, Titus B. VII, fols. 10–10v printed in Leslie Hotson, 'Who Wrote Leicester's Commonwealth,' pp. 481–83 and cited in Peck, p. 8.
14. Lee, p.41.
15. CP, vol III.

his parents' relationship as well as his own existence. It is impossible not to wonder if he read a copy of the Commonwealth during his childhood or his time as a student at Oxford.

Leicester continued to live his life between court, Wanstead, Leicester House and Kenilworth. Robin recorded in his memoirs that his father visited him on occasion. Even these brief visits were about to be curtailed. During the summer the earl went to Buxton to take the waters for recurring stomach and bowel pain[16] but there was trouble in the air. William of Orange, the Protestant champion of the Low Countries, was shot by a Catholic assassin on 10 July 1584. The Dutch offered Elizabeth the throne in return for continuing a military campaign against the Spanish. Leicester wanted to lead an army against the Duke of Parma who began a siege on Antwerp. Elizabeth prevaricated, refused to accept the proffered kingdom but was persuaded to offer military support to the Dutch in the form of an expedition led by Leicester.

Elizabeth did not want Leicester to go and she certainly did not wish Lettice to accompany him. It was the end of October by the time she agreed and December before the official order was handed to the earl. Leicester raised a loan to pay for the campaign and requisitioned arms from the Tower.[17] He eventually set out for Harwich on 8 December 1585. Amongst the English volunteers was Edmund Sheffield, Robin's step-brother, as well as his cousin Sir Philip Sidney and Lettice's eldest son Robert Devereux, the 2nd Earl of Essex. Leicester would return from the affair chastened and unwell. Whilst in the Netherlands Leicester made the mistake of accepting the title Governor-General in 1586 despite Elizabeth's instructions to the contrary. The queen's temper was not improved when Leicester advised her that she should take formal sovereignty of the Low Countries and spend more on her army. In addition to which, as time elapsed, Lettice decided to join her husband. On 11 February 1586, Leicester learned from his messenger, Thomas Dudley, a distant kinsman of his own and brother of John Dudley of Stoke Newington, that Lettice's plans to join her husband were known at court. Elizabeth, whose antipathy to the countess had not lessened with the passage of time or the loss of Lord Denbigh, was furious. It appeared

16. Wilson, p.336.
17. Ibid, p.338.

to her that Leicester was setting up his own court in the Low Countries. The earl's past ambitions were ready to trip him up and send Fortune's wheel spinning in a downwards motion if he was not on his guard. It was Robin's uncle, Lord Howard of Effingham, who refuted many of the charges that Elizabeth made against Leicester. This raises the question of whether Howard would have been so magnanimous if his sister, Douglas, was legally married and then deserted by the earl?

Worse was to follow. On 13 September the town of Zutphen which had been commandeered by the Spanish was placed under siege. Sir Philip Sidney was renowned for his bravery but on 22 September he was unhorsed during fighting at Zutphen. As he mounted a fresh horse, he was shot in the thigh with a musket ball. The wound turned gangrenous and he died on 17 October. Leicester, wracked with grief, returned to England with the body of his nephew in December. His relationship with the queen was sufficiently repaired for him to be awarded the post of Lord Steward of the Household. Leicester took the opportunity to take Essex to court to help to establish him by Elizabeth's side as a new favourite. As once Elizabeth and Leicester danced and hunted together so now Elizabeth and Leicester's stepson danced and hunted together. On 18 June 1586, Essex took Leicester's place as Elizabeth's Master of Horse.

There is no record of Leicester taking the opportunity to spend any time with Robin in Sussex on his return to England from the Low Countries. During his father's absence, loss of favour and bereavement, Robin continued his education. As well as his lessons, in his free time, he would have explored Cissbury Hill near Offington with its prehistoric monuments and tracks, legends of tunnels and walked down to the sea where he could have watched fishermen on the beach mending their nets and inhaled the salt air with its promise of adventure. At some point during the year, Leicester made a decision about the boy's continuing instruction. Either he saw, or Robin's tutors told him, that his son was interested in maritime exploration and navigation. The lure of the sea was not, Robin admitted later in life, far from his mind during his early years. Leicester set about finding a university tutor who would develop Robin's talents and continue an education that befitted the son of an earl.

As Robin prepared for life at university Walsingham and Cecil became more concerned than ever about Queen Elizabeth's safety. One of the plots to assassinate her involved Robin's step-uncle. Sir Edward

Stafford's younger brother, William, visited him secretly in Paris in 1585 but returned to England when he was found out. In 1587, he contacted the secretary of the French Ambassador Châteauneuf in London. Châteauneuf 's secretary, Leonard des Trappes, dismissed Stafford whose ill-devised scheme involved either gunpowder to blow the queen up in her bed or poison liberally applied to a personal possession. The plot involved a recusant called Moody who was formerly a servant of Sir Edward Stafford in Paris. Châteauneuf should have taken news of the intrigue to Burghley or Walsingham. Instead, he remained quiet which was a mistake. Both Moody and Stafford are known to have been in Walsingham's employment at one time or another. Stafford was arrested and implicated Châteauneuf in the plans to assassinate Elizabeth. The outcomes of the so-called conspiracy were that the guard around the queen was tightened; the French ambassador found his movements restricted and Walsingham was quietly able to raise the pressure being placed on the queen to order the execution of her cousin, Mary Stuart, without French intervention.

There was also the matter of Sir Edward Stafford himself. His ambassadorial role in Paris which spanned the years 1583 to 1590 was no sinecure being a crossroads for Protestant and Catholic ambassadors and exiles. It has been claimed that shortage of funds, latent Catholic sympathies or a desire for political prominence may have led to him being recruited by the Spanish in France.[18] He took money from Henry of Guise and also from the Spanish agent, Bernardino de Mendoza. He made contact with Mendoza through Douglas's cousin Charles Arundell in January 1587. It's probable that Stafford was the agent codenamed 'Julio'[19] by Mendoza or 'the new friend'.[20] The difficulty is knowing whether he was a double agent working on behalf of the queen or whether he actually did supply useful information to Philip II. It has been claimed that he passed information about Drake's Cadiz expedition, though it arrived in Spain too late to be of any use and besides which it is now accepted that Drake's attack on Cadiz was not planned so far in advance that Stafford could have known of it. In addition, he provided Spain with Lord Howard's instructions for the English fleet in December 1587. The

18. Leiman and Parker, p.1139.
19. Read:1915, p.107.
20. Ibid.

extent to which he might have known of his brother-in-law's plans are uncertain although according to Mendoza, Julio knew of the proposed strategy to defeat the Spanish in the winter of 1587 because Howard told him of it. The only difficulty with that is that Stafford was in France and Howard was in England.

Sir Edward was close to the privy chamber given the esteem in which Elizabeth held Stafford's mother, Lady Dorothy, who was one of her favourite companions. He was also protected by Burghley. Walsingham suspicious of Stafford, and wishing to control the flow of intelligence, had his own agents in Paris watching the ambassador's household. Amongst his spies were Sir Edward's own chaplain, Richard Hakluyt.[21] Walsingham is known to have intercepted the ambassador's correspondence on occasion and also to have kept him in ignorance of what was happening in England. Suspicions about Robin's stepfather are tangible but shrouded in a fog of double-dealing.

In 1587, Robin, fourteen years old, entered Christ Church College, Oxford. His status was entered as *filius comitis* or an Earl's son. Leicester's expenses for his son's education would have been greater than before, somewhere in the region of £250. One of the first things Robin was required to do was assent and subscribe to the Thirty-Nine Articles of the Anglican Church. The articles are the liturgical and doctrinal statement of the Church of England. The beliefs expressed in the Thirty-Nine Articles were agreed upon by a Church Convocation in 1563 based on the articles of Thomas Cranmer written in 1553. The articles upheld the supremacy of scripture for salvation and rejected various Catholic beliefs including transubstantiation or the change of the bread and wine into the body and blood of Christ during the Eucharist. In 1571, Parliament made adherence to the Thirty-Nine Articles a legal requirement for all clergymen. From 1573 onwards, this test of Anglican orthodoxy was applied to students taking their degree. After 1576, all students sixteen years and over were required to subscribe to the articles and from 1581, the rules were tightened so that all students made a declaration of their Anglican faith.

Leicester, who had been Chancellor of Oxford University since 1564, placed Robin in the care of Sir Thomas Chaloner the Younger who was

---

21. Haynes, p.41.

widely travelled. Of dubious legitimacy himself, Chaloner must have understood Robin's predicament. Chaloner's father was the English Ambassador in Spain from 1561 until 1565. He began his career under Protector Somerset. His support of Northumberland's plan to put Lady Jane Grey on the throne was well known. In 1558, when Elizabeth became queen, Chaloner the Elder benefitted not only from the fact that Elizabeth had known him when she was a young girl in Catherine Parr's household but because of Chaloner's friendship with Cecil. By 1563, as the relationship between England and Spain deteriorated, an increasing number of merchant seamen found themselves detained by the Spanish authorities having been captured at sea and their cargoes confiscated. It was Chaloner's responsibility to try and help them. He delayed his return to England in 1564, despite poor health, in order to remove some of the obstacles to their freedom. One strategy included a letter to Leicester asking for his intercession. The pair had previously encountered one another when Chaloner was required to bring back four horses for Elizabeth at the start of her reign.

Chaloner the Elder's delay in returning to England resulted in his son being born outside wedlock. Audrey Frodsham travelled to Spain in 1563 to meet him. She returned to England that summer whilst the ambassador delayed his journey in order to help the English prisoners. Chaloner was aware of his poor health and wished for an heir. A Protestant wedding could only occur on his return home. It is likely that the wedding took place in October 1565 but Chaloner the Younger was probably born towards the end of 1564. Chaloner the Elder, as Leicester would choose to do, wrote a will leaving his estate to his natural son. His brother Francis would have inherited the family estates had Chaloner not married Audrey who was pregnant with their son when she left Spain. In order to avoid a costly legal case and questions about the validity of the will, Cecil and six friends became trustees of Chaloner's estate to ensure that Audrey and young Thomas were protected from Thomas's thwarted uncle. Cleary then, Robin's tutor was a man who understood the difficulties of a complicated family and would have been able to offer a friendly ear to Robin whose own parents could be read about in the scurrilous *Leicester's Commonwealth*.

Chaloner the Younger, educated initially at St Paul's went on to study at Oxford but did not take his degree, preferring instead to travel. It was during this time in his life that his ties to Leicester began to develop. He accompanied the earl to the Low Countries on campaign in 1585 as a volunteer but there were already family connections. Henry Frodsham who was identified as a witness at Douglas and Leicester's wedding in 1573 was Chaloner's uncle. As well as learning mathematics, marine engineering and navigation from Chaloner, Robin's interest in science was also stimulated by his tutor. Chaloner took a particular interest in alum which was used as a mordant for fixing colours in woollen cloth. Whilst visiting Italy, Chaloner visited alum mines and recognised the shale deposits in which the alum was found as similar to the geology of his Guisborough estates. He would remain Robert's mentor and lifelong friend.

Chapter VII

Tilbury and Leicester's Death

The Spanish, irritated by England's interest in the New World and its policy of licencing piracy, edged closer to war. Matters were not helped when Sir Francis Drake burned twenty Spanish ships in the port of Cadiz. The execution of Mary Queen of Scots at Fotheringhay Castle on 8 February 1587 proved to be the tipping point. Philip II intended that his armada commanded by the Duke of Medina Sidonia would sail up the Channel to meet forces in the Spanish Netherlands led by the Duke of Parma. The combined navy and army would then invade England using 300 flat-bottomed barges to transport the Spanish army across the Channel. The armada would not invade when it arrived off the south coast of England. Medina Sidonia's job was to provide cover for Parma. The armada also had on board 18,500 troops from Spain who were to be held in reserve until the Duke of Parma landed his men.

By November the Privy Council had a plan to defend England from the Spanish. Elizabeth's cousin Henry Carey, Lord Hunsdon would protect London; the Earl of Huntington was charged with raising an army to protect the North of England; a third force would prevent a landing from the Channel whilst Leicester's role was to lead the men protecting Kent and Essex. In December there was a rumour that a Spanish fleet was in the English Channel. Before Christmas, Robin's uncle, Howard of Effingham, was appointed Lord Admiral. The fleet was put on standby. Edmund Sheffield, Robin's half-brother, captained the *White Bear* which was commissioned by Lord Howard and was later knighted by his uncle for his part in the campaign. Howard was to patrol the North Sea to protect the east coast whilst Drake's vessels were to keep watch on the west coast. Orders were issued that harbours and ships should be repaired. By the early summer of 1588, Elizabeth's financial reserves had declined to the extent that the fleet stood down and sailors were sent ashore to fend for themselves until the Spanish danger became more real.

The Spanish Armada set sail from Coruna on the 12 July and was sighted off the Lizard in Cornwall on 19 July. It was composed of approximately 150 vessels. Philip II thought that it would be unbeatable. As English seadogs readied themselves for war, England's militia which had been on standby since May began to assemble. Leicester took command of 8,000 men from the home counties at Tilbury. He sent instructions for his son to travel from Oxford. Robert Devereux, Earl of Essex and Robin's cousin, Sir Robert Sidney were also present. Leicester orders were to defend the Thames Estuary. He gave orders to barricade the Thames where it narrowed. Earthwork forts were thrown up at the same point.

The English fleet was forced back into harbour because of the wind but by 21 July Elizabeth's navy began to fire on the Spanish ships. Although they had fewer vessels, the English had the advantage of long-range guns. Lord Howard of Effingham, Robin's uncle and the commander of the English fleet, pursued the Spanish up the Channel until they reached Portland Bill where the Spanish were able to turn with the wind and counter-attack the English. On the evening of 27 July, the armada anchored off Calais. Medina Sidonia intended to wait for news of Parma and his army. They were shadowed by the English fleet. Unfortunately for the Spanish, Parma's men would not be able to embark for another week. And in any event, the flat-bottomed barges that Parma had requisitioned were not sturdy enough to withstand the rigours of a sea crossing. The following night the English sent eight fireships in amongst the armada still anchored off Calais. The Spanish cut their anchor cables but, in the darkness, ships collided with one another and scattered.

Much of the armada including the vessel carrying Medina Sidonia were driven north-west by the winds towards Dunkirk. The English took advantage of the disorganisation the following morning and engaged the Spanish. The Battle of Gravelines was hard-fought and lasted most of the day. Both fleets used all their ammunition. That afternoon the wind changed direction. The Spanish fleet found itself being blown towards the North Sea pursued by the English. During the next two days, the armada regrouped but when they tried to turn on the 31 July to make another attempt to join with the Duke of Parma, the prevailing winds prevented them.

1. *The Dudley family crest* carved by John Dudley, Earl of Warwick during his imprisonment in the Tower 1554 (engraving, Nineteenth Century) J Fry, after a drawing by F Nash.

YOW THAT THESE BEASTS DO WEL BEHOLD AND SE
MAY DEME WORE EASE WHERFORE HERE MADE THEY BE
WITE BORDERS EKE WHERIN
4 BROTHERS NAMES WHO LIST TO SERCHE THE GROUND

2. Title page, book six, *Dell'Arcano del Mare* (engraving, 1647) by Antonio Francesco Lucini.

3. *Robert Dudley, 1st Earl of Leicester* (engraving, 1586) by Hendrick Goltzius.

4. *Queen Elizabeth I 'The Ditchley Portrait'* (oil on canvas, circa 1592) by Marcus Gheeraerts the Younger.

5. *Thomas Cavendish* (print, c.1595–1597) by Jodocus Hondius.

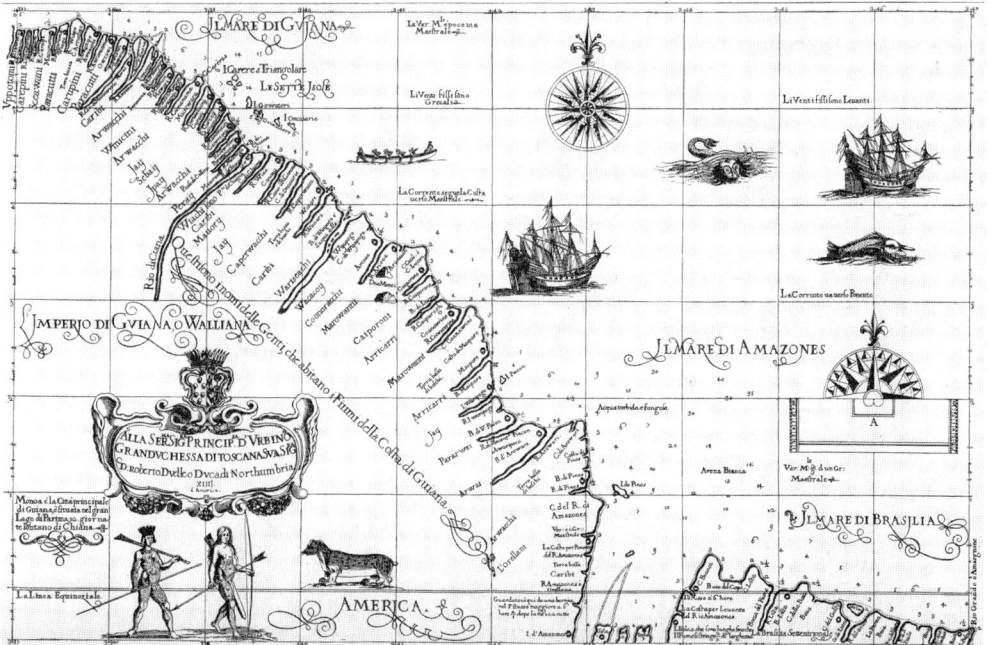

6. Map for the North East coast of South America covering Guiana in *Dell'Arcano del Mare* (engraving, 1647) by Antonio Francesco Lucini.

7. *Battle of Cadiz* (printed on paper, 1600–1601) by Bartholomeus Willemsz.

8. *Astrolabe*, (brass c.1597) by Johannes Bos.

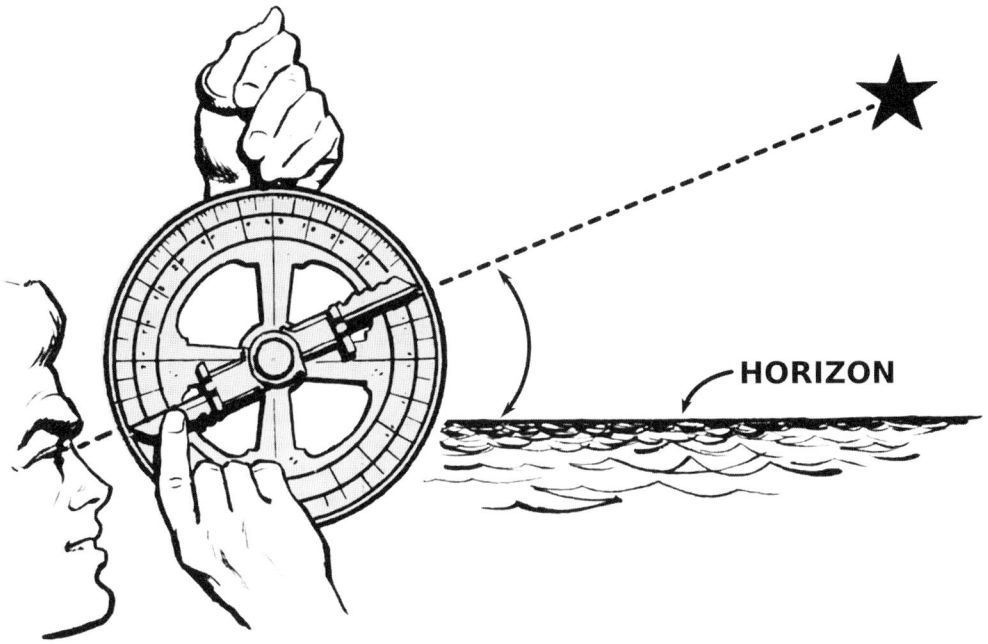

9. *Diagram showing the use of an astrolabe.*

FERD. MED. MAGN. DVX ETRVRIÆ III.

10. *Ferdinando I de Medici, Grand Duke of Tuscany* (printed, circa 1589) by Agostino Carracci.

11. *Restoring the Aqueduct in Pisa, from the Life of Ferdinand I de' Medici* (engraving, 1614–1620) by Jacques Callot.

12. *Cosimo II de Medici, Grand Duke of Tuscany* (oil on canvas, 1597–1681) from the Workshop of Justus Sustermans.

13. *Lady Frances Kniveton*, St-Giles-in-the-Fields (chest tomb in white marble, c.1663) by Joshua or Edward Marshall.

14. *Lady Katherine Leveson*, (oil on canvas, 1625) by Cornelius Jansen.

15. *Countess Teresa Dudley de Carpegna*, (oil on canvas, 1654), by Justus Sustermans.

Leicester took the opportunity afforded by his appointment as commander of the queen's army to commission his son as a Colonel of Foot under the supervision of another officer.[1] Warfare was part of a nobleman's education and by now the earl had taken steps to ensure that Robin would inherit his estates if not his titles. Leicester appointed Essex as commander of the cavalry in 1585 when he was just twenty years old. It may have been that Leicester intended to promote his natural son's interests at court in exactly the same way that he had promoted his stepson's a few years earlier but time was no longer on Leicester's side. The earl who had been going to Buxton for years to cure his ailments was increasingly unwell.

Elizabeth I arrived at Tilbury by barge at the invitation of Leicester on 8 August. Earlier in the month, she moved from her palace at Richmond to St James' which was more defensible but now Leicester wanted her to be seen. She was clothed in white velvet and wore a silver cuirass. On disembarking from the royal barge, she mounted a grey gelding and was led through the camp by Leicester on one side of her and the Earl of Essex on the other so that she could inspect her army. Robin both saw and heard the queen that day and the next when she gave her famous speech, the words of which were recorded by Leicester's chaplain, Lionel Sharpe. According to Burghley, the ranks of soldiers were so moved by Elizabeth's words that they broke into spontaneous applause. Leicester, the creator of courtly pageants, created a spectacle that would be remembered for centuries.

Afterwards, the queen went to dinner in Leicester's tent with her women. Just as the meal began, George Clifford, Earl of Cumberland, arrived with the news that Lord Howard had pursued the Spanish beyond Harwich where he had to turn back when his supplies and shot were exhausted. By 12 August, the Spanish fleet had no option but to continue to sail north, around Scotland and home. Storms pursued them and many ships foundered either off the coast of Scotland or Ireland. It was October before the surviving vessels managed to make their way home. The night after the defeat of the armada, Leicester presented Robin to Elizabeth. She had promised to protect him as a child when she learned of the earl's

---

1. Lee, p.43.

marriage to Lettice. It was a timely reminder of Robin's existence and the fact that he was turning into a handsome young man with many talents.

As the camp at Tilbury disbanded Leicester took his son with him. At London, their ways parted. Lettice awaited the earl at Leicester House and Robin was never welcome in Lettice's presence. One of Robin's extended family may have provided him with somewhere to stay. It is plausible that he could have lodged with the Earl of Pembroke. Henry Herbert was married to Leicester's niece, Mary Sidney. Robin is known to have visited the couple on other occasions as an adult. On 20 August Robin would have gone to St Paul's to attend the service of thanksgiving and on 26 August been at a military review in Whitehall which included jousting. The Earl of Essex was paired against the Earl of Cumberland. It was Sir Henry Lee's job, as Queen's Champion, to organise tilts and the pageantry which accompanied them. Robin, along with the rest of the spectators would have enjoyed the sight of the best of Lee's 'sons of chivalry' competing against one another.

Robin travelled back to Oxford. Leicester set out to take the waters at Buxton once more. His health was still deteriorating. His plan was to stop at Kenilworth before continuing his journey. He became increasingly unwell and broke his journey at Rycote where he wrote a brief note to Elizabeth in which he described himself as 'your poor old servant' before moving on to Cornbury House. The story was told in a letter by the Genoese merchant Marco Antonio Micea sent to Philip II:

> On the 27th [of August 1588] the earl of Leicester started for the baths of Buxton, but on the way, in the house of a gentleman near Oxford, it is said he supped heavily, and being troubled with distress in the stomach during the night he forced himself to vomit. This brought on a tertian fever, which increased to such an extent on the third day that on Wednesday, 4th [September], at ten o'clock in the morning, he expired.[2]

The official cause of Leicester's death was malaria but the recurring stomach condition that troubled his later years has led some historians to consider stomach cancer as a potential cause of death.

---

2. Whitlock, p.252 and CSP Simancas, p.481.

As Leicester's body was washed and wrapped in its shroud before being placed in a coffin, a messenger spurred his horse towards London. The Spanish ambassador described Elizabeth's grief when the news reached her:

> The Queen is sorry for his death ... She was so grieved that for some days she shut herself in her chamber alone, and refused to speak to anyone until the Treasurer and other Councillors had the doors broken open and entered to see her.[3]

The note that Leicester sent from Rycote became a treasured memento labelled, 'His Last Letter'. At the end of nearly four decades of friendship and mutual loyalty, despite the bickering, the depths of Elizabeth's love for Robert Dudley, Earl of Leicester, was finally revealed. His letter did not need to bear a name or a title. For the queen, there was no one else but him.

The previous year Leicester expressed a wish to lie in Warwick along with his ancestors and his legitimate son. He was buried in the Collegiate Church of St Mary in Warwick near the tomb of Lord Denbigh on 10 October. The funeral cortege included the scullery maid from Wanstead but neither Elizabeth nor Robin attended. For Elizabeth, it would have been against protocol but there was the consolation that Lettice would not be in attendance either as it would have been against the conventions of the period. The Earl of Essex, who was Leicester's chief mourner, and Leicester's brother-in-law, the Earl of Huntingdon, are recorded as being present but there is no record of Robin.

Once it became clear that Lettice would have no more children, Leicester might have considered acknowledging his only living child as his legitimate son but to do that he would have had to admit that he was guilty of bigamy. There was also the small matter of both Lettice's and Elizabeth's reaction to such an eventuality. Leicester was in the habit of referring to Robin as his 'base son and the badge of my sin'.[4] His will used similar language but an indenture of February 1588 refers to Robin as his 'reputed bastard son' which leaves some room for doubt.[5]

---

3. CSP Simancas, pp.425–432.
4. Lee, p.34.
5. Temple Leader, pp.159–166.

Chapter VIII

The Bear's Whelp

Elizabeth grieved for Leicester. Her 'Eyes' as she called him was gone. She transferred some of her affections to his handsome stepson, Robert Devereux, the 2nd Earl of Essex. Gristwood describes Essex as 'Leicester's stepson and surrogate'.[1] Despite being thirty-four years younger than Elizabeth, Essex deployed flirtation and flattery in exactly the same way that Leicester once did. Many historians have pointed out that Elizabeth indulged the flamboyant and ambitious Essex forgiving him on many occasions when other men might have found themselves in a prison cell. She also kept an eye on Leicester's natural son. It helped that on the very day that Leicester died, Robin's mother Lady Douglas Sheffield returned from Paris to resume her life at court. Catherine de Medici wrote to Elizabeth commending Douglas to her and took the opportunity as well to wish that Elizabeth and her subjects might be good Catholics. More practically, Charles Howard made arrangements for his sister to be escorted home. Aboard *The Rainbow*, Lord Henry Seymour wrote to the admiral that since Douglas was expected at Dieppe after 26 August, a command had been issued for *The Achates* 'to clear the coasts of some pilling knaves, and to transport my Lady'.[2] Seymour did not convey Lady Sheffield home himself because sickness broke out on his ship. Douglas, accompanied by her husband's chaplain, Richard Hakluyt, arrived home in September and took up the reins of her old life.

The earl's death did not soften Elizabeth's attitude to his widow. Lettice found herself in financial difficulties because she was her husband's executrix and so liable for Leicester's debts, totalling £50,000, much of which he accrued financing the campaign in the Low Countries. She was assisted by Warwick who bore some of the liability, Leicester's old friend

---

1. Gristwood, p.433.
2. CSP Domestic, Elizabeth, pp.529–541.

Sir Christopher Hatton who became Lord Chancellor in 1587 and also by Charles Howard.[3] Whatever passed between Leicester and Douglas did not impact on the friendship that existed between the two men.

Elizabeth required that the £25,000 Leicester borrowed from her for the Low Countries campaign should be returned. She focused her attention on Lettice who inherited the manors of Wanstead, Drayton Bassett, Balsall and Long Itchington as well as jewellery and half the contents of Leicester House. The other half of the contents being Robin's. Elizabeth's bailiffs sequestrated lands that Lettice expected to control and sold off Leicester's art collection. Wanstead, which was heavily mortgaged, was taken as well. In theory, Leicester provided Lettice with a jointure worth £3,000 a year along with £6,000 of plate and furniture but as well as Leicester's debts, there were also a series of costly legal battles to be fought. She sold Leicester House on the Strand to her son even though it was only hers during her lifetime. In future, it would be known as Essex House. By contrast, although the Earl of Warwick faced some debt as an executor of his brother's will, the queen released most of the land which was destined for Robin without financial constraint.

Leicester had made a settlement on 6 February 1586 providing for Robin's future. The greater part of his estates, including the castle and estate at Kenilworth as well as the Lordships of Denbigh and Chirk, were bequeathed to Robin although Warwick would enjoy them during his lifetime. This avoided Robin becoming a ward of the Crown. Leicester began Elizabeth's reign with very little but ended his life as one of the most important landowners in the country. Elizabeth granted him lands in the Midlands, Wales, York, Essex, Hertfordshire, Middlesex and Bedfordshire – these would come into the hands of Robin when he came of age or when his uncle died. In the event of Robin dying before he reached twenty years of age and without heirs of his own, everything went to Leicester's nephew, Robert Sidney, and his stepson, the Earl of Essex. In the usual course of things, Sidney would have been the earl's principal heir rather than Robin. In matters of common law illegitimate children had no inheritance rights. In both Robin's case, and Chaloner the Younger's, their respective fathers named and specifically provided for their natural sons by legal settlement. There are other examples of

---

3. Lee, p.50.

leaving the bulk of an estate to a base-born son where there were no legitimate children to inherit. In 1558, for instance, Sir John Byron left his estates to his illegitimate son John. Nor was it uncommon for some settlement to be made for natural children but analysis of a set of northern wills covering this period in history suggests that illegitimate beneficiaries were more likely to benefit from fixed amounts of money rather than land.[4] Besides which, Leicester was not simply a local magnate whose son would be absorbed into gentry life. He was one of the most powerful men in the country with extensive land holdings. Despite the fact that he describes Robin as illegitimate in his will, it is impossible to avoid speculation about Leicester's motives in naming Robin rather than his nephew Robert Sidney who would have been the more conventional beneficiary.

The significance of Robin's inheritance is further amplified by the contents of his uncle's will written on 28 January 1590. Ambrose Dudley, Earl of Warwick, left dower lands to his third wife Anne, the daughter of Lord Russell and arranged for trustees to pay his debts. Like Leicester, Ambrose regarded Sir Philip Sidney as his heir. After Sidney's death at Zutphen, much of Ambrose's estate along with the lands that had passed to him from Leicester were bequeathed to Robin rather than Sir Philip's brother Robert. Warwick had always been close to his brother and was one of Robin's guardians when he was a child but for Ambrose to also bypass his nephew Robert Sidney, who was ten years older than Leicester's boy, must have been as surprising at the time as it is today.

It is thought that Elizabeth I, who was fond of him, visited Ambrose at Bedford House in the Strand before he died, having had his leg amputated when gangrene set in. He had been shot by the French at Le Havre in 1562 and by the end of his life could barely walk. No one knows what they discussed. Two days before he died on 21 February 1590, Ambrose received a visit from Robin's stepfather, Sir Edward Stafford. Warwick entrusted Stafford to look after Robin's interests. Lord Howard of Effingham, Robin's maternal uncle, was nominated as the boy's other guardian. Later Stafford would say that Ambrose selected him rather than Sir Henry Lee who was Robin's godfather because Lee was too preoccupied with his own pleasures.

---

4. Carlton and Thornton, pp.23–40.

After Warwick's death, it did not take long for an inheritance dispute to bubble to the surface. Lettice's new husband Sir Christopher Blount forced his way into Kenilworth which Lettice thought ought to be hers and remained there until the Earl of Huntingdon reported the matter on his nephew's behalf. An order from the Privy Council was issued to the justices of the peace for Warwickshire requiring the eviction of Blount and his servants. Lettice's jointure included several manors surrounding Kenilworth but she removed belongings from the castle including, it was later claimed, records from the so-called 'evidence house'. The dispute rumbled across the next decade.

There is no known record of Robin ever being a Ward of Court which is unexpected as his inheritance was large and he was a minor. Elizabeth was entitled, as a feudal due, to take a profit from his wardship and potential marriage. The Court of Wards' role was to extract revenue for the Crown from the sale of wardships which included the right of marriage and to arrange leases for wards' lands. Burghley was the Master of the Court of Wards. He bought only two wardships himself but he held several important wardships during his life including the earls of Oxford, Surrey, Southampton and Essex. He did not retain possession of a wardship for Robin. Hatton, the Lord Chancellor, may have taken a hand in matters as might the Howard family but it seems just as likely that Elizabeth, from a distance, looked after the financial wellbeing of Leicester's boy.

Whereas Leicester's acknowledged widow was not welcome at court, Elizabeth made sure that Robin's mother Douglas was in her presence. She took up service as a Gentlewoman of the Privy Chamber. If Robin had lost one line of access to the queen, another opened up. Douglas obtained permission for her son to come to court to visit her, enabling Elizabeth to keep her eye on him. Robin may have resumed his Oxford studies after his father's death but he now began to live in Kenilworth Castle. Robin was Leicester's son in both looks and intelligence. He was welcome at court but did not receive the preferment that he might have enjoyed under his father's patronage. Instead, his education as a courtier began. Sir Henry Lee, Robin's godfather and the queen's own champion, may have taught the boy to joust when he stayed at Lee's Oxfordshire home of Ditchley. Now during the annual Ascension Day tournaments, Lee introduced the boy to the Tudor court's tilting fraternity and the chivalric codes of the tourney. He may have grown to know the Earl of Essex better as well. Devereux remained devoted to Leicester's memory and he was a tournament champion.

Robin, a handsome and wealthy seventeen year old, was soon smitten by Frances Vavasour of Coppenthorpe who came to court as one of Elizabeth's maids.[5] He would have known Frances' sister Anne from his visits to his godfather at Ditchley. Sir Henry Lee and his wife, Anne Paget, were not happily married. However, at some point in the 1580s, Lee became enamoured of Anne Vavasour describing her as 'his dearest deare'.[6] One clue to the exact date for the start of their relationship is the monogram AV which appears on the armour that Lee used in his role as Master of the Horse in the north of England.[7] He was in his fifties. She was scarcely out of her teens; the ex-mistress of the Earl of Oxford and a disgraced maid-of-honour having given birth to Oxford's child in the Maidens' Chamber opposite Elizabeth's own quarters.[8] Lee never seems to have faced the queen's wrath for separating from his wife, who died in 1590, and living with Anne who was married for appearance's sake to a sea captain called Finch alias Freeman. Sir Henry kept all his appointments and was visited by Elizabeth at his home in Ditchley during the summer progress of 1592 when he presented her with the so-called Ditchley Portrait during a pageant that explored the twists and turns of love. Anne's misalliance with Oxford and its associated scandal meant she would never be welcome in Elizabeth's presence but she and Lee lived together until his death in 1611. Their son Thomas did not take Lee's name in the way that Robin took the name Dudley but Lee did acknowledge Thomas and secure him a position as Yeoman of the Armoury in 1608.

The proposed match between Arbella Stuart and Robin came to nothing after Leicester's death. Charles Paget, a double agent in exile, wrote to London to find out about the girl's marriage prospects 'seeing that Leicester's intention to match his bastard son with her is by his death made frustrate'.[9] Robin was free to ask Frances to marry him. She

5. Temple Leader, p.166 and Warner, p.ix.
6. Simpson, p.148.
7. Ibid, p.152.
8. Lee, p.52.
9. Ibid.

agreed and after some hesitation, the queen accepted the proposed union on condition that they wait until Robin, who was younger than Frances, was older. Later Robert would testify that the couple had engaged in a verbal contract to marry in the presence of witnesses making his own first and second marriages bigamous as she was still alive when he contracted them. Whatever happened in private, the marriage did not go ahead in public. Sir Thomas Shirley, a soldier and adventurer, recently returned from a campaign in Ireland, began an affair with Frances. It was him that she married. The pair kept their union so well hidden that Shirley was able to court Frances Brooke, Lady Stourton, the daughter of Lord Cobham and sister-in-law of Robert Cecil, without suspicion. In September 1591, Frances' marriage to Shirley was uncovered. Suffice it to say, Elizabeth was unamused by their behaviour. Frances was banished from court for her conduct and Shirley, having offended the queen, the Cobhams and the Cecils, found himself imprisoned in the Marshalsea for fourteen weeks. Robin's thoughts are not recorded but he does not seem to have been much affected by his disappointment.

Robin was soon attracted to Margaret Cavendish, the cousin of explorer, Thomas Cavendish, who became the second Englishman to circumnavigate the globe in 1586. This fact might have been part of Margaret's initial charm to Robin. She was also the sister-in-law of Richard Hakluyt, the chaplain who spied upon Sir Edward Stafford whilst he was the English Ambassador in Paris. Hakluyt's family connections to Robin were complex. On his return to England, Hakluyt became the rector of Wetheringsett and Brockford in Suffolk. The living for these parishes lay in the hands of Robin's mother, Lady Sheffield. Hakluyt's first wife was Douglas Cavendish, and, perhaps, a goddaughter of Douglas herself. Robin's intentions towards Margaret were very publicly demonstrated in October 1591 when he kissed the young maid-of-honour in the presence chamber in front of the queen which was against all protocol. Elizabeth banished Robin from court for two months having chastised him for his actions.[10] He, undeterred by his sovereign's wrath, explained that he wished to marry Margaret. Given that his exclusion was only two months, and that he was given a chance to explain himself without having his ears boxed or anything thrown at him, Elizabeth must have approved both

10. Ibid, p.53.

the match and Robin. It also demonstrates that Robin, who was at the margins of court life, was not required to be eternally devoted to Gloriana in the way that the Earl of Essex relied on his flirtation with the queen for both financial and political gain.

Robin's offence in kissing Margaret was mild in comparison to that of Sir Francis Darcy who seduced Katherine Legh. The unfortunate girl gave birth the week after the queen caught Robin kissing Margaret. Mrs Elizabeth Jones, the so-called 'Mother of the Maids' whose job it was to supervise the maids-of-honour, was dismissed and sent to the Tower along with Katherine and Darcy who was one of Essex's cronies. Elizabeth's exasperation with the love lives of her courtiers rose a notch in May 1592 when it became clear that Sir Walter Raleigh, who was in Falmouth preparing for a voyage, was secretly married to Elizabeth's lady-in-waiting, Bess Throckmorton, and that she had given birth in secret to a son before resuming her duties. Raleigh did not help matters by delaying his return to court and when he did, he compounded his offence by lying. Like Leicester before him, Raleigh was reliant on his relationship with the queen for his position and wealth but like Leicester, his thoughts turned to marriage and an heir. Raleigh fell in love with Bess, they married in secret as Leicester may have done with Douglas, and had attempted to do when he married Lettice. It was not long before the new parents found themselves under house arrest and by August, in separate cells in the Tower, demonstrating that Leicester's fears for his own private relationships had not been unfounded. Nor can it have helped that Raleigh who was supposed to be devoted to Elizabeth had been rewarded with Sherbourne Castle at the beginning of the year. Raleigh was saved only with the capture of a Portuguese treasure carrack from which the queen took a massive profit and by Raleigh's suddenly wealthy and somewhat riotous sailors who refused to take orders from anyone but him.

Robin began his career as a maritime backer during the same period as his youthful romance with Frances Vavasour withered and his love for Margaret Cavendish blossomed before he got himself into trouble for kissing her. Thomas Cavendish and Robin became friends. He told Robin stories of the China trade, the walled Muslim city of Manilla and a hold full of plunder. Before long Robin offered to back Cavendish's next voyage to the South Seas, the Philippines and China. One of the vessels that he equipped was the 400-ton *Leicester*. John Davis, the inventor of the Davis quadrant, joined with Cavendish in the venture as part of his continuing search for the North-West Passage through the Arctic, linking the Atlantic and Pacific Oceans. The voyage of 1591 was disastrous. Five ships containing 350 men left Plymouth in August 1591. The *Daintie* returned to England laden with plunder after Cavendish and his men sacked Santos in Brazil. The rest of the fleet reached the Strait of Magellan by March the following year. They faced fierce storms that Cavendish described as 'not durable for Christians'.[11] After two months they were low on provisions, forty of the crew died and the rest were ravaged by sickness. The men mutinied and Cavendish set a course back to Brazil. The *Leicester* and *Roebuck* went in one direction whilst the *Desire* and the *Black Prince* were separated from Cavendish one dark night. Cavendish died at sea near Ascension Island in May 1592 having written his will and an account of the voyage. Davis returned home aboard the *Desire* which Cavendish bequeathed to Sir George Carey who also happened to be Lettice's first cousin.

Robin's interests in the sea were no doubt nurtured by Margaret Cavendish's brother-in-law, Richard Hakluyt, as well as the stories of Thomas Cavendish. Hakluyt's writing, supported by Sir Francis Walsingham in the first instance, promoted a strong navy and English colonisation of the Americas. He was fascinated by cosmography, maps and accounts of voyages to new lands. He would have been able to provide Robin with a core of knowledge. As well as being able to access information about Thomas Cavendish's circumnavigation, Hakluyt was also in correspondence with Mercator and John Dee who also promoted the concept of empire. Robin's desire to become an explorer grew stronger than ever. He later recorded that:

> He determined at any cost to enter the marine army, on which at that time the reputation and greatness of England depended … he gave himself to the study of navigation, and of marine discipline and war.[12]

The *Leicester* and *Roebuck* limped back to Portsmouth with news that Cavendish's venture had failed. The Privy Council issued a warrant with

---

11. Quinn, ed., p.16.
12. Warner, ed., p.xiii.

a letter on 18 March 1593 for Robin, an executor of Cavendish's will, to present to the Mayor and officers of the Port of Portsmouth.[13] Not only was Cavendish dead but Robin must have lost a great deal of money in the venture. The disaster was not enough to deter Robin, now married to Margaret, from sharing his plans for a voyage of his own with the queen. Perhaps if he had a guardian to restrain his youthful enthusiasm, or his friend Chaloner had been at hand to counsel him, he might have waited. As it stood, Robin was independent and Chaloner was in Scotland in the Court of James VI where he had been sent by Burghley.

13. Lee, p.56.

Chapter IX

An Adventure

R obin was not yet twenty years of age when he asked Elizabeth's permission to undertake his own voyage to the South Seas. His early years had been spent by the sea at Offington; Leicester and Warwick were the patrons of cartographers and explorers; his friends and family shared his interests in navigation, ships and exploration. Robin began his account of his own voyage of 1594 with the words, 'Having ever since I could conceive of anything, been delighted with the discoveries of navigation, I fostered in myself that disposition until I was of more years and better ability to undertake such a matter.'[1]

At the end of his life, he would recall that he came from a family line that included three Grand Admirals of England; on his mother's side of the family his grandfather William, Lord Howard of Effingham, and more famously his uncle, Charles. John Dudley, Duke of Northumberland, on his father's side also held the title. Leicester and Warwick shared a passion for discovery and adventure that potentially had its roots in John Dee's childhood cosmography lessons. Dee was convinced colonial expansion was essential to safeguard England's future as it was a way of keeping Spain in check. The Crown and Privy Council were also persuaded on the importance of exploration and settlement by men such as Richard Hakluyt. William Cunningham's *The Cosmographical Glass, Containing the Pleasant Principles of Cosmography, Geography, Hydrography and Navigation* written in 1559 was dedicated to Leicester whilst John Montgomery dedicated a text on the navy to him.[2] Surviving inventories from Kenilworth reveal that Leicester owned twenty-three maps. Navigation and scientific instruments were not only of interest mathematically but politically as well.

---

1. Warner, ed, p.67.
2. Stedall, p.118.

Warwick and Leicester also invested in colonial expansion because the profits could be lucrative. In 1576, both of them invested £20 each in Martin Frobisher's voyage in search of the North-West Passage to the Pacific. Leicester backed John Hawkins' voyage in 1562 to Sierra Leone. Hawkins was commissioned by Elizabeth as a privateer looking for Spanish ships to plunder but profited by shipping slaves to the West Indies in return for sugar, pearls, hides and ginger. His foray into the triangular trade resulted in Leicester joining with the Earl of Pembroke to invest in Hawkins' second voyage in 1564. Spanish colonists were encouraged to trade with Hawkins at gunpoint. In 1577, Leicester provided financial backing for Drake's circumnavigation of the globe. In 1581, the earl commissioned a forty-gun vessel named the *Galleon Leicester* from Matthew Baker at the royal dockyards in Deptford.[3]

Having inherited maps, knowledge, contacts and wealth from both his father and his uncle, Robin was able to undertake an expensive voyage of exploration without the need for numerous investors. He sought out Matthew Baker, Master of the Shipwright's Company. Howard of Effingham was also one of Baker's patrons. Both Robin and his uncle were interested in Baker's galleon designs. Robin had the means to build his own fleet as well as inheriting Thomas Cavendish's vessels. Rather than outfitting his ships at the busy dockyards, Robin opted for Southampton in order to complete the outfitting of his fleet of four vessels more quickly. He acquired ships and men so that by the summer of 1594, he was ready to follow in Drake's and Cavendish's wake with the intention of rounding the Strait of Magellan into the South Seas and from there to circumnavigate the globe. In addition to outfitting his fleet, he also had the support of his uncle Lord Howard of Effingham. At court, Douglas and Catherine Howard, the admiral's wife and Elizabeth's lifelong friend and companion spoke to the queen on Robin's behalf.

At the beginning of the year, Elizabeth's memories of Leicester had caused her to worry about another of the earl's scions. Sir Robert Sidney, on an embassy to France, aboard the *Tramontana* experienced a stormy crossing followed by a narrow escape due to the arrival of 5,000 Spanish troops in Brittany. There were a number of Spanish bases on the coast including Brest and Blavet. They were seized by Catholics and the

---

3. Wilson, p.294.

Duc de Mercoeur during the Wars of the Three Henris which erupted between the Catholics and the Protestants in France during the summer of 1584 when Henri of Navarre, who was a Protestant, became heir to the French throne. Philip II took the opportunity to garrison coastal bases with Spanish troops and harass English and Dutch shipping in the Channel. The English deployed ground forces in order to dislodge the Spanish from a position that would be useful to them for a renewed invasion attempt. Elizabeth wrote:

Robin, when I remember from whom you be descended and to whom you appertained, I cannot but yield my humblest thanks to Him from whom all goodness comes, for your narrow escape from so dangerous mischance and do wish that this may be your last hazardous danger.[4]

If she worried about Leicester's nephew, how much more precious to her was his son? In October 1594, Robin came to court accompanied by Captain Wyatt. Elizabeth, it transpired, did not think that Leicester's boy was old enough to voyage into the South Seas and bid him wait. No matter how much the queen would have liked to be involved in a lucrative trade in silk and spices, she would not endanger Robin with either a voyage around Cape Horn or through the Strait of Magellan with their associated risks of storms, disease and starvation.

Robin later recalled that 'I could not be suffered to hazard more of her Majesty's subjects upon so uncertain a ground as my desire'.[5] Instead, recognising the amount of money already spent on the venture and perhaps not wanting to disappoint the young man who looked so much like her own Sweet Robin, she agreed to a shorter and less dangerous voyage to the West Indies which would take him to Trinidad and Guiana. She noted 'that experience might work a most excellent perfection in him'.

The voyage was no sinecure. Sir Walter Raleigh was planning an expedition to explore Guiana and the River Orinoco in search of the fabled city of El Dorado that would depart at the same time as Robin's venture. It is possible that the queen envisaged that the two fleets would

4. CSP Foreign, List 5, pp.378–380.
5. Lee, p.59.

link up and that Robin would be mentored by her erstwhile favourite. Raleigh's voyage was delayed at the last minute. Later, well versed in the art of self-promotion, he made little or no mention of Robin's maiden voyage which charted the same seas as his own. Raleigh followed in Robin's wake three months behind him, arriving in Trinidad ten days after Robin's fleet left the island for the last time.

Robin became one of Elizabeth I's seadogs when she issued him with a Letter of Marque. It meant that he could take and plunder vessels belonging to the enemy. Any return that Robin made on his voyage would be shared between him, his captains, his crew and the Crown. Privateering subsidised crown income and meant that Elizabeth did not have to maintain a navy commensurate to the Spanish fleet. Privateers weakened Spain by attacking its boats and stealing its wealth and so far as Elizabeth was concerned even paid for the privilege. There are three accounts of the voyage that spanned six months; Robin's own account, Captain Wyatt and Abraham Kendall's. Wyatt's account desired to proclaim Robin's virtues. It was a commendation for future voyages. Kendall's version of events stated that the purpose was 'to explore Guiana' but Robin's own explanation suggested that the voyage was to gain the experience that Elizabeth deemed that he lacked. He said that he was not in search of profit but the 'lure of a Spanish prize should not be underestimated'.[6] As with most things the truth was probably more complicated. Robin wanted prizes and fame of the kind associated with Drake and Raleigh but he also wanted to be the master of his own ship and sail into uncharted waters.

Robin enlisted his crew of 140 men. They included Captain Wyatt who kept his own account of the voyage and Captain Thomas Jobson of Colchester, a cousin of Robin's who served as his lieutenant. The Duke of Northumberland was Jobson's maternal uncle. He was older than Robin and more experienced. He served under Drake at San Domingo. Other officers included Captain Benjamin Wood who had been the master of the *Wild Man* when John Chudleigh made an unsuccessful attempt to circumnavigate the globe in 1589. He had also sailed to the Americas on previous occasions including the Roanoke Expedition. In 1592, he commanded four ships sent on a privateering expedition by Lord Thomas

---

6. Warner, ed., p.69.

Howard off the coast of Cuba which cemented his reputation as a privateer. Abraham Kendall was a veteran navigator who mentored Robin's own course-plotting skills during the journey. Kendall, who sailed with Drake as well as Frobisher, was one of the best-known navigators of his time and was the Earl of Cumberland's principal sailing master. In 1589, he deserted from a voyage off of the Guiana coast with a pinnace which he and his crew sailed home to Barry in Wales where he sold the vessel. He was a ruthless privateer who kept his and his captains' secrets. It was said that in order to prevent someone from dying on one of his vessels that he marooned the man on St Helena in 1591.

The largest of the four vessels, commanded by Robin, was called the *Bear* – a reference to Leicester's heraldic device – the bear and ragged staff. Robin's captain, Wyatt, called the same boat the *Peregrine*. Accounts of the *Bear*'s tonnage differ. Dudley gives her size at 200 tons; Wyatt makes the boat smaller at 180 tons and Kendall states it to be much larger at 300 tons. Robin described the *Bear* in more detail in the *Arcano del Mare*, his atlas of the sea, saying that she was a '*galeone riformato*' carrying thirty guns. Both he and Wyatt commented on the *Bear*'s speed in their separate accounts. In later years, Robin would use his experience of the *Bear* to work on designs for faster galleons. The second vessel in Robin's little fleet was the *Bear's Whelp* commanded by Captain Monck. The ship, perhaps named with a wry nod to Robin himself, was somewhere between 80 and 140 tons. The other two vessels were pinnaces named the *Earwig* and the *Frisking*. These boats were to serve as tenders. Wyatt's account mentions a fifth vessel, the *Mermaid* of 100 tons which was left at Southampton. There is no further reference to it.

Having prepared for the expedition and sent his servants on ahead, Robin travelled from London to Southampton where he and his companions received Holy Communion on Sunday 3 November. Afterwards, his officers dined with him. The fleet weighed anchor on 6 November 1594, crossing to Hythe on the Western side of Southampton Water. Whilst there the fleet took on supplies. The weather was rough so Robin remained until 16 November when the wind changed direction. Even then he delayed departure until the following day because it was the anniversary of the queen's accession to the throne. As the fleet sailed from Southampton Water into the Solent, they fired their cannon in celebration. The queen's own ordinance replied from Calshot Castle.

The *Bear* anchored under the castle because of the ebb of the tide. The *Earwhig* and the *Frisking* went ahead.

The last of Robin's fleet arrived in Plymouth on 19 November. Whilst they waited, possibly for Raleigh, Robin arranged to rendezvous with George Popham, a cousin of Anne Dudley's husband Francis Popham, at Trinidad if possible. On 21 November, Robin's crews set a course for the Canaries. Robin noted his passage through the Needles in his memoirs and the fact that he was driven back to port by storms. The *Bear* and her pinnace returned to Plymouth whilst the *Bear's Whelp* found safe harbour in Falmouth. Robin sent instructions to Monck by land that he should meet with them in the Canaries or failing that Cape Blanco on the Western coast of Africa.

Robin set off once more on 1 December, this time losing his pinnace when it was swamped. The crew successfully transferred to the *Bear*. With blue water ahead of him and the wind behind him, Leicester's son felt the exhilaration of the adventure. He writes of sailing along the coast of Spain, sighting Cape Finisterre and Cape St Vincent. He gave orders to pursue prizes as his fleet sailed down the coast towards the Canaries. The decks of the *Bear* were cleared for action. The optimism and enthusiasm of youth gave little thought to the fact that many of the vessels he sought to take as prizes were larger, more numerous than he or that they turned out to be English merchantmen. The one Spanish vessel they did meet hoisted English colours as a way of escaping.

Robin's excitement with the thought of being at sea was tempered by the realities of life. His sleep would have been broken. He would have often been cold and wet. The bread they took on board would soon have gone mouldy and there was the constant need to resupply fresh water and food when it was possible. Stores for the kind of voyage Robin and his men undertook included flitches of bacon, beef and other meat, dried stockfish or hake which was known as 'poor john' as well as wheat, cheese and beer. Drake calculated that one hundred men would need twelve hogsheads of beef and pork in 1585.

On Christmas Day, with no sign of the *Bear's Whelp*, they were becalmed near Tenerife near a ship from Weymouth. It was a hot day according to Wyatt and the men swam from ship to ship to 'make greate cheere to each other'. Robin tried to convince the Weymouth vessel to join with him but they were later separated by contrary winds. As the fleet continued on its journey, they encountered two caravels which Robin cornered in shallow waters. Once the two caravels had been taken as prizes Robin put men from the *Bear* aboard, reducing the overcrowding which led to sickness. Wood and Wentworth became the captains of the caravels renamed *Regarde* and *Intent* whilst Robin saw to it that their Spanish crews were set ashore without being robbed of their personal possessions.[7] There was still no sign of the *Bear's Whelp*. Having waited for Monck to meet with them in vain, the fleet of three departed the Canaries for Cape Blanco. Robin landed with Wyatt and others of the crew during their wait for Monck but described the landscape as a 'barren and sandie place, the sand running in drifts like snow, and very stony'.[8] He also described it as being full of 'blacke venomous lizards'.[9] Ultimately Robin continued with his voyage leaving letters for his missing captain. Monck, failing to find the rest of the fleet, returned to England with a couple of prizes of his own but Robin did not know what became of the *Bear's Whelp* until his return to Plymouth.

Robin plotted their path across the Atlantic, remembering much later that he had always loved the science of navigation 'I practised the science of navigation by grand circles with practical longitude'.[10] Great circle sailing required Robin to plot the shortest route between where he was and Cape Blanco. The shortest route is the arc along a circle that divides a globe into two equal halves. All lines of latitude are great circles. This is only helpful if travelling along a north-south line. The most obvious east-west example of a great circle is the Equator. The problem for navigators is that the further away that two points are from the Equator, the smaller the circles become so that the globe is not divided equally. Great circle sailing relies on the mathematics of circles bisecting the earth equally. In order to achieve a great circle and the shortest distance, Robin needed to plot a course that followed a great circle. This would have involved a series of calculations taking account of prevailing winds and tides and adjusting position accordingly without the benefit of a coastline to take an accurate reading. Wyatt's account of the voyage expressed praise for Robin's skill as a navigator. It was an easy passage with good weather and

---

7. Lee, p.63.
8. Warner, ed., p.69.
9. Ibid.
10. Lee., p.65.

the water changed colour showing that they were approaching a coast exactly as the mathematics and accurate measurements predicted.

Robin gave orders to Kendall to set a course running past the Cape Verde Islands in the night. The wind was fair and it was a clear run of twenty days. Robin spotted Trinidad on 31 January and sent his caravels to explore the coastline. The *Bear* sailed to Cape Curiapan and anchored in a bay that Robin named Pelican Bay because of the number of birds that he saw there. Robin's safe anchorage was modern-day Cedros Bay. Trinidad lay in the hands of Antonio de Berrio y Oruna. Columbus discovered the island in 1498 and by 1588, the Spanish established their control. De Berrio saw the island as a base camp for exploring Guiana and finding the legendary city of El Dorado. Robin's arrival did not cause alarm and he remained anchored off the bay for the next forty days.

Robin found no Spanish prizes off Trinidad but he did encounter the indigenous Arawak population which he described as 'a fine shaped and a gentle people, all naked and painted red'.[11] Both he and Wyatt took the opportunity to make a list of words in Arawak – the earliest to be recorded. Robin described the trading that took place including the sight of canoes crowding around his fleet. Having planned his expedition carefully, the hold of the *Bear* contained 'knives, beads, fishing hooks and hatchets with which to trade'.[12] Ever the 'son of chivalry', Robin took care to issue orders that the Arawaks were to be well treated and no women were to be molested. His attitude was different to that of the Spanish. Most of the native population had already been destroyed by the time the *Bear* dropped its anchor. Eventually, Robin found an Arawak who could speak Spanish and began to make enquiries about gold. Unlike Raleigh, Leicester's boy did not set out with the aim of finding fabled gold. Despite this, he did need to see some sort of return for the venture. He decided that if there was gold on the island that he should find a mine that was not under the control of the Spanish as it would yield a profit. Balthazar, the Spanish speaking Arawak, was taken on board the *Bear* as a guide.

There was a mine, Robin was told, some eight or nine miles down the coast in an easterly direction. Captain Jobson made the journey on 2

---

11. Vaughan, p.30.
12. Ibid.

February and found what he believed to be gold. The next day Robin led more men to the mine from where they returned laden with ore. Wyatt wrote about the way in which Robin was willing to share the hardships of his men. Robin claimed the territory for Elizabeth by the simple device of having a lead plate fixed to a nearby tree even though there was a Spanish presence on the island. Raleigh, passing the same way, also found the mine but he immediately realised that the ore was of no value. What the *Bear*'s crew discovered was marcasite or white iron pyrites. Raleigh made some cutting comments about those who were less astute in their observations. By then he had come to believe that Robin's departure for Trinidad before his own fleet was an attempt to steal the glory and the gold that were rightfully Raleigh's. Robin, writing for Hakluyt about his West Indies adventure, recognised his folly and coined the phrase, 'all is not gold that glistereth'.[13]

The *Bear* and its attendant vessels moved north to the Bay of Paracoa and its settlement of San Paracora, modern-day San Ferdinando, on 6 February. Robin and his officers planned to assault the town which was held by a small Spanish force numbering about 300 men. This assault was prevented when the town sent a flag of truce and de Berrio sent a letter which Robin declined even to read so great, he said, was his contempt of the Spanish. Even so, there was no attack. There was too much risk for too little reward. Robin decided that he did not want a confrontation with de Berrio. What he wanted was the opportunity to explore the interior of Guiana. His position was a good one and he needed to caulk his fleet using pitch from an asphalt lake he found at Cape Curiapan.

Repairs complete, the fleet split up. Two carvels under Wentworth and Wood set off to find plunder leaving Robin with only fifty men. None of the three narrators of the voyage complete the story of the carvels. Captain Benjamin Wood reappeared in Robin's employment back in England so at least one of the caravels returned home. Robin decided that he wanted real riches and possibly to out-explore Raleigh whose stated purpose before leaving England was to venture up the Orinoco. The famous explorer was fascinated by the mythical golden city of El Dorado, as indeed was de Berrio who believed he had reached the edge of its territory in 1585 at the end of an eighteen-month-long expedition.

---

13. Warner, ed., p.70.

Robin made enquiries. He wrote in his account of the voyage, written at Hakluyt's behest, that at least 100 men confirmed the presence of a valuable mine at the head of the delta of the Orinoco. The location can be identified according to Raleigh's description as 'Arrriacoa', where the Orinoco divides itself into three branches. The gold, if it was ever there, must have been washed down from higher ground through the river basin.

The *Bear*'s draught was too deep to sail up the Orinoco. Robin decided to send the ship's longboat in search of the mine on 20 February. He did not go himself although that was his initial plan. Jobson and Kendall protested against 'soe worthie and hopefull a gallant' being hazarded in 'soe small and simple vessel'.[14] Robin's own account stated that the company did not want to be left in Abraham Kendall's care during his own absence. Jobson went with a crew of twelve men which included two master's mates and two Dutchmen. Robin's expedition was technically the first English venture to explore at least part of the delta rather than the better-known Raleigh quest. They reached Orocoa where they traded some goods for four crescents of gold and a silver bracelet. Jobson also learned of a tribe who powdered their bodies with gold. The difficulties of the return journey included heat, lack of provisions and little fresh water. Balthazar, their guide, escaped into the night leaving an Arawak that Jobson and his men could only communicate with by sign language. He also tried to escape and was 'striken by a brown bill'.[15] Having murdered their remaining guide, the long boat had to find its way through a maze of crocodile-filled channels back to the coast. By the time Jobson got back to the *Bear*, everyone except Robin thought that they were dead. In his account of the voyage, Robin expressed the desire to immediately make the return journey himself but he had to give up the project when not one man would go with me (no, albeit I had had commission to hang or kill them).[16] The truth was that the men who returned were almost dead from starvation and lack of fresh water.

Robin, having had his own brush with the legend that obsessed Raleigh for the rest of his life, decided to 'discover the main' following conversation with Captain George Popham who joined him off Paracora. The day after Jobson's return 'being wonderous desirous to see the end of

---

14. Ibid, p.35.
15. Ibid, p.75.
16. Ibid.

this discovery',[17] Robin and Popham advanced some twenty miles inland on Trinidad itself with seventy men. They travelled 'in good order' with drums playing and flags flying in hope of finding gold but there was little reward for their efforts aside from evidence of small-scale smelting. The local inhabitants fled at the approach of the English. Wyatt described Robin refusing to allow his crew to loot their homes. Leicester's son was an unusual conquistador in his approach to the indigenous populations he encountered, although Balthazar's flight and the murder of his substitute demonstrate a darker side to the relationship.

It was Popham whose arrival alerted Robin to the news that Raleigh's fleet was not far off Trinidad. He did not sail from Plymouth until the beginning of February 1595 and did not arrive until six or so weeks after Robin might have first expected him. Raleigh's account of *The Discoverie of the Large, Rich and Bewtiful Empire of Guiana* ignores Robin almost entirely. Sir Walter needed to impress Elizabeth. He was still in disgrace because of his secret marriage to Bess Throckmorton. He did not want to promote the maritime career of Leicester's son nor did he want Robin to outshine him. He wrote that he undertook the journey in the 'winter' of his life to restore his reputation without giving credit to Robin for making much the same journey before him but as a maiden voyage. The information would have deterred potential investors in future ventures. It would not have done for him to publicise the fact that Robin was the first Englishman to build a fort on Trinidad, to take a force inland or lay claim to the territory for Elizabeth.

Raleigh finally arrived off Trinidad on 22 March, captured the town of San Jose and took de Berrio prisoner. Having found out from his captive as much as he could about El Dorado, he left his ships anchored off the island and took only one hundred men and stores to the mainland of Guiana. Neither Jobson or Raleigh found either a real mine or El Dorado. Raleigh described the latter in his account of Guiana. El Dorado began with the story of chieftains whose rule began with a ceremony at Lake Guatavita. Accounts reported the new ruler covered with gold dust and that his people threw gold and precious jewels into the lake to appease the god who lived there. The Spanish who heard the story began to call the chief 'the gilded one' or El Dorado. The man turned, over time, into

---

17. Ibid, p.76.

a lost city of gold. De Berrio and Topiawari, a tribal chief who Raleigh met at the end of his own river journey, confirmed the explorer's belief that El Dorado really existed.

By 11 March 1595, Robin knew it was time to leave his base in Trinidad for the last time. The *Bear* became separated from Popham's craft when it was carried off course from Granada. Robin decided to make for Puerto Rico instead where prizes might be had. On the afternoon of 13 March, Robin found a Spanish vessel. It was four leagues from the *Bear* when they first spotted its sails on the horizon. The *Bear*'s crew gave chase and captured their prize in the night having only to fire three shots. Jobson went aboard to discover a cargo of wine, linen and hats meant for trading with Puerto Rico's population.[18] The contents of the hold were transferred to the *Bear* and the merchant craft set alight because it was too small to complete a journey back to England. The captive crew was put ashore in an isolated spot with supplies. Wyatt wrote sourly that 'Our General used them so kindly, they forgot they were prisoners'.[19]

From his captives Robin learned that the Spanish Silver Fleet, comprising 150 ships, was due to leave Havana for Spain. He plotted a course north-east towards Bermuda hoping to run into stragglers from the fleet with its precious cargo of precious metals, sugar, spices and other exotic merchandise. Instead of rich pickings, all the *Bear* discovered were storms and 'a sea swallowing wherlepoole'.[20] For a month the ship and its crew were tossed around the ocean by gusting winds and swelling seas. Wyatt's account described them running up the American coast of Florida and Virginia before finding themselves off Labrador which Wyatt recognised by the 'great abundance of whales'.[21] Kendall's account placed them lower down the coast when their sails caught the wind and carried them from the Atlantic to the Azores.

The journey continued eastwards before a howling gale split the *Bear*'s sails and broke the shrouds. The *Bear* bumped and rolled across the waves with her planks springing and her mast cracking. On 28 April the crew finally spotted the green and white islands that make up the Azores archipelago in the middle of the Atlantic. By that time supplies were running low. After a day's rest, Robin set a course for home. The

18. Lee, p.71.
19. Warner, ed. p.51.
20. Ibid, p.54.
21. Ibid, p.53.

adventure was not yet over. On 6 May Robin, taking his turn on the quarter-deck keeping watch, saw the sails of a Spanish man-of-war. The battle that followed filled two days. The *Bear*, a much smaller vessel than the Spaniard which was somewhere between 300 and 600 tons depending upon the account, worked to keep the wind in their sails.

Robin used his boat's greater agility to pour shot at the Spanish vessel with its four remaining guns and nine barrels of powder. On the morning of the second day, sails trimmed and colours flying Robin 'came forth unarmed, having only his leading staff in his hand, saluted, and took his standing on the open deck, where he might best see and be seen of his enemies'.[22] Later that morning a Spanish shot struck Robin's staff, tore the sail near his head and sent splinters of wood flying. 'Yet,' said Wyatt, 'would he not budge or move by any means.'[23] The *Bear* only stood off when it ran out of powder, the remainder of the barrels being water damaged. Fifty or so exhausted men on the *Bear* would not have been able to board the man-of-war and the Spaniard had no intention of striking its colours. It was Robin's first battle. It is impossible to avoid the irony that had Leicester acknowledged a marriage to Douglas he would have had a legitimate heir of whom he might be proud.

The *Bear* arrived off the English coast towards the end of May 1595, narrowly escaping the rocks off of Scilly in a fog. Robin made landfall at St Ives in Cornwall with the experience that Elizabeth felt that he lacked for a South Seas voyage but very little in the way of prizes despite the fact that he claimed to have taken or destroyed nine Spanish ships. Robin now only had to travel back to London. He broke this journey at Wilton House near Salisbury where his cousin Mary Herbert, the sister of Sir Philip Sidney, and her husband Henry Herbert, Earl of Pembroke lived. Amongst the news was the fact that Thomas Chaloner, his university tutor, mentor and friend had fought at the siege of Rouen as part of King Henri IV's attempt to control Normandy and been knighted by the king. The poor harvests of the previous year two years had resulted in famine at home and prices were increasing. Robin may not have cared. Mary and Henry also had to break the news that Margaret, his wife of a few short months, was dead from plague.[24]

---

22. Ibid, p.59.
23. Ibid.
24. Lee, p.76.

Chapter X

Cadiz and the Earl of Essex

Despite his grief, it was not long before Robin wrote to Sir Robert Cecil who had taken his father's place as Elizabeth's most trusted advisor. He might have done this on the Earl of Pembroke's advice as the letter was sent from the Herberts' home in Wilton. Robin wanted to return to sea and to do that he needed the goodwill of the Queen's Secretary. His letter sought to establish a prior connection between himself and the Cecil family as well as revealing that the travails of his adventure had taken a toll on his health:

> How much I honour you and how infinitely I think myself tied unto you for your many favours, which I understand by my mother! I cannot choose but make myself your vowed servant. Let me entreat you not to take me as a complimental courtier, but as a plain dealing sailor that hath learned to love them honestly and unfeignedly that he is so much bound to. The discourse of those matters I have seen, I leave till I wait upon you, which shall be when I have in some reasonable sort recovered my health, which hath been not altogether the best since I came; I am strong enough, but somewhat dulled with the sea fare. The best things I know I shall be glad to make known unto you.—From Wilton, 11 June, 1595.[1]

Robin knew something of Sir Edward Stafford's association with the Cecils during Stafford's time as English Ambassador in Paris between 1583 and 1590. There is no record of what happened when Sir Robert met Robin in London.

Leicester's boy had shown himself to be a seafarer of promise. It was unfortunate that his return coincided with Raleigh who was more of a self-publicist than Robin. Raleigh was able to boast of destroying the

---

1. CP, p.225.

Spanish settlement in Trinidad and capturing de Berrio. All Robin had was some marcasite which he had mistaken for gold and Monck's captured ships which were more than Raleigh whose fleet took no prizes. Raleigh sought to scupper his young rival. He wrote to Cecil at the beginning of November 1595 that if Robin returned to Guiana:

> Farewell all good from thence, for although myself like a cockscomb, did rather prefer the future in respect of others, and rather sought to win the kings to Her Majesty's service than to sack them, I know what others will do when those kings shall come simply into their hands.[2]

For the time being Robin's desires for further exploration and a return voyage to Guiana were thwarted. In the meantime, he wrote a dutiful account of his journey for his brother-in-law Richard Hakluyt. Robin himself thought that his voyage was so little out of the ordinary that it was not worth recording. Raleigh's account of his own journey was written with colourful detail, including the information that one of his men was eaten by a crocodile. Not that it made much difference to Raleigh even if he did conclude his account by urging the queen to colonise Guiana. Cecil sent neither one of them back to the West Indies in search of fabled gold or Spanish prizes.

In August Drake and his cousin Sir John Hawkins set off for the Spanish Main and the Indies with a fleet of twenty-seven ships. Robin's sailing master Abraham Kendall went with them. They intended to raid the Spanish treasure fleet on its journey from South America to the Spanish mainland. Hawkins' galleons proved unable to outpace the Spanish vessels. The venture was a disaster. He died off of Puerto Rico at the beginning of November. Sir Francis Drake died from dysentery in January 1596 whilst the fleet lay at anchor in Portobelo Harbour, Panama. Kendall died at the same time. News of the deaths spread slowly. It was 20 June 1596 before Andres Armeneros, part of the Spanish Council for the Indies, wrote to tell the Duke of Medina Sidonia that his old enemy was dead. The same letter described an Anglo-Dutch fleet that was under

2. Ibid, p.437.

the command of the Earl of Essex and Lord Howard of Effingham that was on its way to attack Spain.

The previous year, in November 1595, Sir Walter Raleigh warned the Privy Council that Spain was once again preparing an invasion fleet. It was thought that sixty or so vessels intended to land in Ireland where they would find support from the Earl of Tyrone who had risen in rebellion against the English. Elizabeth agreed to attack the Spanish first in March 1596. It was agreed that her fleet would assault Spain's richest port – Cadiz. The Earl of Essex and Charles, Lord Howard of Effingham, Robin's step-brother and uncle respectively, were appointed as joint commanders. In addition to the English, the Cadiz expedition was also composed of twenty-four Dutch vessels under the command of Jan van Duyvenvoord. Robin, with the experience of his West Indies voyage, was given command of the *Nonpareil*.[3] Elizabeth's enthusiasm for the campaign waned with the passage of time but the usually parsimonious monarch was prepared to pay for her fleet to be outfitted on the understanding that her commanders would salvage supplies and equipment from Cadiz that the English could use.

Plymouth Sound was full of vessels awaiting their sailing orders by 23 May 1596. Anthony Standen's letters to Anthony Bacon describe 'tall handsome men'[4] and 'green headed youths covered with feathers, gold and silver lace'.[5] The fleet, Robin amongst them, finally set sail from Plymouth on 1 June. Prayers for the fleet filled churches across the country. Each night the fleet gathered into squadrons and a watch was set. When dawn approached the vessels fanned out to capture any boats that might send news of their approach to Spain. Howard, aboard his flagship the *Ark*, wanted to maintain the element of surprise. Amongst the men Robin knew on the campaign was Essex who captained the *Repulse*, Raleigh on the *Warspite* and Tom Wyatt commanding 'a hundred men out of Kent'.[6]

With the wind behind them, their target came into sight on 20 June. By then the news had spread around the fleet from a captured Irish merchantman that the garrison was weak. The harbour was full of more

3. Lee, p.81.
4. I.P.I. MSS 647–662 (the papers of Anthony Bacon) cited in Hammer, p.621.
5. Ibid.
6. Ibid, p.81.

than seventy merchant ships including three treasure ships bound for the Indies. The following day the fleet's commanders decided that there should be a full-scale assault on the town led by the Earl of Essex beginning by landing several regiments of men simultaneously on the beach near the town. Howard would concentrate on the merchant fleet. The English Armada was spotted as it crossed the horizon. Citizens of Cadiz were alerted to their danger by the frenzied ringing of church bells and bark of signal cannon from the fort that defended the harbour. As the English prepared to launch their attack on the town the wind rose and the waves became increasingly dangerous. Essex's attack was eventually aborted but not before fifteen men drowned when their longboat was overturned.

Essex continued to press for an immediate attack on the town but Howard refused because of the fort guns and the dangerous height of the waves. He had no wish to lose any of Elizabeth's expensive fleet. It was decided that Essex should land on the beach nearby. Raleigh, who had been absent chasing some merchantmen, returned in time to discover Essex's plan and reject it. It was, he announced, better to attack the Spanish fleet at anchor first. Essex countered that a night attack on the town was a more viable option but this was vetoed as well. The discussion moved to who should lead the attack. Essex thought that he should but Howard refused because Elizabeth wanted nothing to happen to her favourite. Raleigh claimed the vanguard. Lord Thomas Howard demanded that he should have the position because he was superior in rank to Raleigh. However, his ship the *Merhonour*, was too much of a risk in shallow waters so he came aboard Robin's vessel the *Nonpareil* whose draught was shallow enough to manoeuvre safely.[7]

Meanwhile the Spanish moved their merchant ships to Cadiz's inner harbour. Four galleons known as the Apostles guarded the entrance in a defensive line. At sunrise, Raleigh ignoring his orders sailed across the outer harbour straight at the galleons which blocked the way into the inner bay. By flouting the precedence agreed upon, Raleigh instigated a rush amidst the English to get to grips with the enemy. From the start of the voyage, the leadership of the expedition had been troubled by jealousy, personal conflict and two chains of command. This now erupted into an unedifying scramble to get to close quarters with the

---

7. Ibid, p82.

enemy. He was closely followed by the *Nonpareil*, Sir Robert Southwell aboard the *Lion* and Sir Conyers Clifford in *Dreadnought*.[8] The fort batteries opened up but were too far away to do any damage. Two of them would explode when their gunners overcharged them with gunpowder in an attempt to compensate for the range. The ensuing battle lasted for eight hours. Raleigh demanded that he should be allowed to board the Apostles that fired broadside after broadside at the English. Whilst he was arguing with Essex about this Sir Francis Vere on the *Rainbow* pushed ahead of the *Warspite* only to be overtaken by the *Nonpareil*. Essex on the *Repulse* pushed his own way to the front of the battle fouling the *Dreadnought* as he did so. Raleigh, not to be outdone, made his way once more to the front of the English fleet and anchored so that no one could pass him without risking being grounded. Vere was so angry that he had a grappling iron fastened to the *Warpsite* but Raleigh had the rope cut. During the resulting argument, Essex took the *Repulse* in front of both of them. The Spanish galleons were still firing as the English commanders closed up behind Essex and Raleigh. Thomas Howard returned to *Merhonour* whose guns had already joined the action, leaving Robin in sole charge of *Nonpareil* with its thirty cannons. His was still one of only four vessels in the van of the fight. Raleigh wrote 'the volleys of cannon and culverin came as thick as if it had been a skirmish of muskets'.[9]

Although the English were struggling for position between themselves and their firepower was lighter than that of the Spanish fleet, their firing was more accurate. Aboard the Spanish galleons splintering wood and shot created a deadly storm of shrapnel. After five hours of fighting Raleigh boarded the *St Philip*, one of the four Spanish galleons protecting the harbour, swiftly followed by the *Nonpareil*. All four of the Spanish galleons cut their cables and drifted shoreward where they were caught by the tide and grounded on sand bars off the beach. The *St Philip* and the *St Thomas* were fired by their own crews who threw themselves into the water where many of them drowned or became stuck in the mud. The majority of the Spanish fleet moved deeper into the inner bay. In the aftermath, which sickened Raleigh, the Dutch fleet took the opportunity

---

8. Ibid, p.82.
9. Ibid, p.83.

to kill wounded Spanish sailors who sought help. Robin witnessed the hell of burning ships and drowning men.

Essex finally got his wish to attack Cadiz itself. He, Sir Francis Vere and about 2,000 men landed to the south of the city whilst oarsmen were sent to the Suazo Bridge which linked the peninsula upon which Cadiz stood to the mainland to prevent reinforcements from arriving. There was hand to hand fighting in the streets. Citizens hurled tiles from the rooftops and bones from the ossuary in a bid to repel the invaders. Meanwhile, as the troops began sacking the town, the wealthiest of Cadiz's inhabitants retreated to the citadel to avoid surrendering to the English. Howard, ignoring the need to capture the merchant fleet, joined the attack on the town. Looting lasted through the night. Only the churches were not attacked because Essex gave an order that they should not be desecrated.

The campaign's commanders in their haste for glory and spoils ignored something extremely important to the queen – the cargoes aboard the merchantmen. The Duke of Medina Sidonia gave orders that these should be removed as secretly as possible and when Lord Howard refused to ransom them for two million ducats had the vessels fired rather than allow them to fall into English hands. Robin would have caught the acrid taste of smoke at the back of his throat and seen the billowing columns of black smoke as the prizes which they so eagerly sought were consumed by flames. The inferno raged for three days. It was a costly mistake on the part of the English commanders. Their investors, Elizabeth in particular, expected a financial return for engaging in war.

The seizure of the city was a victory which Essex intended to claim as his own. On Sunday 27 June, he conferred knighthoods upon sixty-six of his men. Amongst the men knighted by Essex was Francis Popham, who would later gain his place in history for his opposition to Charles I. Popham was also part of the wider Dudley affinity. His wife, Ann Dudley, was John Dudley of Stoke Newington's daughter, Robin's childhood companion. His cousin, George Popham, joined in Robin's West Indies voyage of 1595–1595. Noticeable by his absence from the list of those knighted was Leicester's son. Was it because of the difficulties between Robin and Lettice? Or was it simply that he was still on board the *Nonpareil* and overlooked?

In London, a prayer of thanksgiving was in the hands of the queen's printer by 3 July. Four days later the English fleet left Cadiz having swapped its captives for English galley slaves. A vessel carrying Sir Anthony Ashley and Sir Robert Cross, two of Essex's new-made knights, went on ahead. They reported a great victory for Essex and talked of soldiers with their arms full of treasure which raised the queen's expectations as to her share of the spoils. He was followed by George Buck who also made his way to the queen at Greenwich where he was made to repeat his story several times. A month after the prayer of thanksgiving was penned the fleet arrived back in Plymouth. By that time Elizabeth had heard enough to believe that the soldiery had taken more spoils than was justly theirs. She ordered an immediate investigation. Meanwhile, the Privy Council sent instructions that ships were to be searched before their men disembarked. The Plate Fleet had not been captured; the fruits of victory were not as great as Elizabeth, Cecil or the Privy Council hoped. The Spanish fleet arrived in Lisbon two days after the English departed. Essex was eager to get his account to the queen before anyone else could report that he failed to instruct English sailors to take loot from merchant cargoes. Ashley, who was commissioned by Elizabeth to oversee her interests, was not only incompetent but was soon found to have taken his share of the loot. A diamond that should have been the queen's was broken up before the truth could be discovered. Ashley found himself in the Fleet Prison as a consequence.[10] Elsewhere the bells rang and there were bonfires in the streets to celebrate Essex's victory.

Although Elizabeth was angry with Essex for knighting so many men in the celebrations after the capture of Cadiz, there was a man who had been forgotten. The queen rarely dubbed knights because she regarded the honour as an important one. Nonetheless, after attending a church service of thanksgiving in Plymouth on Sunday 8 August, Robin was 'knighted in the open street'[11] and became Sir Robert Dudley. His brother-in-law Hakluyt wrote of Robin that he was 'of so many good parts of a worthy gentleman as the like are seldom seen'.[12]

A month later Burghley and his son Sir Robert blamed Essex in public for the loss of plunder. Raleigh, by contrast, seemed to be rising

---

10. Meyrick, S. Rush. (1829). Report of the commissioners appointed to inquire into the amount of booty taken at Cadiz in 1596, with the charges preferred in consequence, by Sir Gelly Meyricke, against Sir Anthony Ashley, *Archaeologia 22*. Vol 22, pp. 172–189.
11. Lee, p.86.
12. Ibid.

once again in Elizabeth's favour. This impacted on Robin in a small but significant way when the official account of the campaign came to be written by Sir Anthony Ashley. He wrote under the supervision of the Cecils. Sir Robert Cecil's amendments to one of the existing copies of the account played down the role of Essex and developed the importance of Raleigh and Howard. Originally a list of officers who played a prominent part in the battle included 'Mr Dudley'. Cecil's pen deleted the sentence containing Robin's name and replaced it with 'Sir Robert Southwell and one or two more gentleman'.[13] Southwell was Lord Howard's son-in-law. At a stroke, Robin was deleted from popular history because he was the Earl of Essex's step-brother.

---

13. Hammer, pp. 621–642.

Chapter XI

Marriage, Misadventure and Mathematics

In 1596, shortly after his return from Cadiz, Robin married Alicia, or Alice, Leigh, the daughter of Sir Thomas Leigh of Stoneleigh in Warwickshire. Leigh hunted regularly at Kenilworth which was only a few miles from his home and had been acquainted with Leicester. The earl's household accounts reveal that he visited Stoneleigh in August 1585. The bride was seventeen years old when she stood at the altar of the little church of Our Lady of the Assumption at Ashow, a short walk from her childhood home. Stoneleigh had once been a Cistercian abbey. Its post-dissolution owner was a former Lord Mayor of London and a Merchant Adventurer. His new house was still under construction when he died in 1571. Thomas Leigh, named after his father, continued with the project and looked for suitable matches for his family to improve his standing in the county. He did this by marrying into the Spencer family of Althorp.

Thomas's older daughter Catherine, named after her mother, married in 1592 into an eminent family with estates based in Northamptonshire and Gloucestershire as well as Leicestershire. The groom's name was Robert Catesby. He left Oxford before taking his degree in order to avoid the oath of Supremacy because of his Catholic beliefs. Sir Thomas, a Protestant, seems not to have been unduly bothered that the family he married his daughter into were recusant in their sympathies. Ten years prior to Catherine's marriage there was a court case before the Star Chamber involving the Catesbys which included charges of harbouring the notorious Jesuit Father Edmund Campion. Catherine's new father-in-law paid fines for his religious beliefs and spent many years in prison. Catherine who came with a dowry of £2,000[1] as well as giving Robert a Protestant association, died in 1598. After her death, Catesby became more radical in his beliefs. He was fined 4,000 marks for his part in

---

1. Fraser, p.111.

the Essex Rebellion of 1601, funded Jesuit priests and in March 1603, may have sent a messenger to Spain to enquire whether Philip III would continue to support English Catholics once James Stuart was on the throne. Catesby went on to conspire to blow up the Houses of Parliament along with King James and his family.

Leigh, who was one of the Warwickshire justices who evicted Sir Christopher Blount from Kenilworth in 1590, did not regard Robin's illegitimacy as an impediment. Rather, he saw a wealthy and eligible nobleman who was part of the Warwickshire landowning elite and welcome at court. It was an opportunity for advancement so far as he was concerned. Alice and Robin's marriage was witnessed by her parents and her Aunt Alice whose husband the 5th Earl of Derby was a claimant to the Tudor succession. Robin's future looked bright. He had the favour of the queen and was beginning to make a name for himself as one of her seadogs. The marriage was cemented the following year with the birth of the couple's first daughter who was baptised at Kenilworth on 25 September 1597. Her name was Alice Douglas Dudley.

Robin, part of the Warwickshire gentry, a courtier and a father of a growing family, still dreamed of adventure. He hankered after an expedition bound for the South Seas. The *Bear*, the *Bear's Whelp* and the *Benjamin* were outfitted for another journey. Robin received the queen's bounty of five shillings per ton for the building the *Benjamin*, a merchantman.[2] Despite the experience gained during his West Indies expedition and as a captain who fought with valour at Cadiz, the venture was still not one that Elizabeth would permit Robin to take.

One example that might have come to her mind, aside from the death of Thomas Cavendish, was the example of James Lancaster's expedition. On 10 April 1591, four ships slipped out from Plymouth Sound. On board were 200 men under the command of Captain James Lancaster. The voyage they were setting out upon was the journey that Robin pleaded with Elizabeth that he should be allowed to make. Lancaster's mission, on behalf of his backer the London merchant Thomas Cordell, aside from privateering, was exploration and to open up trade routes to the East Indies. He was also to weaken any Portuguese trading posts the expedition might encounter. It was a hard voyage. The fleet found

---

2. 28 May 1604, Dudley Papers, in Warner, p.vii.

itself becalmed in the Doldrums. Disease, especially scurvy, weakened the crews. Men's gums ulcerated. Their skin, already made raw by ocean-going conditions began to bleed. Their teeth fell out. One vessel rounded the Cape of Good Hope only to founder a few days later with the loss of all hands. To the men aboard Lancaster's ships, it may have felt as though God had abandoned them especially when four men were killed by lightning. The survivors eventually reached the island of Penang in June 1592, remaining in the Pacific for three months until September. Lancaster set about robbing every merchant vessel he encountered. Finally, forced by food shortages and mutiny to turn for home Lancaster finally arrived in England in May 1594 with only twenty-five men remaining from his original crew.

Robin, like his father before him, was required to remain at home and take on the role of investor whilst Captain Benjamin Wood, the captain of the caravel that made its way back to England from Robin's West Indies voyage, led the mission to China via Magellan's Strait and the Philippines. The queen was persuaded to provide Wood with a letter to the Emperor Shen Zong of China recommending Richard Allen or Allot and Thomas Bromfield, two London merchants who joined the expedition. The letter dated 16 July 1596 offered the 'fullest protection to the subjects of China, should they be disposed to open a trade to any of the ports in Her Majesty's dominions'.[3]

The presence of merchants and the contents of Elizabeth's letter suggests that the voyage was principally about trade and expanding the boundaries of the nation's economic influence. The queen was motivated by trade and diplomacy as well as the immediate financial gains of privateering. By the end of her reign, English merchants and explorers would have opened links with Russia, Persia, Morocco and the Ottoman Empire. Elizabeth exchanged letters with Ivan the Terrible and Murad III. Her letter to the Emperor of China was the latest in an ongoing strategy to take English trade east beyond traditional networks both for reasons of trade and for the acquisition of political power. Robin, driven by an interest in navigation and exploration, anticipated a significant return on his investment duration of the proposed voyage. Crews signed up to

---

3. CSP Colonial, pp. 97–98. 'The unfortunate voyage of Capt. Benjamin Wood towards the East Indies in 1596,' is printed in Astleys Collection of Voyages, 1745.

arduous voyages in the expectation of gold. Portuguese vessels carried valuable cargoes that would recoup Robin's costs, make the dangers of the voyage worthwhile to the men who sailed aboard his vessels and, so far as the State was concerned, any successful attack would weaken the hold of competitors on the Spice Islands to allow English merchants a foothold.

Robin provided Wood with detailed sailing orders before his little fleet departed on its long voyage. But rather than navigating the Strait of Magellan as instructed, Wood sailed around Cape Horn sometimes called the Drake Passage. Like Lancaster before him, Wood was intent on taking as many prizes as possible rather than delivering Elizabeth's letter to the Emperor of China. The *Benjamin* floundered during a storm soon afterwards sinking with all hands. The *Bear* and *Bear's Whelp* seem to have worked their way up the coast of East Africa. Evidence suggests that they were attacked by Portuguese men-of-war off Mozambique before crossing the Indian Ocean to Sri Lanka. In September 1598, Sir Robert Cecil received a letter from Gyles Van Hardwick in Lisbon stating that two English ships in 'the India' had captured two Portuguese ships on their way from Goa to China and plundered them. The writer assumed that 'it is Captain Wood in Mr Dudley's ships'.[4]

After February 1597, there was no certain news of Robin's ships, 'not one of the company ever returned to give an account of the rest'.[5] Reliable intelligence proved difficult to locate both at the time and after. Some clues were provided in letters like the one received by Cecil. De Villa, captain-general of New Andalusia, wrote to Philip II of Spain describing a party of English privateers, their ill-gotten gains and the sickness which struck them. From this it is possible to deduce that Wood arrived at the Malay Peninsula in January 1598 and that his crew suffered from scurvy in much the same way as Lancaster's had done. Portuguese records of the same period, written by Couto, reveal that the voyage of the *Bear* and *Bear's Whelp* ended in the Indian Ocean due to storms, disease and the enemy. Somewhere in the Strait of Malacca, Wood encountered a Portuguese fleet. There was a running battle that lasted eight days. The last of Wood's gunpowder blew up in the hold. The survivors broke off the engagement to repair their vessels at Old Kedah. There were

---

4. CSP Colonial, p.99.
5. Danvers, p.8.

insufficient men to crew both ships, so the smaller of the two remaining boats, the *Bear's Whelp* was abandoned. Whilst the crews transferred their cargo from the *Bear's Whelp* to the *Bear*, they came under attack. Many badly wounded men were left behind in Wood's haste to escape. The last of Robin's fleet, the *Bear*, began its homeward journey crewed by men who had faced storms, injury and disease only, it has been suggested, to founder in the Gulf of Martaban during a storm. The problem with this version of events is that the Portuguese talk about 'Hollanders' rather than English vessels.

Mandelslo's Travels published in 1662 includes a description of Mauritius which may yield the last part of Wood's story. When the Dutch arrived in 1601, they found a naked, half-starving, fever-ridden Frenchman who told them about three English ships: the first sank off the Cape of Good Hope; disease killed so many that the second boat was set afire and the remaining men sailed on in the last boat. The third vessel was wrecked and all hands lost apart from seven men in a longboat. These seven sailed for Mauritius. Two of the men tried to kill their companions. On being discovered they cast themselves into the sea and drowned. The four Englishmen in the party took the longboat thinking they might be able to continue their journey and the last man, the Frenchman, remained on Mauritius where both his physical and mental health deteriorated until he was discovered by the Dutch. There are discrepancies in the different accounts. All of them are fragmentary. Robin suffered a major financial setback from the failure of the venture but it did not affect his overall fortune which demonstrates how wealthy he was at the time.

At home, Robin became a patron of London's scientific instrument makers, maintaining his passion for mathematics and navigation even if he was not able to go to sea for the time being. As with much else about Robin's life, there was an echo of Leicester in his interests. The earl presented Elizabeth with an astrolabe made by Thomas Gemini, one of London's leading scientific instrument makers, shortly after she became queen. This gift, and images such as The Ditchley Portrait, project an image of Elizabeth not just ruling her own kingdom but reaching out across the globe. Scientific instruments of the kind that interested Robin were symbolic of power and empire. In 1595, Robin commissioned Charles Whitwell to make an astrolabe of the kind described by the mathematician John Blagrave in *The Mathematical Jewel* published in 1585. Whitwell has been described as the 'most skilled and versatile'[6] instrument maker of the period; demonstrating not only Robin's wealth but also the superiority of the navigational instruments that were commissioned by him. An astrolabe is made from four movable parts. The mater, which is the body of the astrolabe, has an edge called a limb upon which are marked the degree scale and a scale of hours. The rete is sometimes called a star-net. This is a plate that rotates around the mater to show the position of the stars. A bar called a rule rotates across the front of the astrolabe to locate positions on the rete and relate them to the hours marked on the limb. Another rotating bar called a label is fixed to the back of the astrolabe. This is used to measure the altitude above the horizon of the stars and planets. The label often also contains a calendar and divisions of the zodiac. By using the information on both sides of the astrolabe and careful measurement of the positions of celestial objects, it is possible to work out both position and the correct time. Whitwell's astrolabe was the first of several instruments made for Robin during this period. He might have been in Warwickshire but his heart was still set on exploring the high seas.

Soon after the astrolabe was completed, Whitwell made Robin an instrument for lunar measurement. It gave the moon's position over a period of thirty years at different periods. The instrument measured conjunctions between the moon and the stars and planets. A chart could be used to compare the measure conjunction with the same conjunctions at known longitudes. The user could work out their position longitudinally by calculating the time difference between the measurements taken and the measurements given on the chart. It was an expensive purchase demonstrating the maker's talent and the designer's understanding of the science. Turner describes Robin's lunar computer as 'the most complex instrument made during the sixteenth century'.[7] Robin's involvement with its design speaks of his superior understanding and abilities.

Navigational purchases continued amidst Robin's life as a landowner and courtier. He divided his time between Kenilworth and London. The British Museum holds an Azumoth dial for the latitude 52 degrees, the latitude of London, ordered from Whitwell by Robin in 1598.[8] He

---

6. Turner, p.29.
7. Ibid, p.80.
8. Azimuth Dial, unsigned circa 1600, with an inscription that attributes the invention of the instrument to Robin. MLA 1894, 6–15.2.

would later have the dial illustrated in Book V of his maritime atlas. In addition to seven instruments made by Whitwell, Robin also owned instruments by Humphrey Cole. These may have been made before his West Indies voyage or commissioned by Leicester as part of his backing of the Muscovy Company. Cole, a goldsmith turned instrument maker, worked as a moneyer in the Tower mint before supplying instruments for Martin Frobisher's voyage in 1576. Robin had other instruments made by James Kynvyn including a folding rule, a plane table, a quadrant, a graphometer, a geometrical compass, a graduated circle and an astrolabe. Kynvyn was part of the Merchant Taylor's Guild having moved from his home in Wales to Fleet Street where he set up his business. By the time he made Robin's acquaintance, he had already made instruments for the Earl of Essex.

There is evidence in the form of later navigational instruments made when Robin was an exile that as well as designing his lunar disc, he worked on other designs at his desk in Warwickshire or London. He may have improved existing instruments or adapted designs he read about in mathematical treatises. It is difficult to be certain of the provenance of the ideas that he claimed as his own in Tuscany because by that time his livelihood depended on publicising his expertise. In 1596, Robin finished his diagram for a wind rose and the following year drew a horary quadrant used for finding the time by the sun. Whilst Robin may well have designed the wind rose, horary quadrants were used by the Ancient Greeks and improved upon by Islamic astronomers before their use spread to Europe during the medieval period.

Abraham Kendall died at sea off Porta Bello, Panama on 28 January 1597, the same day as Sir Francis Drake. Kendall's sea chest was carried home and its contents dispersed. Some navigational papers were passed into the hands of the Earl of Cumberland who thought that the manuscript was Kendall's own work, but which was in fact a copy of Edward Wright's work on longitude and latitude. Robin may have already seen the calculations and taken his own notes given that Kendall mentored him during his voyage to the West Indies. He was deeply interested in the methodology of scientific navigation. During the year that followed Kendall's death, Robin began to assemble his papers and charts, to write the story of his West Indies voyage at the behest of his brother-in-law Richard Hakluyt and to write down all that he knew about modern navigation.

It is difficult to know the extent of Robin's relationship during this time with the Earl of Essex. His friend Chaloner was still in Essex's employment. It would have been impossible for Robin to ignore the increasingly hostile factions at court. One group under the leadership of Robert Cecil and the other headed by the Earl of Essex clashed over appointments to public offices and the way that England's foreign policy should be directed. Cecil favoured continuing a policy of piracy which conserved Elizabeth's finances as well as weakening the enemy. It was a strategy that Essex opposed, in part because Cecil supported it because Philip II of Spain began building a fleet to take revenge for the humiliation of Cadiz. In the summer of 1597, against her better judgement, Elizabeth allowed Essex and Raleigh to take the English fleet to destroy the Spanish fleet at Ferrol and their possessions in the Azores as well as to capture the Spanish Plate Fleet. The failure of the so-called Islands Voyage and the arrival of a Spanish Armada off the English coast in October that year, when the fleet was otherwise engaged, weakened Essex's position with the queen even though some of the catastrophes which befell the English were thanks to storms at sea as much as Essex's behaviour. It was a venture that Robin had not taken part in. Fortune still seemed to be favouring him.

Robin and Alice became parents again in 1598. A daughter called Katherine joined her sister in the nursery. In total, the couple would have seven children of whom five survived infancy. The period concluded with several bereavements. The deaths included his aunt, Frances, Countess of Hereford. It was her infatuation with Leicester in 1573 which brought Douglas's entanglement with the earl to the queen's attention. Sir Robert Southwell, his cousin-in-law who had taken part in the Armada campaign of 1588 as well as the Cadiz expedition in 1597, also died. In 1599, one of the queen's maids-of-honour, Margaret Ratcliffe, pined for a brother who died in Ireland and subsequentially starved herself to death. A new maid-of-honour was appointed. Her name was Elizabeth Southwell, a daughter of Sir Robert. She was thirteen years old and not to be confused with her aunt of the same name who had an affair with the Earl of Essex and bore him an illegitimate son called Walter in 1591. Young Elizabeth Southwell, whose grandmother was Katherine Carey and whose grandfather was Lord Admiral Howard of Effingham was one of the queen's goddaughters as well as a royal cousin. Like the rest of Elizabeth's ladies, she dressed in silver and white. Robin was making his own mark at court but history does not record whether he noticed his young cousin. Dugdale describes him as, 'a person of stature tall and comely…also strong, valiant and famous at the exercise of tilting'.[9] This is confirmed by the cabinet miniature of Robin painted by Nicholas Hilliard at some time between 1590 and 1599 which depicts Robin with his right hand resting on his tourney helm in much the same manner that Zuccaro depicted Leicester in 1575.[10]

Fate played an unkind trick when Owen Jones, Robin's boyhood servant, reappeared in his life. He was destitute and in search of alms. He divulged the story of Leicester visiting Offington and telling Owen, 'Thou knowest that Robin, my boy, is my lawful son; and so I do charge thee to keep it a secret, so I charge thee, be careful of him and forget it not.'[11] Until then Robin had no reason to believe that his parents were married but now there was room for doubt. If the stigma of illegitimacy were to be removed from Robin's name, he would be able to inherit both his father's and his uncle's titles and Fortune's wheel would carry him upwards.

---

9. Lee, p.93.
10. The National Portrait Gallery also holds a probable portrait of Robin by an unknown artist, oil on panel, 1590s, NPG 2613.
11. Lee, p. 101.

Chapter XII

Essex's Rebellion

T hings were becoming more complicated at court. Essex and Raleigh formed opposing factions in the aftermath of the Islands Voyage, each blaming the other for the expedition's failure. There had always been a rivalry between Burghley and Leicester but it was nothing in comparison to the hostility that grew between the next generation. Tensions magnified. Essex and Cecil's son Robert became increasingly antagonistic to one another with the passage of time. It did not help that when Essex was absent from court in 1596 that Elizabeth promoted Robert Cecil to the position of Secretary of State. The following year he became Chancellor of the Duchy of Lancaster. Each man wanted power to be concentrated within himself. In 1598, Essex demanded to know of Lord Grey whose man he was – either Essex's or Cecil's. There was more than a hint of paranoia in his demands.

Essex took offence wherever men took precedence from him. Elizabeth created her cousin, Robin's uncle, Charles Howard, Earl of Nottingham, together with a pension of £100 a year on 23 October 1597. This meant that Nottingham took precedence over Essex on State occasions and in the House of Lords. The wording of the patent included fulsome praise for his part in the raid on Cadiz. Essex was furious. The glory of Cadiz, as Essex saw it, was his own. His immediate response to his demotion was to challenge Nottingham's sons, Robin's cousins, to a duel and then to leave court complaining of illness. When he returned, he refused to attend Privy Council meetings unless the queen was present. Nottingham left court for his home in Chelsea pleading sickness of his own and taking his wife with him. Elizabeth was not amused that her good friend and cousin Catherine Howard née Carey was no longer by her side but rather than punish Essex, she chose instead to promote him to the post of Earl Marshal which gave Essex precedence over Nottingham in the House of Lords.

Elizabeth was adept at managing factions using rewards and favours to ensure that no single group became dominant but by the end of the 1590s, factionalism poisoned the atmosphere at court. The faltering dynamics of power and politics of patronage had consequences for Robin and his wider kinship. His extended family network was largely affiliated to Essex. Robert Sidney, Robin's cousin, had been named governor of Flushing in 1589 but throughout the 1590s Sidney's progress at court was blocked by the Cecil faction simply because Sidney was one of Essex's adherents. Sidney took the opportunity provided by his role in the Low Countries to correspond with Cecil and to distance himself from Essex who had proved unable to advance his interests but his change of allegiance produced no immediate benefits. Robin owed his loyalty to Essex even though Lettice had never welcomed him into her household. The only alternative was Raleigh who had written so disparagingly of Robin in the aftermath of his West Indies venture. One of the consequences of his relationship with his step-brother was that Robin's name had been struck from the official account of the Cadiz expedition by Sir Robert Cecil even though he played a significant role. Essex's role, as a meaningful power at court, was essential if Robin was to achieve his own ambitions to go on another voyage.

Any calm which Elizabeth managed to establish at court and within her Privy Council by appointing Essex Earl Marshal vanished when Thomas, Lord Burgh, the Lord Deputy for Ireland, died from typhus. Sir William Knollys, Lettice's brother, was selected to replace Burgh. Essex wanted to appoint Sir George Carew. During the course of the ensuing argument, Essex turned his back on the queen. Elizabeth's temper exploded and she cuffed him around the ear. The earl tried to draw his sword on her. Nottingham threw himself between his monarch and the point of the sword. Two guards hauled Essex, swearing, from the room. In Raleigh's account of events, Essex compounded matters by telling the queen that 'her conditions were as crooked as her carcass'.[1] Raleigh's relationship with Essex had already broken down due to recriminations over the so-called Island Voyage of 1597. The petulant earl, who believed that he had the right to advise the queen and make military decisions as a birth right, was not incarcerated for his behaviour, instead, he left court in a sulk and waited for Elizabeth to make the next move.

The death of 2,000 English soldiers at the massacre of Yellow Ford drew the episode to a conclusion. Elizabeth provided Essex with

---

1. Guy, Elizabeth, The Forgotten years, p.ix.

an army in 1599 and sent him to Ireland as her Lord Deputy.[2] The expectation was that he should use the force to regain control of Ireland. Essex, who left London at the end of March, believed that his rivals in England would poison the queen against him unless he could win a speedy victory. Instead of victory over the Irish, Essex arranged a secret meeting with the Earl of Tyrone, negotiated a truce and hurried home. He arrived in Whitehall on a cold November morning just before dawn. Discovering that the queen was at Nonsuch he took some horses and hastened to find Elizabeth before anyone else could break the news of his insubordination. He arrived there at 10:15 am. The queen, suffering from toothache, rheumatism and increasingly depressed by bereavement, was still getting dressed. Essex burst into her chamber to discover her without her wig or makeup. Elizabeth stayed calm. Once she was properly attired and was assured that this was not the opening gambit in a coup, Essex was arrested but only after the queen treated him to a royal tongue lashing.

An enquiry was held. Essex was stripped of his offices and the grants that Elizabeth had bestowed upon him were withdrawn. In August 1600, Essex was released. He was determined to win back his former influence and favour. In September Elizabeth refused to renew the patent on Essex's control of sweet wines which left him with no means of servicing the huge debts he had accrued. Essex, increasingly desperate in the face of financial ruin, blamed Cecil and conspired to seize Whitehall and force the queen to dismiss both Cecil and Raleigh.

Essex had maintained a secret correspondence with James VI of Scotland through David Foulis since 1598. At best, Essex maintained that he would support James after the death of the queen. At worst, he appears to have discussed the possibility with Lord Mountjoy of raising an army and of James crossing the border with an army of his own to depose Elizabeth. It transpired that Essex sent Sir Henry Lee to find out the Scottish king's intentions only for James to backtrack. Robin could not have known that Essex had written once more to James declaring that Cecil wished to put the Infanta of Spain upon the English throne. James sent the Earl of Mar to speak with Elizabeth about reinstating Essex to his former offices but by then it was too late.

---

2. Lacey, p.216.

At the beginning of February 1601, Essex was summoned to appear before the Privy Council. He not only refused to attend but on 8 February took to the streets of London with 200 men. Cecil, in a pre-emptive strike, sent heralds to proclaim Essex a traitor. The earl rose expecting that the citizens of London would be on his side. Instead, he found himself locked in the city, the streets behind him and his followers blocked by the same heavy chains that had been placed in preparation for a Spanish invasion and his stepfather Sir Christopher Blount was seriously injured during fighting.

By four in the afternoon, Essex and fifty or so of his more loyal followers had retreated to Essex House on the Strand and were preparing for a siege. The Earl of Nottingham arrived with two cannons from the Tower. He threatened to blow Essex House and its inhabitants up unless they surrendered. With Nottingham was Robert Sidney who had distanced himself from the earl as his fortunes waned. He now found himself playing the role of negotiator because both sides trusted him and knew him to be a man of honour. He was also Essex's brother-in-law; the earl having married Sir Philip Sidney's widow, Frances Walsingham.

Ottaviano Lotti wrote to his employer the Grand Duke Ferdinando of Tuscany detailing the uprising. He named only three of the hundred men arrested and sent to the Tower for their part in the rebellion. They were Essex, his stefather Sir Christopher Blount who would go to the executioner's block for his treason and Robin.[3] It has been suggested that rather than being a ringleader, as his inclusion in the letter might infer, that Lotti knew Robin personally. It is feasible that Robin exchanged letters with Chaloner who spent some time in Tuscany gathering intelligence for Essex in 1596 via Lotti. Robin is not on the list of those who were fined for their part in the rebellion suggesting that his involvement was marginal. Any written evidence pertaining to Robin's participation in the events that unfolded in February 1601 was destroyed by Essex who took the opportunity to burn his private papers whilst Essex House lay under siege. A list of his supporters and letters sent to him by King James went up in flames as the gates of Essex House were forced and snipers took potshots at the windows.

---

3. Lee, p.99.

Essex was tried and executed for treason on 25 February 1601. Like so many traitors before him, his head was parboiled, dipped in pitch and displayed on London Bridge. If Fortune's wheel slipped and threw the earl down, it began to slip downwards for Robin as well. The rebellion and his short imprisonment seemed to coincide with Robin chafing against his status as the illegitimate son of the Earl of Leicester. Although Leicester had provided financially for Robin, there was no chance that he could inherit the titles of either his father or his late uncle. He had much to think about when, upon release from the Tower, he made his way home to Kenilworth where Alice was about to give birth to another daughter.

Chapter XIII

Surprised by Time

Elizabeth continued to dance, to ride and to rule her kingdom but she suffered from bouts of melancholy as her ageing family, friends and loyal servants began to die around her. Her old enemy Philip II of Spain died on 13 September 1596. Burghley died in 1598. William Campden attributed the queen's own good health to her diet despite it being evident at the beginning of 1603 that 'human infirmitie'[1] was bringing the queen's reign to its conclusion.

Alice Dudley was pregnant again during the winter of 1602. Another daughter, Anne, was born in 1603. In London, Elizabeth spent a despondent Christmas. She caught a cold and developed a painful boil on her face. In January 1603, after the New Year's festivities came to an end, she decided to go to Richmond because it was where Elizabeth could 'best trust her sickly old age'. She and her ladies travelled from Westminster. The queen insisted on wearing 'her sommer like garments'.[2] It was a cold and wet journey. She caught another cold and had difficulty swallowing. Elizabeth's melancholy deepened when word reached the court that Catherine Howard, Countess of Nottingham, Robin's aunt, died on 25 February. Catherine, the granddaughter of Mary Boleyn, served the queen for forty-five years. Elizabeth lost her appetite. She was unable to sleep. By March the queen's throat was so sore that she would not speak. She was sixty-nine years old.

Elizabeth's lady-in-waiting, Elizabeth Southwell the younger, told her story of the queen's final days in April 1607.[3] By then she had served not one but two queens and caused a scandal by eloping with her cousin,

---

1. John Harington to Mall Harrington, 27 December 1602, in John Harington, Nugae Antiqueae, (1779) cited in Loomis, p.482.
2. Roger Wilbraham, the Master of Requests quoted in Loomis, p.488.
3. Elizabeth Southwell's account was recorded by the Jesuit Robert Persons, Stonyhurst Ang. Iii.77 Stonyhurst College Lancashire, the Very Reverend F. J. Turner archivist, printed in full in Loomis.

Robin, a married man with five young daughters. Historians still regard her account with suspicion because she was a woman who had turned Catholic and because her version was used by the Jesuits to tarnish Elizabeth's reputation.[4] Equally her story contains details that can be found in no other version. Hers is the only report which has the queen calling Cecil 'Little man' and reminding him that 'must' was not a word to be used to Princes when he tried to persuade her to go to bed.[5]

The queen, it was said by Elizabeth Southwell, had not looked into a mirror for a full twenty years. Now she demanded a looking glass and responded with fury when she looked in it to see an old woman who had lost her teeth and her hair. Other accounts described Elizabeth's overwhelming guilt stemming from the deaths of Lady Katherine Grey who starved herself into an early grave in 1568 and the execution of Mary Queen of Scots in 1587. According to Sir Robert Carey, 'She shedd many teares and sighs, manifesting her innocence that she never gave consent to the death of that queene'.[6] She stopped eating and sat all day on cushions scattered about the floor. The queen refused to speak. She stared silently at the ground and sucked her index finger. Elizabeth Southwell's account dispenses with the cushions and places the queen on her toilet stool for two nights and three days. She refused to go to bed. She was afraid that if she lay down that she would never get up again. She had always been afraid of the dark and now she was frightened by ghosts and hallucinations. She told Lady Scrope, in confidence, that she was seeing fiery visions. Hallucinations can sometimes occur in older people with delirium. They may be caused by infection so it is not beyond the bounds of possibility that the queen's final days were tormented ones. If Elizabeth did confess to Philadelphia Scrope that she was being tormented by flames, it is unlikely that the information would have been missing from Robert Carey's own account of the queen's death. Philadelphia was Carey's sister. More likely then, that visions of fires and by inference Hell, were a later Jesuit addition to the story.

The Lord Admiral, Elizabeth Southwell's grandfather and Robin's uncle, came from his home where he was mourning for Catherine his wife. He sat with the queen, talked to her, convinced her to go to bed

---

4. Loomis, p.483–484.
5. From the Southwell manuscript printed in full in Loomis, p.485.
6. Carey in Nichols, ed., p.603.

and persuaded her to take a little broth. During a brief conversation, Elizabeth said that she was 'tied about the neck with a chain of iron'.[7] This offers some circumstantial evidence that has drawn some historians to conclude that she was suffering from dental abscesses which resulted in an infection and severe dental sepsis. It would explain the pneumonia-like symptoms that Elizabeth suffered, the fever, the painful mouth, tongue and inability to swallow and even the confusion which might have resulted in hallucinations. Despite the physic that her doctors administered, her throat was not eased. It was clear that the queen did not have much longer to live. Her Privy Council gathered in the rooms outside her chamber. Preparations began for the transfer of power. And the queen's bishops came to comfort her. In most accounts, they found Elizabeth in a receptive frame of mind. In her goddaughter's account, Elizabeth was furious at their arrival and sent them away.

Elizabeth died in the early hours of 24 March 1603. Cecil was quick to put it about that in the final hours of her life she identified, by gesture, James VI of Scotland, the son of Mary Queen of Scots as her successor. Robert Carey, Southwell's great-uncle, described Elizabeth holding her hands above her head to signify a crown when her ministers asked if she wanted James to succeed her. In Southwell's account, Elizabeth died refusing to name an heir. After the queen's death, a small packet of letters was found beside her bed tied with a ribbon. One of them was Leicester's final letter to his beloved Elizabeth. The queen's body was wrapped in costly waxed linen cloth and placed in a lead-lined coffin that was draped with velvet. Her ladies took turns, in groups of six, to sit with the coffin to keep watch over it.

On 26 March, Elizabeth's coffin was moved from Richmond to Whitehall. The coffin was never left unattended. Lady Anne Clifford's diary records her own mother sitting with it for several nights. According to Elizabeth Southwell, the royal corpse burst with 'such a crack'[8] in exactly the same way that her father's corpse disintegrated. Southwell described the explosion within the coffin as so great that the queen's head exploded causing the coffin to break. Elizabeth was not buried for a full thirty-five days, so perhaps it is not so strange that gases might have

---

7. Ibid.
8. Ibid, p.486.

built up. However, this element of the account is generally accepted to be unreliable as other sources do not describe it but Elizabeth Southwell, providing her testimony in 1607, said that the matter was suppressed by Robert Cecil.

Queen Elizabeth I was buried on 28 April. She could no longer protect the Robin who might have been her own son had she followed her heart. Robin missed his chance to prove his legitimacy. Elizabeth never forgave Lettice for marrying Leicester and the opportunity to humiliate her would have been one that she enjoyed. King James I arrived in London on 7 May 1603. Whereas in the past Robin had Elizabeth's favour because he was the son of Leicester and her ear through Douglas, he now found himself on the margins of the new court as men scrambled for position, power and influence. Kinsmen who might have helped him like his uncle Nottingham and godfather Lee were no longer prominent courtiers. Fortune's wheel sped its downwards trajectory. Despite his wealth, Robin was a mere knight of illegitimate descent with the whiff of rebellion about him. Even worse, his father was the Earl of Leicester, the man who James I chose to blame, along with Sir Francis Walsingham, for the execution of his own mother Mary Queen of Scots.

Chapter XIV

A Trial

Since he was a child Robin understood that his parents were not married. He could not inherit his father's, uncle's or grandfather's titles. Their nearest legitimate claimant was Robin's cousin Sir Robert Sidney, a courtier and a soldier. Throughout the 1590s, he had been involved with the conflict in the Low Countries including the battle of Zutphen in 1586 which claimed his brother, Sir Philip Sidney's, life. It was Sidney who negotiated with Essex and persuaded him to surrender in the aftermath of the earl's ill-advised rising. Even so, Elizabeth did not elevate him to the peerage with either Leicester or Warwick's titles despite his petitions that she should do so. There were no other claimants. John Dudley, Duke of Northumberland and Jane Guildford had thirteen children but their sons died without heirs. Ambrose married three times. His first wife bore him a child called Margaret in 1552 but the young mother and child died from the sweating sickness soon after. His second wife, Elizabeth Tailboys, died in 1563. His third marriage to Anne Russell was also childless.

Owen Jones' revelation about Robin's legitimacy lacked legal solidity. It was just enough to make Robin think that he might be Leicester's lawful son. As the end of Elizabeth's life approached a man called Thomas Drury contacted Robin.[1] They were kin of sorts. Drury's cousin Lord Robert Rich married the Earl of Essex's sister Penelope, whilst his brother, William Drury, was married to Sir Edward Stafford's sister Elizabeth. It's thought that Stafford's man 'Dewry' in Paris may well have been Thomas. He claimed that he could provide Robin with two witnesses who would substantiate the truth of his parents' wedding. Early in 1603, Drury and Robin's proctor, a man called Thomas Ward, arrived at Kenilworth with a woman called Magdalen Salisbury. In her youth, as Magdalen Frodsham, she served Lady Sheffield. She was also

1. Lee, p.100.

kin to Thomas Chaloner which must have added to her credibility in
Robin's mind. She was prepared to testify that Douglas and Leicester
were married secretly before Robin's birth. There were doubts even then.
Mrs Erisa, now Lady Parker, who was present during Douglas's laying-in
stated that Magdalen entered Douglas's service after Robin's birth rather
than before. The evidence was contradictory. Salisbury said that Douglas
gave birth to a child two days after the marriage. Robin wasn't born
until 1574 and the counterfeited tale of the secret child born at Dudley
Castle was earlier – besides which Douglas was adamant during her own
testimony that she only ever bore one child by Leicester.

Robin's father-in-law took a hand in matters. How much better would
it be for an ambitious man to have an earl as a son-in-law rather than
an illegitimate knight? Dr Creake was appointed as Council.[2] The
Archbishop of Canterbury was approached with a plea that he should
hear the depositions for himself. John Whitgift, archbishop since 1583
declined but authorised a Commission of the Court of Audience to take
witness depositions. The authority was dated 20 May 1603. One of
Leigh's chaplains took the statements at Alice's family home in Stoneleigh.
Leigh's involvement is enough to suggest that he and Alice encouraged
Robin's hopes and it also goes some way to explain the subsequent family
breakdown. There was an outbreak of plague that delayed the sitting of
the Court of Audience. The case was moved to the Consistory Court
of Lichfield. If Dr Zachary Babington, the archbishop's chancellor,
concluded a wedding had taken place at Esher then the matter would
have progressed to the College of Heralds to decide which title belonged
to whom. Douglas would not even be required to testify about the alleged
marriage.

Robin wrote to his father's secretary, Arthur Atye, in search of
additional information to support his case. Atye became friends with Sir
Philip Sidney whilst they were both at Oxford and gained Leicester's
patronage at the same time. He was a trusted courier whilst Leicester was
in the Low Countries.

I am sure you hear of my proceedings to prove my legitimation and the
Council's authority for me to proceed in the Court of Arches; for as

---

2. Ibid, p.103.

much as I understood by Mr Barker's deed that you were acquainted with an instrument my father made, of this last reputed marriage, under the hands and seals and oaths of them that were at it, and it is thought that he might procure sentence of the same secretly from Doctor Aubrey to colour aught better which afterward he seriously repented that matter. Now because this point being known, is of little effect; a marriage proved good before it, yet not nown, might do harm in proceeding, wherefore I pray you most earnestly that you will acquaint this bearer, Mr Ward, my proctor, with your directions therein, of the substance of the deed.[3]

Ayte transferred his service to the Earl of Essex after Leicester's death and was knighted in 1603, like many other of Essex's followers who returned to favour after James became king. It was unlikely that Ayte would find it politically expedient to produce evidence to support Robin's claim. And like so many other of the players in the putative marriage between Leicester and Douglas, he was reaching the end of his life. He died and was buried at St Dunstan-in-the-West on 4 December 1604, taking any knowledge of Leicester's marriage to Douglas with him to the grave.

Sir Robert Sidney regarded himself as the rightful beneficiary of his uncles' estates as well as their titles. He had pursued the titles of Warwick and Leicester throughout the 1590s but Elizabeth refused to grant them to him. It was not Elizabeth's policy to make new peers. Fourteen titles died out during her reign. With Elizabeth dead, opportunities presented themselves to both Sidney and Lettice. She and Sidney agreed to support one another against Robin. Counter charges were levelled against Robin. He was accused of using his uncle's title – something that was in King James' gift alone. He had to deny that he had ever called himself the Earl of Warwick and Leicester or that his watermen wore coats emblazoned with the Ragged Staff. A charge of criminal conspiracy was brought against Robin which resulted in an order in council being issued on 18 October 1603. Robin's case in the ecclesiastical court at Lichfield was halted and all the evidence he collected impounded. Even worse, Sidney's supporters included some of Robin's extended family. Sir Edward Stafford was prepared to testify against his stepson. He had an obvious interest in

---

3. Adlard, p.285.

maintaining his stepson's illegitimacy. He claimed that Robin terrified Douglas into testifying. Before his death in February 1605, Stafford provided evidence as to the content of both his and Douglas's interviews with Elizabeth I about whether or not Douglas was married to Leicester. He said of his wife in 1585, 'her conscience be no further touched than an honourable intent and a weak woman deceived'.[4]

Lettice also charged Robin with defamation – if his parents were legitimately married then Lettice's subsequent marriage was bigamous. The charges were suggested by the attorney general, Sir Edward Coke. Robert Sidney applied to the court of the Star Chamber and the case was moved there. Elizabeth, with no love of Lettice, might well have been sympathetic to Robin's cause but Sir Robert Sidney had smoothed James Stuart's path to the throne. Robin perhaps should have remembered that Sidney had been created Baron Sidney of Penshurst by James I in 1603 and named Lord Chamberlain of Queen Anne's household. In addition, the Earl of Essex's rebellion expressed the aim of inviting James to England. James' gratitude to the executed earl could be demonstrated through support of Essex's mother. It did not signify that Robin spent time in the Tower in the aftermath of the rebellion. The fact that he was Leicester's son became a misfortune because James chose to blame Elizabeth's favourite for his own mother's execution. As the case progressed Douglas appealed to her brother, the Earl of Nottingham, for support. Howard was non-committal. He had recently acquired preferment at court by taking for his second wife Lady Margaret Stuart who was part of James I's own extended family.[5] Men who Robin counted as his friends were too busy cementing their own positions to risk disfavour on his behalf.

Robin's trial began in the Star Chamber on 22 June 1604 with Sir Edward Coke leading the prosecution. By the end of the day, the trial was adjourned for eleven months and reconvened in May 1605. Robin protested that since he had evidence that Douglas and Leicester were married that he should have the right to have that evidence tried within a court of law. The case came to be described as 'the greatest cause now in England'.[6] Nottingham might not have had stood by his nephew but his eldest son Lord William Howard came to Robin's aid as did his

---

4. CSP Foreign, p.378.
5. Lee, p.107.
6. Ibid, p.109.

second cousin Baron Dudley. His own half-brother Edmund Sheffield risked losing a much-needed allowance of £1,000 a year from the king to support Robin, demonstrating that even with the king against him that the case was not clear-cut.[7]

Robin produced five witnesses, including the bride, to testify that the marriage took place and a further ninety to support his case. Other witnesses were ill or, like Dr Julio, long dead. When the case came to trial Magdalen panicked and said she could remember nothing. A servant called Roose testified as to her alarm before she provided her account of events. It transpired that Thomas Drury, who first approached Robin about the matter, coached Magdalen before meeting with Robin. Evidence was presented that found Magdalen living in the house of Thomas Ward in 1602. Drury made her promises, wrote down a statement and sent it to Robin on 8 August 1603. Drury undertook to provide more information in return for payment. Robin accepted Magdalen's statement and that of her brother Henry without considering that Coke would turn them into rogues or himself into a fool for believing them.

Thomas Drury, a life-long swindler, did not profit from his involvement with Robin. He died at the Swan Inn, Southwark, from plague on 26 August 1603, but like so much in the story of Robin's life it leaves unanswered questions. Drury began a career of swindling when he was at Cambridge University where he encountered the Earl of Oxford and Sir Walter Raleigh. By the summer of 1585, he was in the Fleet Prison. Two years later he was in Paris in the service of Sir Edward Stafford. It is likely that he was involved in a world of intrigue and spying though it is hard to say for whom or why. In any event by May 1591, he was back in England in the Marshalsea Prison where he spent the next two years. Drury was released on the request of Sir John Puckering, the Lord Keeper of the Great Seal, to do 'some service' overseas in November 1592. Early the following year he resurfaced in London. He was one of the men who accused Christopher Marlow of heresy and seditious atheism. In 1605, Coke called Drury a 'man of mean condition and notoriously evil character' but no one thought to enquire whether Drury, who worked as a spy for both Burghley and Cecil, was still employed by Sir Robert.

---

7. Ibid.

In July, Coke insisted that Douglas provide a sworn statement. She testified at her home in Sudeley in Gloucestershire. She was adamant that a marriage to the Earl of Leicester had taken place, that her life had been repeatedly threatened, and attempts had been made to poison her, and that her hair and nails had fallen out.[8] She did not adequately explain why she did not tell the truth when she was questioned before her marriage to Sir Edward Stafford. The libel contained about Leicester's murderous tendencies in *Leicester's Commonwealth* may have promoted her assertion that she feared for her life and provided a ready excuse for her own actions. Douglas's words were a demonstration of love for her son. She risked execution. In 1604, at the same time as Robin's case got underway, Parliament passed a law that made bigamy a capital offence unless a spouse went missing and remained unheard of for seven years. Before then it had been a matter for the ecclesiastical courts which did not execute people for their crimes. After the Bigamy Act of 1604, it was something for the common law courts. Both the timing and the wording of the act are an indicator of the importance of Robin's petition and the determination of the State to injure Leicester's son.

Another witness, Owen Jones, the servant employed by Leicester when Robin was a child, also gave his testimony. Lettice and Robert Sidney made much of the fact that Robin gave him money. The majority of Robin's witnesses were dismissed because they were servants, 'the baseness and meanness of the defendant's witnesses'[9] was emphasised by Coke time and again. Coke stated that the Frodshams' account was 'not worth a frieze jerkin'.[10] Magdalen Salisbury would eventually be fined £100, as was Henry Frodsham. Robin was fined a similar amount because he was 'indiscreet in his proceedings'.[11] No doubt Coke's venom was enhanced by the promise of payment from Sidney upon the collapse of Robin's case.

Sidney's evidence given on 3 May consisted of establishing his own family tree and presenting the depositions taken at the time of Lettice's marriage which did nothing to disprove Robin's claims. The following day James created Robin's cousin Viscount Lisle of Penshurst. Sir Robert

---

8. Report of the Barony of Lisle: 254.
9. Lee, p.113.
10. Ibid, p.111.
11. Ibid, p.114.

Cecil became the Earl of Salisbury. Salisbury cemented his authority at the beginning of James' reign by bringing Raleigh, who was a potential threat to his own power, down with the so-called Main Plot of 1603. Robin was small fry compared to Raleigh, but like Sir Walter, Robin was a loose end to be tied up. His name was mentioned during the course of the Bye Plot trial of 1603. Anthony Copley, one of the defendants in the case who sought to force James I to grant religious toleration to his Catholic subjects, named Robin as being interested in joining future conspiracies.[12] Rowland White wrote to Gilbert Talbot, now Earl of Shrewsbury, in his father's place expressing the view that the court had queried Robin's legal methods rather than exploring the legitimacy of his claim.[13] Given that White was employed by Sir Robert Sidney after a long association with the Sidney family, he probably ought to have been more circumspect with his opinions.

On 10 May 1605, judgement was passed. Douglas's wedding to Leicester was deemed never to have taken place though Salisbury admitted that it was 'natural for him (Robin) to want to prove his legitimacy'.[14] The court ordered that all of Robin's evidence should be suppressed. Having lost his court case and been denied the opportunity to test the validity of the assertion that his parents were married, Robin, his mother, his wife and his father-in-law found themselves facing criminal charges. So far as the Star Chamber was concerned, Robin's belief that his parents were married stemmed from wishful thinking and his mother's testimony said more about her imagination than reality. Without more evidence, the truth of the matter cannot be proven beyond doubt. Sir William Dugdale, the seventeenth century antiquary, expressed the view after seeing depositions retained in the Cotton Collection that Leicester was married to Douglas, meaning that their subsequent unions with Lettice and Sir Edward Stafford were bigamous. A fire in 1731 destroyed the Cotton manuscripts including the documents relating to the trial that might have resolved the matter more certainly. In 1899, Sir George Warner made a study of papers he could find. His introduction to *The Voyage of Sir Robert Dudley* expressed the view that no marriage had been undertaken. Conyers Read rejected the proposition in 1936 as does Adams in his entry for the *Oxford*

12. De Lisle, p.281n.
13. Lee, p. 114.
14. Ibid.

Dictionary of National Biography. Robin's case was resurrected in the nineteenth century when Sir John Shelley-Sidney inherited Penshurst. He claimed the baronies of Lisle and Dudley by right of descent. The Committee of Privileges in the House of Lords reviewed the case and having done so refused to give Shelley-Sidney the titles because he was unable to prove that Douglas had not married Leicester in Esher. So far as they were concerned, Robin's parents might well have been married.

Part III

Chapter XV

Exile

Robin's reaction to the suppression of his evidence and the court's determination of his illegitimacy was to ask permission to travel abroad for three years. A licence was issued on 25 June 1605. It permitted Robin, three servants and four geldings, or nags, to board ship. Robin took the £80 that the State permitted him when he left England on 2 July. No doubt there were more gold and valuables secreted about his person. In his luggage were his charts, his notes and a selection of scientific instruments made by the finest makers in England. Evidence in the Medici archives suggests that he may have taken the precaution of transferring a considerable share of his wealth to France before leaving England, implying that he saw the tilt of Fortune's wheel before the Star Chamber delivered its verdict and decided to take matters into his own hands. A French informant, viewed as unreliable, suggested that Robin managed to move 40,000 ducats prior to his flight.[1]

There were a number of ways that Robin might have achieved the transfer of funds out of England through his contacts. Medici bankers operated internationally from the fifteenth century onwards. The London branch of the family bank closed its doors in 1478 making a direct transfer of funds by letters of exchange from England to Tuscany more difficult. There were also German banking houses that worked as intermediaries between centres of commerce using letters of exchange amongst other things. Goldsmiths lent and changed money. In 1564, the Spanish ambassador reported that Spinola, a wine merchant from Genoa, acted as Leicester's banker. For a man of Robin's wealth and contacts, moving money was not an insurmountable problem.

A second scandal was about to break. Robin left his wife and daughters who were all under eight years old at Kenilworth but he did not travel alone. He was accompanied by a beautiful woman disguised as a page.

---

1. Lee, p.123.

Elizabeth Southwell, Queen Elizabeth's cousin and witness to her last weeks, was now one of Queen Anne's maids. She was a beautiful and wealthy nineteen year old, Robin was thirty years old. He had been the subject of speculation and gossip for months but no breath of scandal attached to Elizabeth Southwell during that time nor any hint of a romance. The King commanded Sir William Monson, Admiral of the Narrow Sea, to prevent the couple crossing the Channel. It was too late. The Governor of Calais briefly halted their escape but Lotti, the Tuscan agent, reporting London's gossip, wrote that Elizabeth explained that she came with the 'object of entering a monastery, and serving God in the true religion'[2] and the pair were permitted to leave.

King James demanded that the French return both his wife's maid-of-honour and Robin, only to be informed that they claimed sanctuary in France having converted to Catholicism. King Henri IV said that it was impossible to return them as they would face persecution for their beliefs in England. It is difficult to know what Robin's religious beliefs might have been even if he did later claim that his 'opinion' did not change upon his departure from England, rather he concealed his true beliefs for many years. A distant cousin, Richard, from the Yanwath line of Dudleys, fled an agreement to marry in order to become a Catholic priest. The Howard family had much closer ties to the Old Religion which could prove uncomfortable on occasion. Elizabeth's cousin once removed, the Jesuit Robert Southwell, was regarded as a Catholic martyr following his death in 1595. A tendency towards Catholicism may have resulted in Sir Francis Walsingham setting spies upon Douglas's husband Sir Edward Stafford whilst he was in Paris. Most significant, on 5 November 1605, Robin's brother-in-law Robert Catesby, increasingly fanatical since the death of his wife Catherine in 1598, attempted to blow up the Houses of Parliament.

In early October the errant couple arrived in Lyons with its covered passageways or *traboules* that connected noisy weaving workshops to the River Saône. The streets were filled with bustle and many different languages. Along the water's edge cargo vessels loaded and unloaded their wares. Robin and Elizabeth paused. It was a crossroads in their journey. Robin took the opportunity to contact Captain Robert Eliot, an English

2. Ibid, p.118.

exile with connections to the Vatican. He petitioned the papacy for a dispensation to marry Elizabeth. There was no petition for an annulment of the marriage to Alice. The petition was for a dispensation from the laws of consanguinity to marry Elizabeth because they were cousins. The marriage to Alice that had taken place in a Protestant church was no marriage at all and besides which Robin claimed that he was contracted in marriage to Frances Vavasour in 1591 meaning that his subsequent marriages were not legal. In a few words, he rendered his young family illegitimate. Frances' death a few months before his elopement meant that he was free to marry Elizabeth. Fortunately for Robin's daughters, Robin's subsequent marriage to Elizabeth in France ran contrary to the Bigamy Act of 1604.

Robin made some provision for Alice and their children. His desertion of his wife, who according to some sources offered to turn Catholic and join him in Europe with their children, did not reflect well upon him. He 'conveyed his estates in trust to certain relatives and allies'.[3] Two of his trustees were his father-in-law and Alice's brother Sir John Leigh.[4] It was a wise precaution. King James sequestrated Robin's estates leaving Alice and her children to make a home in Dudley House in London. The question of ownership of Robin's estates, Kenilworth Castle in particular, would reverberate down the coming years.

Robin needed to provide for himself and his new wife. Any funds he transferred from England would not last forever and besides, he had expensive tastes. He determined that he would go to Tuscany. There were long-standing mercantile and cultural connections between England and Italy. Sir Thomas Shirley who married Frances Vavasour when the world thought she was in love with Robin sought to repair his fortunes there in 1602. More significantly, Robin's old friend and university tutor Sir Thomas Chaloner served as the Earl of Essex's agent in Tuscany in 1596. Much of Essex's paperwork for this period was destroyed by Essex himself during the final hours of his rebellion. The extent of Robin's own dealing with Florence or his knowledge of Essex's transactions with Florence are unknown. There is circumstantial evidence of Lotti's letter to the Archduke of Tuscany following the 1601 rebellion that suggested

3. Ibid, p.130.
4. Ibid.

Robin was known to him personally. Nor is it unreasonable to suggest that Lotti continued to operate as a postal service between Robin and his family in England.

The Grand Duke, Ferdinando I, wanted men who knew the sea. He needed to strengthen the Tuscan navy to protect his trade routes from piracy which was rife in the Mediterranean. He followed the expansion of the Spanish and Dutch empires and wanted to develop trade, even an empire, in the Indies which in turn would boost Tuscan commerce. The problems lay in cost and expert knowledge.

He was not alone in wanting vessels and crews. The Venetians were also in the market for English maritime knowledge. Robin felt sufficient to the challenge posed. In later years he would recall 'Having now as I live, no country, nor means to raise myself, but my knowledge'[5] he calculated that Tuscany would provide him with both refuge and an opportunity to rebuild his life. By bringing a selection of navigational instruments with him, he was able to demonstrate where his expertise lay. He approached the grand duke via Eliot.

Robin may also have felt confident about travelling to Italy because he had a grasp of the language. Leicester provided shelter for expatriate Italians including Dr Julio the Italian doctor who, Robin believed, had been a witness to his parents' wedding as well as the man accused of poisoning Leicester's enemies by the author of *Leicester's Commonwealth*. In addition to the doctor, Leicester gave refuge to Alberico Gentili, a notable jurist and Giacomo Concio, the queen's Italian tutor. At the beginning of 1603, when Elizabeth met the Venetian secretary Scaramelli, she insisted on speaking with him in Italian. It was politically wise for Elizabethan courtiers to speak some of Elizabeth's favourite language. Leicester was also a patron of the arts. As well as portraiture of the kind by Zuccaro displayed at the Kenilworth entertainment of 1575, the second-generation Italian resident in England, John Florio, dedicated his work *First Fruites* to Leicester. The Anglo-Italian instruction manual published in 1578 targeted merchants and their buyers. Whilst history does not record when Robin began learning the language, it is not unreasonable to suggest that Robin knew sufficient to make himself understood.

---

5. Adlard, p.306.

In the meantime, Robin explored Lyons which was a centre for silk manufacture, a monopoly having been granted to the city for its production in 1540 by King Francois I. For more than sixty years, all the silks coming into France from Italy or the East passed through the warehouses of Lyon. Now the technology for dyeing, spinning and weaving silk was evolving. Robin, interested in everything, spoke to the Lyonnais manufacturers and learned all he could about silk manufacture before his journey resumed.

Chapter XVI

Shipwright

Grand Duke Ferdinando I of Tuscany concluded that Robin had the skills that he needed, but arranged for Lotti, the Florentine agent in London, to report on Leicester's son before proceeding. In a letter dated 23 September 1606, Elliot wrote that 'courteous and loving offers,' had been made to Robin. A letter from Belisario Vinta, the First Secretary of State to the Grand Duchy to Robin dated 8 January 1607 shows that Vinta was impressed with the book about maritime matters written by Robin and sent as part of his application to Ferdinando.[1] Robin borrowed £200 and departed Lyons along with his wife and two servants.[2] Another letter from Eliot to Vinta explains that Robin arranged for 'his ship, being of 300 tons' and loaded with merchandise to sail to Ligornia before continuing to Livorno.[3] The vessel was rented by the English merchants who owned the cargo. This suggests both the stratagem by which the vessel left England unimpeded. Robin told Eliot that amongst those on board were 'seafarers, sea carpenters, and other similar provisions, both to build ships and to ship'. Again, suggesting that Robin used his time in Lyons to order his affairs in such a way that he would be welcome in Florence and have additional means of supporting himself. In October 1606, Robin and Elizabeth arrived in Tuscany but the first direct reference to their being in Livorno is February the following year.

It suited Ferdinando to recognise Robin's titles as Earl of Warwick and Leicester but he also sought to ameliorate the hostility that James I exhibited towards his newest employee. In a letter to the Earl of Northampton, the Grand Duke described Robin as a 'loyal and

---

1. Horodowich and Markey, p.219.
2. Lee, p.125.
3. Lee notes that travel from Marseilles to Livorno did not begin for another twenty years p.124.

faithful vassal of the King'.[4] Ferdinando's assurances that Robin regarded him as a 'father and he should be treated as a son,' were not music to Northampton's ears. He rose by dint of clinging to Salisbury's coat tails and courting James Stuart. In due course, he would assist his great-niece Anne Howard to obtain a divorce from her husband the 3rd Earl of Essex so that she could marry the king's favourite, Robert Carr, whose mistress she already was. Northampton would find himself part of a murder scandal as a direct consequence of his involvement.

More practically Ferdinando encouraged Robin to maintain his contacts with English mariners and shipbuilders to invite them to come and work in Tuscany. It helped that men like Sir Thomas Shirley, writing in July 1607, wished to serve the Duke of Tuscany, even though they ran the risk of being regarded as pirates by James I and his ministers:

> As my service was wholly devoted to my Lord your father in his life,
> … I beseech you to hold me in the Duke's good opinions, and it can
> no way be ill for you to have me in those parts, because I am so much
> yours truly.
> My knowledge in Turkey matters may work great honour to me
> and more to your lordship.[5]

Robin also set about buying ordinance from English vessels that docked in Florentine harbours. Sir Henry Wotton, the English ambassador in Venice, complained that Ferdinando, 'protects Sir Robert Dudley and the captain Eliot and other English exiles and traitors'.[6] The ambassador sent a messenger with a letter to Livorno from King James I for Robin but the messenger was arrested. Wotton's concerns sprang from Robin's conversion to Catholicism and his elopement with Elizabeth Southwell. There was also a belated realisation that Robin understood naval architecture and the latest navigational methods learned from England's master shipwrights, adventurers and instrument makers. In London, Lotti's reports to Ferdinando were filled with news of James' displeasure with his erstwhile subject and gossip relating to Robin's relationship with Elizabeth Southwell. Ferdinando's response was to tell Lotti to do his

4. Lee, p.127.
5. CP, p.121.
6. Lorimer, p.31.

best for Robin because he 'shows himself very day more worthy of our protection'.[7]

In 1607, Lotti approached Matthew Baker, the royal master shipwright of Deptford who had advised Robin on building the *Bear* and *Bear's Whelp*. Baker used mathematics to work out the burden and deadweight tonnage of the vessels he built. It was he who built the *Galleon Leicester*, entirely from carefully calculated blueprints making it the first of its kind. Leicester purchased the vessel as his share of the Fenton Voyage in 1581. Baker, in receipt of a pension worth £40 a year from the Crown was in his seventies at the time Robin invited him, through the Florentine Agent, to Tuscany. Baker declined Robin's offer but recommended another shipwright in his place. He sent models and notes via Lotti but it is unclear whether the models in question were three-dimensional models or drawings. He died on 31 August 1613 still supervising his work in the dockyards of Deptford.

Robin began his shipbuilding career in Livorno by planning and building a pinnace called the *Ursa Minor* or *Little Bear*, which was eighty-four feet long and in proportion to the main part of his building project the *San Giovanii Battista*. Construction commenced under the supervision of the superintendent of the Livorno Customs Office, Bernardo Uguccioni, who also collected what information Robin was able to provide about his fellow countrymen. The *San Giovanii Battista* was a three-masted, 600-ton galleon of sixty-four guns. Galleons of the period could serve as warships or merchantmen and sailed into the eighteenth century because their design was so effective. Robin, recognising the need for the Tuscan navy to be built for war rather than having a multi-purpose construction, chose to build a more streamlined boat that was narrower and lower in the water than traditional galleons. His boat was based on the kind of vessel planned by Matthew Baker. He would have been familiar with Baker's formula for working out the proportions of a ship as set out in Baker's handwritten papers entitled *Fragments of Ancient English Shipwrightry*. The total cost of building and outfitting the vessel came to 17,878 ducats. Ferdinando's Court Diary noted that the vessel was launched on 20 March 1608. A drawing by Filippo Napoletano shows the process of launching by which windlasses heaved the galleon down the slipway with the aid of

---

7. Lee, p.133.

tugs at the other end. The sketch also shows that barrels were attached to the underside of the hull for stability during the launch.[8]

Robin wrote to Prince Henry in England, who was interesting in expanding the English navy, extolling the virtues of his design. He boasted that because of her speed that the *San Giovanii Battista* was the terror of Turkish corsairs.[9] He made no mention that there were problems with the galleon or the *Ursa Minor* because of their streamlined design. The vessels sat low in the water if overloaded. However, the launching of the *San Giovanii Battista* in March 1608 proved Robin's usefulness and he was welcome to stay especially when Robin's new ship proved its worth by capturing a 'captain-galleon' twice its size and worth a million ducats. Ferdinando ignored King James I's complaints about harbouring a traitor whilst in England. Salvetti, the Tuscan Ambassador, wrote that 'Little does the King care for the displeasure of the Grand Duke who acts in this unfriendly manner'.[10]

Robin received several offers to buy the *Ursa Minor*. It was suggested that the pair of vessels should remain together and he was loath to sell his pinnace, although he may have hoped that Ferdinando would take it in payment for a debt which he owed. Before that Robin needed to demonstrate its worth and perhaps recoup some of his investment. He and his co-investors, Horatio Erbucci and others, decided to send the pinnace's captain, Stampini, on a privateering voyage licenced on the understanding they would only attack non-Christians. Before the pinnace sailed Robin was called to Florence but left his business in the care of Gasparre Orsi and Tommaso Unt. Differences arose; Robin said that he did not sign the ship's articles as the law required and nor did Orsi and Unt. The *Ursa Minor* sailed, was damaged in a storm off Sicily and entered the port of Trapani where its captain and crew abandoned it. Nicolo Bulgarella, a Tuscan living in Trapani, spent money repairing the vessel. Its owners, including Robin, refused to repay his expenses. The matter was taken before the Consuls of the Sea at Pisa on 21 June 1609 by Robin who sought redress for his losses and the return of the *Ursa Minor* which by then was in the hands of another captain. The

8. Napoletano, Filippo formerly attributed to Tassi, Agostino, A ship in dry dock about to be launched, (pen and brown ink, 1617–1622), British Museum Ff,2.153.
9. Ibid, p.135.
10. Skrine, p.178.

Florentine authorities sought to quash the case because Robin did not fully understand the laws of the court to which he applied for redress.

There were a number of issues to be addressed beginning with whether the *Ursa Minor* was a licenced privateer or not. The court also spent much of its time listening to evidence to ascertain whether or not the ship's articles had been read to the crew. They had to decide whether Erbucci gave the ship its sailing orders without Robin's knowledge. This was important because anyone who sent a ship to sea without the agreement of all the ship's partners became liable for the venture. During questioning, Giovanni Sella, an apprentice at the Livorno arsenal reported that whilst still in harbour some crew refused to board the *Ursa Minor* because they feared it would sink. Other men complained there was nowhere for them to shelter in the event of bad weather. The *Ursa Minor* was proportional to the *San Giovanii Battista* and like the galleon, it sat lower in the water than was usual with a galleon because of the way its sides were shaped. Witnesses for Erbucci recorded that Robin oversaw changes to the boat's superstructure and that all the owners signed the articles which were read to the crew. Further depositions were taken about the value of the pinnace which was two hundred scudi less than Robin's own valuation and whether or not the pinnace was seaworthy. Questions arose about its design, structure, the materials used to build it and who was responsible for advancing a payment of 800 scudi to the ship's crew.

Tommaso di Simone Ghesi, an Irishman, one of Robin's witnesses, said that he was left to guard the pinnace but that 'commissioner Barisione and Oratio Erbucci took me away and sent the *petaccio* away to the east'.[11] He also stated that he saw the *Ursa Minor* again at Messina and then that winter in Naples where he spoke with the captain who claimed to be sailing under the orders of the Spanish who found the boat abandoned in Trapani but still flying the Tuscan flag. In contravention of the laws of the sea, they helped themselves to the boat. It raised the spectre of industrial espionage. It was entirely possible that the Spanish would use the pinnace as a template for their own boats.

In May 1610, the Sea Consuls ordered that the expenses incurred by the *Ursa Minor* during its stay in Trapani should be paid by Erbucci. Robin's former partner challenged the judgement. The case gives

---

11. Erico and Montanelli, p.230.

an insight into Robin's financial difficulties as well as Livorno's cut-throat business world. Questions arose about the Englishman's business methods, his honesty and his capacity as a boat builder. A number of Erbucci's witnesses suggested that the design of the vessel was faulty but Robin continued to oversee the building of a range of different vessels in Livorno's dockyard throughout a long career in Tuscany's service suggesting that the problem of the *Ursa Minor* lay with the novelty of the vessel's design. Erbucci attempted to avoid liability by suggesting that Robin's work was unseaworthy.

By 1611, Robin was in Livorno working on a 300-ton ship of his own invention. He called it a *gallizabra*. It was designed to be effective in combat upwind, carried powerful artillery and required less crew than a galleon. He described it as carrying fifty pieces of artillery, 'and thought the draught of this vessel passeth not ten feet, yet are they good, both in long and short voyages; in swiftness to sail, no ship nor pinnace can arrive near them.'[12] He described it for the benefit of Prince Henry and offered its design along with advice on the construction of a modern navy to the prince. He went on to say that he designed it for use against the Turks and that the Venetians wanted it so badly that they were using espionage and bribery. Robin offered it to the Stuarts in return for which he would like to return to England 'without his (the King's) displeasure'.[13]

12. Adlard, p.301.
13. Ibid, p.306.

Chapter XVII

The Thornton Expedition

The Italian city-states focused on the Mediterranean trade routes which dominated their markets. With the dawning of the seventeenth century, their economies began to suffer while the Atlantic seaboard grew more affluent. Tuscany faced a difficult economic situation not only because of the changing trade patterns but also because of its declining textile industry. Initially, Ferdinando sought to redress the problem by acquiring foreign territories from the Portuguese and the Spanish in Peru and Sierra Leone. His negotiations failed. A Tuscan colonisation programme became the only alternative. Robin would have been familiar with his brother-in-law, Hakluyt's, manuscript *Particular Discourse on the Western Planting* published in 1584, which detailed the colonisation of the Americas. Hakluyt's argument was that an English colony in America would provide a base that could be used against Spain. His work went on to extol the importance of trade. And now, trade was what Tuscany needed if its economy was going to thrive. The latter part of Hakluyt's treatise was easily adapted to Florence's situation. Vinta, Ferdinando's first minister, supported Robin's plan.

In August 1608, the English envoy in Florence informed the Earl of Salisbury that 'Sir Robert Dudley...hoped to have ben an adventurer in it (not with his owne person) with a Pinace of his owne, named the Beare & ragged staffe.'[1] It adds to the information that Robin's fleet was either growing afresh or gradually finding its way to Italian shores from England. Captain Robert Thornton and a Dutchman were commissioned to search for gold, the elusive mines of El Dorado, or a route to gold, minerals and commercial opportunities. Robin wanted the expedition to explore the north channel of the Amazon hoping that it would provide a route to the legendary city of Manoa associated with El Dorado. Thornton was also to search for a good location for a garrisoned settlement that

---

1. Lorimer, p.31.

would eventually serve as a base to export Brazilian timber, rosewood in particular, to Italy.

Thornton worked from Livorno with a house and vineyard close by. He was the owner of the *Mercante Reale* which plied its wares to Genoa. In 1605, he commanded *Il Leon Rosso* as part of an expedition led by the Count of Montecuccoli against the Turks. In England, Richard Cockayne was prepared to swear before the High Court of the Admiralty that he sent Thornton to the Mediterranean in 1604 as master of the *Royall Merchant*. Cockayne signed an agreement with Sebastian Nicolano Demesne of Ragus to lease the vessel to him. Thornton fell out with Demesne and stole Cockayne's ship. Now, just like Robin, he was under Ferdinando's protection because of his nautical skills. Thornton's crew for the expedition included a number of Englishmen who either entered the Duke's service or who had been captured and enslaved by Florentine galleys. One such was a man called William Davies, originally a London barber-surgeon. Davies sailed in search of adventure in 1597 when he left Cornwall on a trading vessel. He saw Algiers and Tunis before his boat was captured by Florentine galleys. He worked as a slave in Livorno for nearly nine years before Thornton asked to take him as the ship's doctor. Davies wrote his own account of the journey including his experiences at the mouth of the Amazon which was published in 1614. Davies' work is the first known description of the area as well as providing an account of Thornton's voyage.

The *Santa Lucia Buonaventure*, a caravel, left Livorno in September 1608 along with a tartane with directions and maps provided by Robin. The tartane was a small ship with a lateen, triangular, rig used for fishing and coastal trading. The lateen would enable Thornton's explorers to tack against the wind making it more manoeuvrable than the caravel as well as able to navigate more shallow waters. One chart that Robin provided for the journey included an image of the north channel of the Amazon and a warning about the spring tides composed of sudden storms and immense waves which Robin described as the 'Burnia'. Their method of navigation was to sail south until the colour of the water changed and became less salty. Thornton discovered that the mouth of the Amazon was as Robin described. The area they explored is modern-day Cayenne. Thornton and his mariners thought that the River Cayenne might have good prospects for accessing the interior of the region.

The voyage lasted a year and, remarkably, returned with the entire crew. There were no losses which were remarkable as there was an attempted mutiny by a small group of disgruntled sailors who purchased a brew from a local 'witch' to kill Thornton. On board the *Santa Lucia Buonaventure* when it docked back in Livorno were some parrots and six tribesmen, five of whom died from smallpox. One man survived and lived at court for several years. He, having learned to speak Italian, reported how fertile the land was and that there were gold and silver deposits in the interior. Thornton agreed that the area was bountiful, as well as rosewood there was wild sugar cane, white pepper, balsam and cotton. He also reported the sighting of Amazons. These legendary women began life as a Greek myth about female warriors living near the River Thermedon. Hercules stole a golden girdle belonging to the Queen of the Amazons. The story remained a popular one throughout the medieval period but was regarded as containing an element of truth so that when the Conquistadors arrived in the Americas they half expected to find the Amazons. California is named after Queen Califa of the Amazons and the River Amazon is so-called because Spaniards exploring the region heard stories of warrior women who lived there. Thornton and his crew mistook local women fishing on the river bank for Amazon warriors. Their interpretation of the scene reflects the underlying desire to find riches further up the river. The local population obligingly provided stories about the legendary city of Manoa and rich mines in nearby hills.

Unfortunately for Robin, by the time Thornton returned from his expedition Ferdinando I was dead. His son Cosimo II was uninterested in establishing a Tuscan colony even though Thornton was prepared to take settlers from Livorno and Lucca back to the proposed settlement site. Cosimo concluded that there was little to be gained in terms of profit. Robin, who in his youth pleaded with Queen Elizabeth to be allowed to go on voyages of exploration to the South Seas, does not seem to have used his position at the Florentine Court to promote further ventures nor does he appear to have invested in exploration in the way that he did in his youth. Of course, part of the problem may have been that he was no longer able to access his English income, lived beyond his means and was the father of a rapidly expanding family.

Robin filed away Thornton's notes about his voyage and updated his own chart of the coastline. The resulting map, XIV in the America series of *Dell'Arcano del Mare*, includes a brief explanation for Thornton's voyage. Robin's original maps came not only from his own voyage in 1595 but also from Laurence Keymis who was closely associated with Raleigh. He was with Raleigh on his 1595 voyage to the West Indies and would accompany him back to Trinidad and Guiana in 1617 after Sir Walter was released from the Tower. Laurence, who died in 1618, describes 'the mouth of the Arrowari, a faire and great river. It standeth in one degree and fourtie minutes'.[2] The River Arrowari is drawn at precisely one degree, forty minutes North on map XIV of the America series with a sounding of three fathoms at its entrance corresponding with Keymis's table.

2. Ibid, p.42.

Chapter XVIII

Working for the Medici

James I continued to demand that Leicester's son return to England. Robin insisted that if he did return that it was Elizabeth who should be recognised as his lawful wife rather than Alice. His licence to travel was revoked on 2 February 1607.[1] Captain Aubrey Yorke arrived in Tuscany with a Royal Warrant of Privy Seal. By the time it arrived Robin knew the message's contents and refused to accept it because it was not addressed to the Earl of Warwick. He insisted that he was his father's lawful son and heir. The withdrawal of the King's permission for his absence and Robin's subsequent failure to return to England rendered him an outlaw. Ferdinando I encouraged him not to give up all hope of a pardon especially as James wished to remain on good terms with the Medici for the sake of his foreign policy. Ferdinando wrote to his own agent Lotti with instructions that Robin's case should be promoted and to Henry Howard, the Earl of Northampton with a similar aim.

Robin wrote to his old friend Chaloner. Fortune's wheel was on an upwards trajectory for Sir Thomas who hastened to Holyrood as soon as Elizabeth I died. Having been sent to Scotland by Burghley during the 1590s, he maintained a secret correspondence with James thereafter and now cashed in on his forward-thinking. In August 1605, Chaloner was appointed governor to Prince Henry, James' son and heir. Robin sent Chaloner drawings for ships of his own design that he thought would please the young prince. He was also part of a wider correspondence between London and Florence that began shortly after James' accession to the throne. The most notable letter writer and key negotiator was Lotti. The Florentine's aim was for a wedding between a Medici bride and Henry Stuart. Robin leant the weight of extended familial and friendship networks to Tuscany's negotiations as well as fostering contacts with the Stuart court that might one day facilitate his own return home.

---

1. CP, pp.397–521.

In April 1607, when they were newly arrived in Italy, Robin and Elizabeth received a visit from Father Robert Persons. He was the rector of the Jesuits' English college in Rome. At some point during the visit Elizabeth gave Persons an account of the queen's last weeks. The Jesuit used Elizabeth's testimony as part of the Jesuits' continuing war of words against Protestantism. Aside from political machinations around Elizabeth's bed ensuring a trouble-free succession, there were ghastly apparitions and a tale of suspected murder by witchcraft involving a nail driven through a card bearing the queen of hearts and left beneath the queen's chair. Then were also terrifying visions of fire. The following year Persons wrote *The Judgement of a Catholicke Englishman Living in Banishment for his Religion* and openly stated that the queen was destined for 'everlasting damnation.' Bishop Barlow of Lincoln, who was one of the clerics at Queen Elizabeth's bedside when she died, described Persons as a 'Carronly Curre' and the Jesuit's sources as 'corner-creeping Reremise'.[2] None of which can have helped Robin's attempted reconciliation with the authorities in England.

Elizabeth's account of her godmother's death, with its elements of Gothic horror, was discredited by the historian J.E. Neale in 1925, not only for its contents which cannot all be verified elsewhere but also because Elizabeth and Robin eloped and become recusants. More recent historians note that Elizabeth's account is corroborated in part by other sources.[3]

At about the same time that Robin was outlawed and Elizabeth gave her account of the Old Queen's death Douglas, Lady Sheffield, was in receipt of an unexpected letter from Sir William Fleetwood, receiver for the Court of Wards. It appeared that Sir Edward Stafford rented land from the Sheffield estate during her son Edmund Sheffield's minority. Now, nearly three decades later, Lady Sheffield was informed that she owed £330 to the Crown on behalf of her late husband. She wrote a heartfelt letter to the Earl of Salisbury:

I have passed my life with many afflictions … I have a new cross fallen upon me … which was strange to me, having never heard

2. Loomis, pp.501–502.
3. Ibid, pp.483–484.

it called in question for 27 or 28 years that I was first married to Master Stafford, during which he might have taken some good course to discharge it. I, poor widow, have not any means to pay it, for I neither have dowry nor jointure, and the little I have is merely out of my son's good disposition, which he need not pay me. I hope it is not unknown to you how little I was bettered by my match with Master Stafford, who left no estate and had all his goods seized for his debt to the King, so as I was constrained to borrow a bed of one of my servants to lie upon, and am at this day beholden to friends for most of the goods in my house.[4]

It is likely that the debt arose in part because of Robin's deteriorating relationship with King. Douglas died on 11 December 1608. She left her 'honourable and beloved son Sir Robert Dudley, Kt. My bed of black velvet embroidered with needlework of thwarts, with bedstead and curtains and the three chairs of the same work and same ground suitable to the bed, and the black leather gilded hanging.'[5] There is no mention of how her bequest was to be transported to Tuscany but the words demonstrate a desire for the record to show her love for Leicester's boy. She also left bequests for her daughter-in-law and Robin's daughters. When Douglas's granddaughter Alice was dying in 1621, she gave her mother, later known as Duchess Dudley, the £3,000 which Lady Sheffield left her.[6] Robin's former wife purchased land in Mancetter, Warwickshire, to augment the livings at parish churches associated with the family.

Grand Duke Ferdinando I died in March 1609. Robin retained the patronage of Ferdinando's widow Christina of Loraine, her son Cosimo II and later Cosimo's wife, Maria Maddalena, the youngest daughter of Charles II, Archduke of Austria. Tuscany was a peaceful and prosperous kingdom thanks to Ferdinando I's policies which sought to redress the economic difficulties that the duchy found itself in when he resigned his cardinalship, having never been ordained a priest, upon the death of his brother in 1587 and took up the reigns of ruling Tuscany at the age of thirty-eight years. He instituted large scale reclamation projects near

---

4. CP, p.124.
5. The National Archives Prob 11/113, ff. 231–2.
6. Lee, p.187.

Arezzo, Pisa and Fuchecchio as well as continuing to develop his father and brother's project at Livorno.

Livorno grew out of a marsh skirting the Tyrrhenian Sea some thirteen miles from Pisa and fifty-eight miles from Florence. Ferdinando's father, Cosimo I, began work on the port to replace that of Pisa which had been silting up since the mid-sixteenth century at the Arno delta. He ordered that a canal should be dug from Livorno to Pisa and had a new customs house built in 1546. This coincided with the building of a shipyard and an anchor factory. He also reformed the way that the town administered customs by implementing low duties making it an appealing place to store goods and as a transit point. In 1569, he gave orders for a new harbour to begin construction. Francis I (1574–1587) planned a simple grid iron pattern for the town beyond the port. The buildings were designed at a uniform height. Where the town was previously home to 12,000, Ferdinando expanded it to accommodate 20,000 households. His plans included a cathedral, governor's palace and an aqueduct. He restarted construction on a harbour that would accommodate 300 vessels and in 1590 a new fortress was built. By 1603, the harbour was deepened and there was a dockyard for the Tuscan navy. Further widening and dredging of the harbour were conducted under Robin's supervision. By 1618, the Porto Mediceo was completed largely by slave labour. Robin's task included building the mole, new quays and the arsenal. The mole at Livorno was completed in 1621. He also drained the marshes northwards towards Pisa.

The Laws of Livorno made all refugees welcome whatever their race or religion. The *Livormina*, as the laws were also known, gave merchants immunity from prosecution for debt contracted outside of Tuscany, tax exemptions and freedom from religious persecution. The port became a cosmopolitan city second only to Genoa with Italians, Greeks, Jews, Moors and, of course, Catholics exiled from England. Artisans were encouraged to come and set up workshops and granted privileges especially if their skills could be of use servicing shipping. During Robin's time in Livorno, the port grew to be a leading centre for commerce and a stopping point for English and French vessels. It was popular not only because it made people from all nations and religions welcome but because it was the world's first free port or *scala franca*. Merchants could warehouse their goods for up to a year without having to pay any customs dues from the mid-seventeenth century onwards provided they did not sell their goods onto someone else. It grew and evolved as a free port during Robin's time in Tuscany as merchants made supplications to the Governor's Court for privileges, licences and exemptions. It is thought that Robin persuaded the Grand Duke of the benefits of Livorno's free port status. The machinery of state worked through the cooperation of traders and grew piecemeal based on the supplications that the merchants and artisans made. By the 1620s, Livorno replaced Genoa as Milan's main port. It was cheaper to unload goods for the Veneto and transport them overland than it was to take them to Venice. In the 1630s, a third of the expensive silks manufactured in Florence were shipped from Livorono to London.

Robin was not a wealthy man by his own standards. His expanding family lived in a rented house in the *Via dell'Amore* in Florence that was soon not adequate to their needs. The Grand Duke paid him 2,000 ducats a year. Maria was born on 7 July 1609 and baptised the same day. Her godmother was Mrs Tracey, the wife of English merchant Andrew Tracey.[7] Maria was followed by Cosimo in 1610. Cosimo II having succeeded his father as grand duke the previous year was the boy's godfather. Another daughter named Anna was born the following October. The family continued to grow until there were seven sons and five daughters. One of them, Ambrogio, named after the Earl of Warwick, had his own tutor to take care of him for fear that he would spend all his month's allowance at once. It was probably just as well that Robin was able to earn an income. In addition to his work at Livorno and his maritime enterprises, he was given a patent in October 1610 for a machine to improve silk weaving. He took the precaution of writing to the governor of Livorno to ensure that his request was settled before any public discussion on the matter.[8] He was granted rights to profits from the new machine for twenty years. He also benefitted from a range of exemptions, indemnities and privileges granted to 'strangers' in Livorno. It was during this period that Robin's engineering capabilities also saw him employed bringing fresh water to Pisa from Asciano by aqueduct and providing a water link from Pisa to

---

7. Tracey was responsible for transporting many of Robin's navigational instruments from England.
8. Tazzara, Corey, 'Managing Free Trade in Early Modern Europe: Instituions, Information, and the Free Port of Livorno' The Journal of Modern History, vol.86, No 3 (September 2014) pp.493–529 p.515.

Livorno. This was achieved by diverting some of the Arno into a canal called the *Naviglio*. As well as engineering and commerce, Robin was welcome at the Florentine court where he and Elizabeth soon established themselves.

In March 1610, Chaloner, now Prince Henry's chamberlain, arranged for the Tuscan envoy to London to forward copies of several books and paintings from the Medici Collection to Henry at St James' Palace. Chaloner was one of several links between Florence and Henry's household. Negotiations commenced for Henry to marry Cosimo II's sister Caterina. Henry, interested in art and the cultural heritage of Florence, recognised that the books and paintings that he requested were part of the negotiations. Eventually, the grand duke sent more than a dozen bronzes including the statuette entitled *Pacing Horse* by Pietro Tacco.[9] Lotti worked tirelessly on behalf of Medici interests. His letters describe the progress of the negotiations for marriage. On occasion, the same letters also outline the ways in which Robin sought to influence events in England and to utilise Lotti for his own ends either to win favour for himself with the aim of returning home or to access income from estates that he still possessed through trustees.

In about 1612, Robin arranged the sale of Kenilworth Castle to Prince Henry for £14,500.[10] The castle and its estates were greatly undervalued but the sequestration process had been halted. It was also arranged that Alice would receive £300 yearly revenue.[11] In 1645, Charles I conceded that they were worth about £50,000. It was entirely possible that Prince Henry's patronage might ultimately have provided Robin with a pardon and allowed him to return home. One of Robin's visitors in Italy was Inigo Jones who inspected the castle on Henry's behalf.[12] Robin agreed to the reduction in price and accepted a down payment of £3,000 which was all he ever received.

Prince Henry was undoubtedly interested in Robin's navigational exploits, the plans for his Tuscan galleons and the lure of the gold that lay somewhere up the Amazon. He and Sir Walter Raleigh were keen that

---

9. Displayed by the National Portrait Gallery in 2013 as part of their exhibition entitled The Lost Prince: The Life and Death of Henry Stuart.
10. Lee, p.149.
11. Ibid.
12. Ibid, p.164.

King James should permit further exploration of the lower Amazon as part of a voyage to Guiana. Raleigh considered that the Amazon might give access to the fabled city of Manoa and its gold mine. Most explorers preferred to investigate rivers to the north because they seemed easier to navigate. Henry and Raleigh were absorbed by the Thornton voyage of 1608 which Robin had directed from Livorno because they thought it would encourage James to release Raleigh from the Tower where he had been since his trial for treason in 1603. The sighting of Amazon warriors only served to whet their appetite. Prince Henry, aside from wishing to be fabulously wealthy, was concerned about exploration as a means to expand English influence. He was involved in ventures to Virginia and New England. As well as being a firm friend of Sir Walter Raleigh, Henry was also a friend of Sir Thomas Roe, one of Elizabeth's seadogs who successfully negotiated the rocky straits between the last of the Tudors and the first of the Stuart monarchs unlike either Raleigh or Robin. Henry sent Roe on a mission to the West Indies in 1610. Like Robin and Raleigh before him, he ventured up the River Amazon into the interior of Guiana. By 1614, the East India Company persuaded the King to send Roe as an envoy to Agra which led to the building of an East India Company factory at Surat. The expansion of English trade and the acceleration of colonisation were the foundations of the empire advocated by Robin's brother-in-law, Richard Hakluyt.

Late in 1612, Robin wrote to James, who was in deep debt and unable to gain the subsidies he required from Parliament, suggesting that he could increase his revenues by imposing fines on his Catholic population. This begs the question of how sincere his own faith might have been. He sent his friend Sir David Foulis, who was in the King's favour, a pamphlet about bridling parliaments. Foulis and Robin had a long acquaintance. Foulis was in London in 1595 on James VI's business, carried letters for the Earl of Essex and may have delivered a diamond ring from the Scottish king to the earl prior to the rebellion which saw his downfall. In 1603, Foulis became Chaloner's brother-in-law. By 1605, Foulis had formed a partnership with Chaloner and Edmund Sheffield that held a monopoly on English alum mining and production. Robin wrote to Foulis frequently from Tuscany. He was one of the men who orchestrated the movement of funds for Robin from his estates including rent totalling some £800 each year and passed Robin's inventions to Prince Henry. On this occasion Robin wanted Foulis to give the pamphlet to Prince Henry with a view to it finding its way to King James. Unfortunately, the copy of the letter to Sir David in the archives in Florence is dated 14 November 1612. Prince Henry died the week before from typhoid. The title of the treatise which Robin thought would help him regain the King's favour was *A Discourse to correct the Exorbitances of Parliaments, and to enlarge the King's Revenue.*

It's unknown whether James ever saw Robin's tract but a copy found its way into the library of Sir Robert Cotton from whence it was recopied without Cotton's permission by Oliver St John of Lincoln's Inn under the more inflammatory title *A Project how a Prince may make himself an absolute Tyrant* and passed around until it reached the attention of Sir Thomas Wentworth who showed it to various members of the Privy Council. Cotton was held under suspicion of writing the dangerous tract along with the earls of Clare, Somerset and Bedford until Foulis confirmed under oath that it was 'contrived at Florence seventeen years before by Sir Robert Dudley'.[13] Despite the truth of the matter being in the public record, rumour turned the tract's writer into Wentworth or even Archbishop Laud. The text which Robin had designed to win favour with the Crown was used to further damage royal interests when it was published in 1641 as *Stafford's Plot Discovered.*

The lives of Robin and Raleigh ran on a parallel course on this occasion as they had during Robin's West Indies' voyage. In 1614, following the fiasco of the so-called Addled Parliament which saw no bills pass and a further deterioration in the relationship between the king and the Commons, Sir Walter Raleigh took up his pen in the hope of promoting his own cause when he wrote *The dialogue between a Counsellor of State and Justice of Peace.* It was an essay on the divine right of kings and the importance of a properly managed parliament. Raleigh being the man to bend parliament to the King's will provided he was freed. His work was widely circulated and by 1628 had been retitled *The Prerogative of Parliaments in England* and was regarded as a thoroughly parliamentary text.

As well as his other commitments and interests Robin found time to develop a medicinal compound called *Pulvis Waricensis,* the Earl of

---

13. Vaughan, p.44.

Warwick's Powder or the Warwick Potion, the recipe for which was first published in 1620. It contained scammony (a form of bind weed), antimony, cream of tartar, cinnamon water and syrup of roses. Pharmacopoeias describe it as a cure-all even though the use of antimony, an element similar to lead, was controversial throughout the seventeenth century. One pharmacopoeia noted that antimony causes heartburn, fainting and vomiting. Hippocrates recommended scammony as a drastic purgative as did Arabic texts. Robin discovered how efficacious his potion was when he suffered from an acute fever following too much hawking and hunting whilst travelling between Livorno and Pisa.[14] Rather than submit to bleeding or any other medicine he took his own brew three times a day until he recovered. He recommended it to Marcus Cornacchini of Pisa having dosed his whole family and claimed to have cured 600 people from a variety of ailments. Cornacchini endorsed a treatise dedicated to Robin. *Methodus qua omnes bumani corporis affectiones, ab humoribus copia aut qualitate peccantibus, genitae, tuto, cito et iucunde curantur* which translates as humours rebalanced safely, quickly and joyfully. It proved to be a popular treatise, not least because Cornacchini was a respected doctor of medicine at the university. The grand dukes developed medicine, the sciences and engineering by offering lucrative salaries. Sir Robert Moray, one of the founding members of the Royal Society, describes Robin's powder in a letter to the Earl of Kincardine in 1658 as well as sending the earl the treatise.[15] The concoction also came to be known as *Poudre Cornachine* because of Cornacchini. It was used, in wine, to treat King Louis XIV in 1657 when he became ill from typhoid in Calais and bleeding proved an ineffective cure.

Sir Edward Herbert of Cherbury, the metaphysical poet's brother and part of the extended family of the Earl of Pembroke, travelled to Venice in 1614. On his return journey, he stopped at Florence where he met Henry Vere, 18th Earl of Oxford, who was to remain there some years and Sir Benjamin Rudyard who are both mentioned in his memoirs. He also met Robin. He recorded the encounter with both Robin and the 'handsome Mrs Sudel (Southwell), whom he carried away with him out of England'.[16] Robin invited Herbert to a 'great feast the night before I

---

14. Ibid, p.33.
15. Moray, pp.129–130.
16. Vaughan, p.2.

went out of town'.[17] During the meal, Robin took the opportunity to offer Herbert 2,000 ducats a year for service against the Turks. Herbert declined the offer.

Robin's plans of returning home from Tuscany unravelled with Prince Henry's death. The sale of Kenilworth remained incomplete. Prince Charles inherited the property but at fourteen years old had neither the authority nor the interest to complete the sale. Henry's funeral was held in December 1612 and his household dissolved. Robin's old friend Sir Thomas Chaloner retired from his life as a courtier and administrator. He concentrated his energies on his home at Steeple Claydon and on his Guisborough estate with its alum mine. If Henry's death was bad news for Robin in Tuscany, it was disastrous for Raleigh in his Tower cell. The explorer made his last journey in search of El Dorado in 1617. He was released from the Tower by King James on the condition that he would not provoke the Spanish. It was expected that he would find a gold mine to ease James's extensive debts. On this occasion, Raleigh remained in Trinidad while his son Wat journeyed up the Orinoco where he was killed when Lawrence Kemys attacked a Spanish settlement at Santo Tomas. Kemys died, probably by his own hand, soon after. Raleigh returned home to be executed for treason, making light of his fate and rebutting the accusations made against him.

In April 1614, Robin recognising that his exile was permanent, purchased a house in the *Via della Vigna Nuova* which was part of the San Pancrazio district of Florence. He paid 4,000 scudi which he could ill afford.[18] The house originally belonged to the Rucellai family and it still bears its arms. The imposing four-storey house was a good size for an expanding family. Carlo, Robin's second son was baptised in September 1614. Another daughter Maddalena, named after her godmother the Grand Duchess Maria Maddalena, was born in 1614. Robin made some internal changes to the *palazzo* and socialised with his neighbours the Rucellai and the Strozzi families.

Despite the fact that his family and career were in Tuscany, Robin still yearned for home. He took the opportunity to write a letter to Sir David Foulis to be presented to the King reminding him that he sent advice on

17. Ibid.
18. Ibid, p.49.

how to grow his income and offered him his design for his *gallizabra*. But Robin's links to England shrank as the years passed. On 18 November 1615, Sir Thomas Chaloner died. The only friends with any influence who remained at court were his cousin William Herbert, 3rd Earl of Pembroke and younger brother Philip Herbert who was something of a favourite with the King. Even the Tuscan Minister, Amerigo Salvetti, was sympathetic to Robin's lack of effective representatives in England when he was recalled to Florence. He said that Robin, was at 'a great disadvantage now because he has no one to take his affairs in hand for him'.[19]

Robin's demonstrated an unfeeling attitude towards his second wife Alice and their surviving daughters when he left them in England in 1605. If his marriage was invalid then his daughters were illegitimate. Fortunately for them, England was Protestant and did not recognise their father's subsequent marriage to Elizabeth Southwell. They would have been heiresses with a substantial dowry had Robin not abandoned them. In 1607, when James ordered Robin home and he refused to return, James declared him an outlaw, which meant that his estates reverted to the Crown. The Sidneys of Penshurst took the opportunity to seize Robin's estates at Balsall near Solihull and Long Itchington. Sir Thomas Leigh was now required to fight for Alice's case against the Crown about who owned Kenilworth. It did not help Alice that Robin continued to behave as though Kenilworth was his to do with what he wished and sold it to Prince Henry in the hope that he might be pardoned.

Sir Thomas Leigh appealed to the privy council on his daughter's and granddaughters' behalf and took legal actions to safeguard their rights against Robin's trustees who held other of his estates, demonstrating that his departure in 1605 was not an impulsive action, rather a carefully planned enterprise. Leigh petitioned that Robin lived with Alice as a lawful wife for ten years, that Alice bore him seven daughters of whom five survived infancy and were still alive in 1616. Robin's attempt to sell Kenilworth and any other lands remaining to him despite their confiscation by the King is described as an 'endeavour' to 'utterly to defeat them of all means of livelihood from him.' Leigh demanded that Robin's agents Foulis and Green who claimed that they were Robin's trustees

---

19. Temple Leader, p.92.

should be halted and that they should be made to reveal which of Robin's lands they held. The family said that the income from those estates should be handed to Alice and her children so that they could live as they should rather than finding its way to Florence. Leigh also petitioned that his granddaughters should have appropriate dowries. It is unlikely that Robin concerned himself with the marriage portions of his English daughters; their family history did not help their marriage prospects. Alice could not remain in Kenilworth after Robin's desertion. She did not have the resources. She moved to Dudley House near London opposite the church of St Giles-in-the-Fields. At that time the house was in the countryside. It had once been the home of John Dudley, Duke of Northumberland. She was a benefactor of the church and parish of St Giles.

On 21 May 1616, the Privy Council ordered that all of Robin's remaining property should be sold for the benefit of Robin's deserted wife and children but as late as 30 July 1621, Sir Thomas Chaloner was able to write to his friend to say that if Robin made proper provision for his English family that a way might be found for him to return home. In 1622, an Act of Parliament was passed which permitted Alice to sell Kenilworth Woods which would have been her jointure in the event of Robin's death. It was valued at £14,000. When she sold it, she received only £4,000 but the law designated her as having the status *femme sole* – she could act in her own right as though she had no living husband. It was only in the summer of 1632 that Robin transferred his interest in Lettice's jointure estates to his four remaining daughters by Alice. Lettice died two years later. Essex House which was part of the countess's jointure should have reverted to Robin, or at least to his daughters, but it remained in the ownership of the Devereux family.

It was Salvetti, in August 1618, who reported that the earldom of Leicester was in the hands of Sir Robert Sidney whilst Robert Rich was created Earl of Warwick, both titles that Robin regarded as his birth right. Baron Rich had been the first husband of Essex's sister Penelope Devereux. He divorced her in 1605 citing her adultery. Penelope's marriage was arranged by her guardian Henry Hastings, Earl of Huntingdon, in 1581 despite her father's wish that she should marry Philip Sidney. To Huntingdon's mind, Sidney's prospects were poor whilst Rich was wealthy. Penelope protested against the marriage, according to one story, right up to the altar. It was only a short time before she began an affair with Charles Blount, Lord Mountjoy. Both she and her lover were implicated in the Earl of Essex's rebellion but escaped imprisonment. The rebellion presented Rich with an opportunity to renounce his wife. She lived openly with Blount until her divorce. Rich's only claim to the earldom, lay not in a disastrous marriage to Leicester's step-daughter, but to the payment of £10,000 into the royal treasury.

Chapter XIX

Duke and Chamberlain

In 1619, Grand Duchess Maria Maddalena appointed Robin to the office of Grand Chamberlain to the Grand Duke of Tuscany. The following year, on 9 March 1620, Maddalena's brother, the Holy Roman Emperor, created Robin both Earl of Warwick and Duke of Northumberland. It was a small dart aimed at James I whose son-in-law Frederick of the Palatinate was engaged against the Holy Roman Emperor in the Thirty Years War. The patent was not a new creation but a recognition of Robin's rights as a legitimate heir of his father and grandfather. The patent also settled the titles upon Robin's heirs. Service to the Medici saw other rewards including a pension and a country residence. The Villa di Castello[1] lay three miles west of Florence. Its assets included a garden filled with statues and fountains. It was surrounded by orchards and vineyards. The Castello estate was part of the Medici landholding acquired in the fifteenth century in the environs of Florence. Cosimo II expanded the estate with the purchase of the Rinieri villa but after he died part of the agricultural land attached to the estate passed to Cardinal Giovan Carlo whilst the villa was given to Robin and his family. It was an area inhabited by the grand duke's courtiers, physicians and artists. Whilst Fortuna's wheel turned against Robin in England, it carried him upwards in Tuscany.

Cosimo II died in 1621, probably from tuberculosis. He was twenty-nine years old. The responsibility for organising the funeral fell into Robin's hands.[2] It was expected that lavish *apparati* or temporary decorations would create a spectacle for the celebration of a requiem mass designed to have maximum visual and liturgical impact. Hundreds of beeswax candles would be lit at the climax of the service illuminating the

---

1. The Villa Castello, also called the Villa Rinieri, belonged in later times to the Corsini family.
2. Lee, p.185.

coffin on its elaborate catafalque, only for them to be snuffed out at the same time at an appropriate moment. Cosimo's heir was a ten year old boy named after his grandfather Ferdinando. His grandmother Christina of Lorraine and his mother Maria Magdalena were nominated as the boy's regents along with a council of four ministers selected by Cosimo II before his death. The two women gave privileges to their nobility and quarrelled with one another. Christina, a devout Catholic, acquiesced with the Papacy and appointed the clergy to all levels of public office and gave pensions to Catholic converts. So far as the Medici Court was concerned, Robin was Leicester's legitimate heir and had lost his patrimony because of his faith. Robin's wife Elizabeth's cousin, Robert Southwell, a Jesuit executed in England in 1595 was a martyr. Consequentially Robin found himself in a more important position in the Medici court than he might otherwise have done.

In 1621, news arrived from England that Robin's eldest daughter by Alice Leigh was dead. She left £3,000 bequeathed to her by Robin's own mother for charitable uses. History does not record whether Robin felt a twinge of regret for deserting his daughters by Alice. The Earl of Nottingham, Robin's uncle, died at the end of 1624. King James I died the following March and Robert Sidney, 1st Earl of Warwick, died in 1626. He was replaced by his own son, another Robert who promptly took possession of Robin's last English manors at Long Itchington and Balsall. King Charles I granted Kenilworth Castle to Robert Carey, 1st Earl of Monmouth. The earl was Charles' childhood governor. Robin had still only received £3,000 for the property paid prior to Prince Henry's death in 1612. During the summer of 1625, Robin wrote to his friend the merchant Andrew Tracey to ask for the scientific instruments which he had left behind in England in 1605. Salvetti mentions 'a quantity of instruments for perspective, and that he (Tracey) would forward the rest as soon as he finds an opportunity'.[3] Robin' Italianised his name to Roberto Dudleo but he intended to have his vengeance on England for refusing to recognise his legitimacy. Word of Robin's intent, though not the detail of his plans, reached Salvetti who was frustrated by Robin's inability to see that claiming his grandfather's title alienated those in

---

3. Temple Leader, p.88.

authority.[4] Salvetti wrote to Dimurgo Lambardi in Florence expressing more practical concerns:

> There are rumours whispered of some sentence which that Sir Robert Dudley, or Duke, as he calls himself has procured from the Ecclesiastical Forum, declaring him the creditor of this kingdom for £200,000. I hope it is not true, or it will prevent merchants from putting into the port at Livorno with their ships and effects.[5]

Having spent years trying to re-establish himself with the Stuarts and to recover his property Robin took England to the Florentine Ecclesiastical Court in 1627. The matter of Robin's legitimacy, which seemed of so little importance during the reign of Elizabeth, shaped his life from the accession of James I onwards. He clung to the view that his parents were legitimately married and that Robert Sidney together with the Stuart monarchy had cheated him of what was rightfully his. England, a non-Catholic country, was promptly condemned and issued with a penalty of £8 million for the estates which Robin lost on departing England, plus £200,000 interest. The information was presented for the world to see on the door of Florence Cathedral. Robin immediately demanded that all English property in Livorno should be impounded to pay towards the costs.

The Medici were quick to let London know that nothing would interrupt trade. Robin wrote to the Grand Duke's secretary but Ferdinando, then seventeen years of age was on his own version of the Grand Tour and not to be disturbed. Robin, implacable in his desire to make England pay, took his case to Rome and the *Camera Apostolica* or Papal Treasury responsible for the administration of justice. It supported the Florentine Court which adjudicated in favour of the Duke of Northumberland. Florentine finances were already straitened thanks to the financial mismanagement and favouritism of the two grand duchesses during Ferdinando II's minority. The Tuscans did the only thing they could do under the circumstances. They ignored the edict and English shipping and goods continued to come and go unmolested.

4. Ibid, p.189.
5. Lee, p.192.

Chapter XX

Losses

In the winter of 1629, the citizens of Tuscany began to hear news of the plague in Languedoc and on the Provencal Coast. By March 1630, the disease arrived in Milan probably brought by German mercenaries. The death rate began to accelerate during the carnival season. Plague killed 46% of Milan's total population whilst in Venice, 33% from a population of 140,000 died. It may have killed up to a quarter of northern and central Italy's population between 1629 and 1631.

Ferdinando II established an Office of Hygiene, the *Sanità*, who wrote to Milan, Verona and Venice to find out about the nature of the pestilence that was ravaging the country. In July, the Grand Duke sent troops to close his borders on the Apennines into Tuscany along the Bolognese border. He and his family moved to their country villa high in the hills to avoid the miasmas which were thought to spread the infection. Then in the same month plague arrived in Trespiano, a village, five miles outside Florence. By August, the first case of plague was reported in the city and the bells of the churches began to toll. In September, the corpses of 600 plague victims were buried in pits outside the city walls and rumours spread through the city about a doctor who deliberately poisoned his patients. Amongst the dead was Robin and Elizabeth's daughter Anna, who died in 1629, buried in the Church of San Pancrazio. Her grieving parents paid for an inscription to be set above her tomb.

By October, the number of plague deaths was more than 1,000. Ferdinando gave orders that monastic houses, private villas and public buildings should be transformed into hospitals called *lazaretti* to isolate and hopefully cure the citizens of Tuscany who fell ill. In Florence, the death toll reached 9,000 or 12% of the population of 75,000. Streets were cleaned and cesspools emptied. People suspected of carrying the plague were rounded up. Beggars were cleared from the streets, brothels and barber shops closed, and washerwomen and Jews were confined. As the death toll mounted so did the number of fires as the mattresses of the victims were burned along with their clothes to prevent their sale on the second-hand clothes market. Plague doctors in their hooded cloaks and herb-filled masks shaped like beaks tended to the sick. By then Robin and his family had fled to their country villa leaving the poor to take their chances. There was little chance to celebrate the fact that Pope Urban VIII created him a *Patrizio Romano* which gave him the authority to form an order of knighthood called the *Ordine Cesareo Armati*.

Robin and Elizabeth's eldest daughter, Maria, left another gap in the family at the beginning of November when she married Don Orazio Appiano Aragona, the Prince of Piombino. The marriage was the work of the Grand Duchess Christina who provided part of the dowry to ensure the match. Maria was part of the Medici inner circle. Robin wrote that she was 'a great favourite'. It reflected the esteem in which Robin was held by the Grand Duke and his wife. This seems to have sprung from his ability to make friends as much as the fact that, thanks to Robin, Livorno's trade saw an annual turnover of eight million scudi. Fortuna blessed Maria only briefly. Orazio was the last member of the family to rule Piombino which included a port and land near to the Isle of Elba. He was invested with the title by Philip IV of Spain in 1626 but was unable to pay the tribute of 500,000 florins. As a consequence, he lost his title in 1635. As Maria set off to her new home another sister, Maddalena, took her place in the Florentine court.

In January 1631, citizens were ordered to stay in their homes for forty days. One member of each household was licenced to go and buy food. Anyone breaking the rules faced fines and imprisonment. Masses were said in the streets so that people could watch services from their windows. Gradually the number of plague victims decreased. In April, there was a new addition to the Dudley family when Enrico was born. The following month Robin's promising oldest son, Cosimo, caught a fever and was dead within the week. He was a Colonel of the Guard at Piombino with his sister and was only twenty-one years old. Robin's heir was now his second son Carlo with whom the family had a difficult relationship. Then Elizabeth became ill; she died in September. Her body was buried quickly and covered in quicklime. She was interred in the church of San Pancrazio next to Anna. Elizabeth and Robin had been married for twenty-five years so far as Florentine society and the Vatican were concerned. Enrico was sent to Olivola where he was raised by his sister Maddalena who married Don Spinetta Malaspina, Marchese d'Olivola. During the autumn of 1631, quarantine was lifted only for the plague to return as people resumed their normal lives.

By this time Robin recognised that he was unlikely to return to England and an agreement was reached in the summer of 1632. By December, Robin transferred his rights to his remaining lands in England to his wife and surviving daughters. In 1633, he received 8,000 scudi from Charles I for the sale of Kenilworth which had not been forthcoming at the time of Prince Henry's death in 1612. As a consequence, it was his daughters who challenged the Sidney claim to the manors which Robin transferred to them. The settlement brought to an end Robin's hopes of ever returning home. Robin sent a gratuity to Salvetti in thanks for his help in the matter. The Italian's response was a recognition of Robin's power in Tuscany:

> …if Dudley wishes to recompense me for all I have done, he might do so by using his influence on the Tuscan Court to get me recalled from exile in London.[1]

Sir Henry Wotton had once proposed swapping Robin for Salvetti who was wanted by the Republic of Lucca for being part of a pro-Florentine party that sought to annex the territory to Tuscany. Under sentence of death since 1596, he faced assassination on several occasions and lived permanently in London. He worked on Robin's behalf from 1616 onwards but was not rewarded by a return to Italy. He died in London on 2 July 1657.

The deaths continued. Lotti died during 1634 and on Christmas Day in the same year, Robin's stepmother Lettice died at the age of ninety-one years. Her widow's jointure reverted to Robin's remaining daughters in England. In 1635, Charles, the sixteen year old son of Philip Herbert, Earl of Pembroke, visited Florence to stay with Robin. Throughout his exile his Herbert cousins had maintained their relationship with Robin. Charles spent the autumn with Maddalena at Olivola before returning to Florence where he became ill. The Grand Duke sent his own physician to tend to the boy but to no avail. Charles was buried in Olivola. The following year Dowager Grand Duchess Christina died. She was an

---

1. Temple Leader, p.205.

important influence on the Florentine court, the Tuscan navy, the seaport of Livorno and had been one of Robin's principal patrons.

In 1638, Robin found himself writing several letters to Balli Cioli, secretary to Ferdinando II, about his son Carlo who stole from him and plotted against him. It appears that Carlo, Robin's heir since the death of Cosimo, was a wild young man who chaffed against life at court. Like his father, he might have been better placed as an adventurer exploring the globe. Instead of finding an outlet he was kept at home where he became a 'scapegrace,' caused a disturbance at a public reception in the Palazzo Strozzi, consorted with outlaws and spent some time in prison. Carlo's behaviour made life difficult for Robin. One Sunday whilst his family and the servants were at mass, Carlo broke into the family home and stole all the plate. Having nowhere to go he, and two armed retainers, sought sanctuary in a church. From there he was sent to the monastery of San Domenico at Fiesole where his brother Ferdinando was a monk. Carlo behaved so poorly that he was forcibly removed. The Grand Duke arranged for him to be confined in Florence's Bargello Prison to bring him to his senses. Maria's mother-in-law, a guest of Robin's at Villa Castello, wrote to warn her host that Carlo, sent to the villa in the aftermath of his imprisonment, showed nothing but ill-will towards his father. Carlo's behaviour stemmed from Robin's conviction that his sons were English rather than Italian.

Antonio, a son of whom Robin was proud, served as a page at the Florentine Court and was elected into the Knightly Order of San Stefano in the autumn of 1638. Part of the process for election required a legal deed proving eighteen year old Antonio's noble descent through all four grandparents. An illuminated genealogical tree was drawn up at Robin's command showing lines leading back to King Henry III on his side and King Edward II on Elizabeth's. Antonio was invested into the knighthood and a career in the Tuscan Navy beckoned but three months later Fortune's wheel dipped once again when Antonio was killed by a pestilential fever.

Chapter XXI

Secrets of the Sea

Grand Duke Ferdinando III's wife, Vittoria della Rovere, was betrothed to him from infancy and was publicly married to him in 1637 when she was fifteen years old. Robin's stewardship of the royal household which had seen him serve and develop friendships with two grand duchesses soon passed into younger hands. Robin was also pensioned from his employment in Livorno. The truth was that a new generation was in control of Tuscany and Robin would never again be so close to the heart of its governance as he had been previously. He retired from court life to the Medici Villa di Castello outside Florence and began to write about the sea and all things maritime. During the course of his writing, Robin described his own life. It took him twelve years to complete six books in three volumes which he called *Dell'Arcano del Mare* or *The Secrets of the Sea* and dedicated to Ferdinando II.

The project was something that Robin started before he even left England. He set down his compiled understanding of navigation in an atlas of the sea using his own sailing notes as well as reports and information from men he knew, had sailed with or who he read about. He drew on his own experiences as well as those of his fellow navigators including Dutch and Jesuit explorers of the Far East and from information provided by an extensive network of contacts and associates. The work included Captain Thornton's report from his voyage of 1608 as well as Robin's own report of his travels in 1594 to the West Indies. He included Abraham Kendall's log and information from Thomas Cavendish's voyage. The chart for Greenland made reference to Martin Frobisher's discoveries in 1578. Wilhelm Barents discoveries of 1595 were also indicated. The completed work also included two charts which showed part of Australia drawing on the 1617 discoveries of Dutch captain Jacob Le Maire who was sent by his father to find a different route around South America into the Pacific to access South East Asia.

It was the first sea atlas ever published and it was the first to use Mercator's projection which transferred the spherical shape of the globe onto a flat surface. This is achieved by drawing lines of latitude and longitude as a grid. Because the grid is made up of equidistant parallel lines, the landmasses represented on the completed map or chart do not necessarily correspond to their actual size. The further away a landmass is from the equator the larger it appears on a Mercator map. The distortions occur because the map is a navigational aid. A compass bearing can be navigated by drawing a straight line between two points. In 1599, Edward Wright published *Certaine Errors* which corrected errors in Mercator's mathematics and claimed that it was his work that translated angular lines into flat surface nautical miles. Abraham Kendall, Robin's navigator on his West Indies voyage, is known to have read Wright's work and it is not unreasonable to suggest that Robin did so as well. It was only in the eighteenth century that cartographers began to use Mercator projections as standard. The *Dell'Arcano del Mare* explains the advantages of Great Circle sailing, that is to say navigating the shortest distance between two points on a globe. It was also the first to show magnetic deviation, currents and prevailing winds.

The first book of the atlas explores the secrets of navigation and in particular the understanding of longitude. The second book contains maps and charts showing longitude, prevailing winds and chapters on tides and currents. The third is about the organisation, discipline and the construction of a navy whilst the fourth book explores naval and military architecture using Robin's own work at Livorno as examples. Book Five is concerned with circular sailing and contains an explanation of practical methodologies and instruments for this kind of navigation. The final book contains 127 charts. They are the first set of published charts to leave out compass lines and replace them with lines of latitude and longitude. It would not be standard practice to show charts like this for another two centuries.

The whole work is beautifully engraved by Antonio Francesco Lucini in the Baroque style. Lucini stated that he required 5,000 lbs of copper to engrave a total of 200 plates and 146 charts. Amongst the illustrations are working diagrams and *volvelles* (diagrams with moving dials). With exquisite attention to detail, the charts include adornments such as an illustration of Mount Hekla erupting in Iceland, finely engraved ships, compass roses and lavish calligraphy. There are also explanations for some charts as well as references to discoveries and the dates on which those discoveries were made. The map for the North East coast of South America covering Guiana is more elaborate than most as it includes Robin's own soundings as well as numerous illustrations including a canoe, two indigenous Arawaks, a puma and sea monsters.

Robin had privileged knowledge about the sea from the days of his childhood. Leicester entertained Drake at his London home and there was a map of the explorer's 1577 circumnavigation of the globe there as well. The *Galleon Leicester*, owned by Robin's father, sailed as a privateer under Drake's command. The earl's ships traded in Africa, Mexico and the Americas. With the crossing of the Atlantic and the development of trade with the Far East, an endeavour of which Robin was a part, accurately charting previously unexplored coastlines became increasingly important as a mathematically based science. Like his father and uncle, Robin was a backer of merchant ventures including the Muscovy Company. In addition to wealth and trading links, returning captains shared their knowledge. As with much else in Robin's life, there was an extended kinship link. Sir Henry Lee, Robin's godfather, had many brothers but his half-brother Sir Richard Lee, was perhaps closest to him. In 1599, Sir Richard was selected by the merchants of the Muscovy Company to represent their interests as Ambassador to Russia. He did not achieve the objectives of his embassy which were to extend trading rights and pursue matrimonial alliances with the tsar's daughters resulting in near financial ruin for Sir Richard on his return to England. However, it was this conduit that may have granted Robin access to the original charts of Henry Hudson. His brother-in-law Richard Hakluyt's *The Principal Navigations, Voyages, Traffiques, and Discoveries of the English Nation* must have been an important source. Even his childhood companion, Ann Dudley, may have provided a link to maritime intelligence. Her husband Francis Popham became a director in the Virginia Company. Edmund Sheffield, Robin's half-brother, was an early investor in the company and also in the New England Company. Robin does not acknowledge his sources but the depth of his study reveals a lifetime of collecting material from every informant that was available to him. His passion for exploration never deserted him.

The atlas is a story of exploration, technology and science. Robin recognised the importance of the science required to support effective exploration of the seas and the mapping of newly discovered coastlines. From the 1590s onwards, he acquired instruments, improved upon them and invented his own. The *Arcano* depicts a number of these instruments, including a nautical hemisphere, which allowed time to be measured and from whence it was possible to calculate the times of high and low tides. Robin's own nautical hemisphere can still be seen in Florence.[1] After his death, Robin left his navigational and astronomical instruments to the Grand Duke. The bequest included wind roses and tide calculators of the kind described in *Dell'Arcano del Mare*. Today, nineteen of Robin's scientific instruments, made by some of London's leading instrument makers, can be found in the *Museo Galileo*. It is a unique compendium.

To navigate successfully, knowledge of two things are required; latitude and longitude. Navigators need to calculate where they are and then chart a course to their next destination. This raised a problem for so-called 'blue water' mariners who had no landmarks to steer by. Sixteenth century navigators could determine latitude with reasonable certainty with a range of instruments and there were a series of tables to help. Astrolabes, which had been in existence since antiquity, measured the height of celestial bodies, the sun and the stars, by measuring the angle between the sun or the Pole Star above the horizon. Elizabethan maritime astrolabes were made from a large brass ring and a sighting rule. The navigator held the ring by a loop at its top, turning the sighting rule until the Pole Star or sun could be seen. Then all that was required was to read the altitude from the scale that was engraved around the ring. The astrolabe may be regarded as a forerunner to the sextant. A calculation known as the declination of the star, taking into account the time of year, was then required which would produce an answer measured in degrees north or south of the equator. The astrolabe required the navigator to look into the sun. Ideally, a measurement should be taken at midday. Robin wrote that the secret of successful navigation lay in finding the longitude. He provided rules for how it could be found and explained how the astrolabe and other instruments should be used.

---

1. Robin's navigational instruments can be found in The Science of Navigation, Room V, Museo Galileo, Florence. https://catalogue.museogalileo.it/section/RobertDudleys Instruments.html

On 12 March 1643, Dudley corresponded with Bernedetto Guerrini, a chamberlain of Ferdinando II. Eight months had passed since Ferdinando gave his permission to print the atlas. Robin wrote about difficulties created by a paper shortage; that his publisher Francesco Rondinelli was slow as was the engraver Lucini. There were difficulties correcting the proofs. His frustrations with his printer spill from his pen. Not only was the proofreader prepared to correct his Italian which Robin felt was imperfect but the mathematician, Evangelista Torricelli, was prepared to help as well if only the printer would allow them. Torricelli, a friend of Robin's, was a student of Galileo whom Robin also knew. The previous year Ferdinando asked Torricelli to succeed Galileo to the Chair of Mathematics at Pisa. Robin was deeply concerned that his *reputazióne* would suffer as a consequence of linguistic errors and tardy printing.

Once the book was ready it needed to be presented to the Inquisition. In Florence, Canon Vincenzio Martelli was presented with the text which he found to be free of any heretical ideas. It was also checked by Padre Alessandro Peri, a theological doctor and by Fra Giacomo Cima, the Inquisitor General of Florence. Finally, it went to the Grand Duke's Inquisitorial censors. It helped that the Medici thought so well of Robin and that his preface began with a recognition that 'The omnipotent God has proportioned the world in regard to magnitude, number and weight'.[2] He went on to say that the infallibility of mathematics was a demonstration of God's work. The first volume of Robin's maritime atlas went to press in August 1645 but it was 1646 before it could be purchased and 1647 before the second and third volumes became available. Robin continued to work to improve the charts that he presented to the world. He wanted the work to be accurate as possible. By then Torricelli was dead, probably from plague.

Shortly before Robin's life work went to press, his former wife Alice Dudley was created Duchess Dudley in her own right on 23 May 1644. This came about because King Charles I found himself in contact with Alice's extended family. He stayed at Stoneleigh Abbey on 19 August 1642 on his way to Nottingham. Among the men who rallied to his cause after he raised the royal standard on Castle Hill was Robert Holbourne who became Charles' Solicitor-General and Sir Richard Leveson. They

---

2. Lee, p.225.

were both Robin's sons-in-law. Leveson was married to Katherine Dudley and Holbourne was married to Anne Dudley. Thanks to the petitioning of these two men, Charles ordered that the evidence from Robin's trial should be re-examined. He became convinced that an injustice had been perpetrated. In May 1644, he issued Letters Patent recognising the wrong that had been done in 1605. Charles acknowledged Robin's legitimacy as the patent confers the precedence of a duke's daughters on his surviving daughters by Alice. For Robin, it was forty years too late even if Charles, fighting an increasingly bitter Civil War, recognised that the dukedom of Northumberland was his by right of birth.

Chapter XXII

Afterwards

Robin died aged seventy-five at the Villa Castello which the Grand Duke granted him for his lifetime, on 6 September 1649. The world he knew as a young man was changing and he was almost a relic of a by-gone age. His coffin was carried to the nunnery at Boldrone.[1] There was no immediate funeral because of Robin's estrangement from Carlo who was his heir. The coffin was still at the nunnery in 1674, twenty-five years after his death. It may eventually have been taken for burial to the church in San Pancrazio in Florence where Elizabeth and Anna were buried but there is no record of an interment. Without a funeral, there was no commemoration of Robin's life or display of his achievements and titles. The tomb and inscription which Dudley had written for Elizabeth and for their daughter were destroyed by the French when they invaded Florence in 1798. There was no mention of Robin himself on the epitaph nor did the Tuscans raise a monument to the English exile who spent forty-four years serving the Medici. Robin outlived his engineering and shipbuilding achievements and the benefits that they brought to Tuscany were already declining.

Robin's place at court meant that he had been able to arrange advantageous marriages for those of his children who survived into adulthood although he was often troubled by the lack of funds available for their education and adult appointments. Despite Robin's efforts to provide his children by Elizabeth with spouses and careers suitable for an aristocratic dynasty, the fortunes of his house were broken within a generation. Ambrogio can be found in the household of the Grand Duchess of Tuscany as a page during his childhood before entering the household of Cardinal Gian Carlo de Medici in his twenty-first year. He died soon after from a fever whilst in Rome. Giovanni also died young. Ferdinando became a Dominican Friar in Fiesole. In 1652, with all his

---

1. Vaughan, p.8.

brothers being dead apart from Carlo who took the title of Duke of Northumberland, Enrico took his father's title as Earl of Warwick.

In 1652, Robin's house in the *Via della Vigna Nouvo* near *San Pancrazio* was passed to his sons and his daughter Teresa who married the Duca della Cornia in 1645.[2] The dowry for such a glittering marriage must have almost ruined Robin. Fortune turned against him and Teresa when her husband died as did their young son, leaving Teresa almost penniless when the Church claimed the Cornia estates. Shortly before his death, Robin arranged a second marriage for his daughter to Count Mario Carpegna di Montefltro. On this occasion, Teresa's dowry was a five-year lease on the *San Pancrazio* house because Robin had nothing else. He also gave Teresa his medicine box, an ebony cabinet filled with silver boxes, and everything in it which he kept until his death.

The family home next passed into the hands of Robin's grandson Antonio whose father Duke Carlo died on 25 October 1686 whilst in the custody of Ferdinando III in Florence's Bargello Prison. Antonio, a canon of the Vatican, died in Rome in 1728. His will, made in 1720, left everything to his nephew Marchese Tommaso Paleotti, but he died soon after he inherited. All the Dudley property that had been acquired across the years and through marriage passed into the hands of Marchese Andrea Paleotti who was the last of Robin's line. Today a blue plaque recognises that Sir Robert Dudley once lived there.

Carlo, Robin's wild second son, married Marie Madeleine Gouffier. Even before Robin died, Carlo wrote that his wife wished to leave him. A petition from Carlo dating from 1676 reveals that he was in Rome separated from his wife and family and had lost his property. The petition sought to provide his daughter, Carlotta, with a dower to facilitate a good marriage. Carlo was unable to fund it so appealed to the Medici to remember the services rendered by Robin to Tuscany. The following year Carlo travelled to England to speak on the subject of his father's titles and estates to the House of Lords who laughed at his claims. He returned to Florence where he was eventually incarcerated once again in the Bargello Prison because of unacceptable public behaviour. He was still there when he died in 1686. Carlo's second daughter, Christina, married the

---

2. Confirmed by an entry in the Arroto made in the Registration Office in Florence, 2 September 1652, recorded in Vaughan, p.17.

Marquese Andrea of Paleotti of Bologna when she was fifteen years old. Christina took up a position as a lady-in-waiting at the court of Savoy. In 1665, during a stay in Rome, Christina bore an illegitimate daughter called Maria but it did not prevent Christina from continuing life as a society hostess or from there being further gossip about her lovers.

Two of Christina's children found their way back to England at the beginning of the eighteenth century. Robin's great-granddaughter, Adelhilda Paleotti visited her great aunt, Teresa di Carpegna in Florence where she met Charles Talbot, the Duke of Shrewsbury. The title was a reward for his part in the Glorious Revolution of 1688 which toppled James II from his throne. Adelhilda, a widow, captured his heart and he married her in Augsberg on their way back to England. The duke later claimed to have converted Adelihilda to Protestantism by lending her a Bible during their homeward journey. She was naturalised by act of parliament in January 1707 and became an active participant at Queen Anne's court, and later in that of King George I where, like her Dudley ancestors, her favour aroused jealousy. Gossip circulated that she was not a widow when she met Shrewsbury, that she had in fact been the mistress of Count Roffeni. It was even suggested that Adelhilda's brother had tricked the duke into marrying her. Lady Mary Wortley Montagu, aristocrat and lady of letters, satirised her as Cockatilla in 1716 when Adelhilda became Princess Caroline's lady-in-waiting:

> Yet Cockatilla's Artifice prevails…
> That Cockatilla, whose Deluding Airs
> Corrupts our Virgins, and our Youth ensnares;
> So sunk her Character, and lost her Fame…[3]

Adelhilda's brother, Ferdinando Marquis de Paleotti, served in Queen Anne's armies and came to England following the Peace of Utrecht. Once in England, he developed a reputation as a heavy, not to mention unlucky, gambler. Fortune did not favour him. Adelhilda finally washed her hands of him but paid his debts one last time so that he might be released from prison. He continued to gamble. One day he asked his servant, John Niccolo, to go and borrow some money on his behalf.

---

3. Pope and Ruffhead, p.18.

Niccolo refused. Ferdinando drew his sword and slaughtered the man. The murder took place between Leicester Street and nearby Lisle Street. Witnesses described a man in a red coat of the same build as Ferdinando. The following morning Ferdinando who had retired for the night to his lodgings and slept, got dressed and tried to claim sanctuary with the Bishop of Salisbury. He was indicted at the Old Bailey for John's murder on 11 February 1718 and hanged at Tyburn on 17 March.

Alice, Duchess Dudley, outlived her errant husband. After Robin's desertion of her and her daughters, she moved to Dudley House near London opposite the church of St Giles-in-the-Fields. At that time the house was in the countryside. It had once been the home of John Dudley, Duke of Northumberland. She died at Dudley House on 22 January 1668 and was buried at Stoneleigh. A funeral sermon preached at St Giles-in-the-Fields by Reverend Robert Boreman on 14 March 1669 demonstrated the extent to which she was a benefactor of the parish. St Giles had fallen into disrepair and had been replaced by a new brick building between 1623–1630. The sermon's contents reveal the extent of the Duchess's contribution to the rebuilding of the church, the provision of an altar cloth, a pair of organs, the altar rail, communion plate and 'the great bell in the steeple'.[4] In addition to the church, she also purchased a house for its incumbents to live in. She gave sums of money to churches which she had an association with including Ashow, Kenilworth and Stoneleigh. She also bequeathed an endowment to generate £100 each year to ransom English prisoners from the Turks. Her tomb at Stoneleigh was surmounted by a Duchess's coronet and recognised that Robin was given the title Duke of Northumberland by the Holy Roman Emperor. It may have been convenient for Robin to disavow their union but Alice remained steadfast to the fact of her marriage even in death.

None of Robin's English daughters had children of their own. Frances Dudley married Sir Gilbert Kniveton of Bradley, Derbyshire. She predeceased her mother and was buried in St Giles-in-the-Fields. When Charles I elevated Alice to the rank of duchess, Anne was one of two remaining daughters to be given the rank and precedence befitting the daughters of a duke. She married Sir Richard Holbourne who was Solicitor General to Charles I. Holbourne's estates were sequestrated in

4. Vaughan, p.90.

the aftermath of the Civil War. Sir Richard Leveson of Trentham and Lilleshall, the husband of Katherine, also faced parliamentary retribution for his support of the king. Like her mother, Katherine became synonymous with charitable giving. She died in 1673 and is buried in Lilleshall with her husband. The Foundation of Lady Katherine Levison continues its work of education and caring for older people in the twenty-first century.

Who's Who

De l'Aubespine, Guillaume, Marquis de Châteauneuf (1580–1653)
Châteauneuf was the French Ambassador at the court of Elizabeth I from 1585 to 1590. He served King Henri III of France.

Arundell, Sir Charles (d. 1587)
Part of the extended Howard family, Arundell was openly Catholic. Following the Throckmorton Plot of 1583, Arundell fled to Paris where he is suspected of writing *Leicester's Commonwealth* which attacked both the Earl of Leicester and the English government.

Bacon, Francis, 1st Viscount St Alban (1561–1626)
Lawyer, politician, philosopher and writer.

Baker, Matthew (1529/30–1613)
Master shipwright who used mathematical calculation to work out a ship's burden and deadweight tonnage. He built the *Galleon Leicester* from blueprints in 1582. It was the first time this method was used in England.

Blount, Sir Christopher (1555/56–1601)
The third husband of Lettice Knollys. Blount, whose family had a tradition of serving the Dudley family, was the Earl of Leicester's Master of Horse. The couple married in July 1589. Blount's loyalty to Lettice's son, Robert Devereux, led to his execution on 18 March 1601 for his part in Essex's Rebellion.

Borgarucci, Dr Julio or Giulio (d. 1581)
Borgarucci arrived in England from Urbino, Italy having studied medicine at Padua. He was a Protestant refugee. He received his letter of denization in March 1562. His chief patron was the Earl of Leicester. In 1573, he became physician to the royal household. He gained notoriety in *Leicester's Commonwealth* as Leicester's chief provider of poisons.

Bray, Sir Reginald (c. 1440–1503)
One of the most influential administrators and statesmen of Henry VII's reign. He entered the service of the King's mother Lady Margaret Beaufort during her marriage to Sir Henry Stafford. As well as becoming her Receiver-General, he played a leading role in the conspiracies of 1483–1485 with the aim of placing Henry Tudor on the throne. Bray developed the Council Learned in the Law and recruited able administrators such as Edmund Dudley to work for the King.

Camden, William (1551–1623)
Antiquarian and historian who wrote the *Annales*, an account of the reign of Elizabeth I.

Cavendish, Margaret (d. 1595)
Cousin of the explorer Thomas Cavendish. She became a maid-of-honour to Elizabeth I by October 1591 when Robin Dudley courted and married her. She died from plague in 1595.

Cavendish, Thomas (1560–1592)
Explorer, navigator and privateer. He sailed in 1585 with Sir Richard Grenville to the colony at Roanoke in Virginia. He is sometimes known as 'The Navigator' following his repetition of Drake's circumnavigation of the globe in 1586.

Cecil, William, 1st Baron Burghley (1520–1598)
English statesman and principal adviser to Queen Elizabeth I.

Cecil, Robert, 1st Earl of Salisbury (1563–1612)
English statesman who served Elizabeth I. He began acting as Secretary of State in 1589 and became the queen's chief minister following the death of his father in 1598. He continued to serve the Crown under James I whose succession he promoted.

Chapuys, Eustace (d. 1556)
Imperial Ambassador to England, serving the Holy Roman Emperor Charles V, from 1529 until 1545.

Coke, Sir Edward (1552–1634)
Coke was appointed Attorney-General in 1594. He led prosecutions against the Earl of Essex, Sir Walter Raleigh and the Gunpowder plotters. In 1606, he became James I's Chief Justice but was removed from office in November 1617.

Commendone, Cardinal Giovanni (1523–1584)
Sent by Pope Julius III to England in 1553.

Cosimo II de Medici, Grand Duke of Tuscany (1590–1621)
Eldest son of Ferindano I and Christina of Lorraine, he ruled Tuscany from 1609 until his death. He married Maria Maddalena of Austria in 1608. He is best remembered as the patron of Galileo Galilei.

Christina of Lorraine (c. 1571–1636)
Catherine de Medici's granddaughter. Christina was raised in France. Her marriage to Ferdinando I was a political one designed to strengthen diplomatic relations between France and Tuscany. After her son Cosimo II's death, she ruled as joint regent with her daughter-in-law on behalf of Ferdinando II. Christina allowed the Church to interfere in Tuscan administration and reduced the treasury.

Devereux, Dorothy, Countess of Northumberland (c. 1564–1619)
Youngest daughter of the 1st Earl of Essex, Dorothy was fostered by the Earl and Countess of Huntingdon following the death of her father. She secretly married Sir Thomas Perrot in 1583, after his death she married Henry Percy, 9th Earl of Northumberland.

Devereux, Penelope, Countess of Devonshire (1563–1607)
The 1st Earl of Essex hoped that his eldest daughter would marry Philip Sidney but the chosen guardian of his children, the Earl of Huntingdon, did not approve the match so arranged a marriage to Robert, 3rd Baron Rich. By 1595, Penelope embarked on an adulterous affair with Sir Charles Blount, Lord Mountjoy. Rich sued for divorce in 1605. Penelope married Blount the same year.

Devereux, Robert, 2nd Earl of Essex (1565–1601)
Politician, courtier and soldier. The Earl of Leicester's stepson and favourite of Elizabeth I. He led an unsuccessful campaign in Ireland in 1599, returning to England without permission he was arrested and stripped of many of the financial favours upon which he relied. He rebelled in 1601 and was executed for treason.

Devereux, Walter, 1st Earl of Essex (1539–1576)
First husband of Lettice Knollys. Walter was created 1st Earl of Essex in 1572 before being sent to colonize Ulster. He returned to England in 1575 before returning to Ireland the following year where he died of dysentery.

Douglas, Margaret, Countess of Lennox (1515–1578)
Daughter of Margaret Tudor and Archibald Douglas married to Matthew Stewart, 4th Earl of Lennox. A friend of Elizabeth Talbot, Countess of Shrewsbury and Robert Dudley, Earl of Leicester. Her eldest son Henry Stuart, Lord Darnley married Mary Queen of Scots while her second son, Charles, married Elizabeth Cavendish, the daughter of the Countess of Shrewsbury.

Dudley, Alice Douglas (1597–1621)
Robin's eldest daughter.

Dudley, Ambrose, Earl of Warwick (c. 1531–1590)
The fourth son of John Dudley, Duke of Northumberland and his wife Jane Guildford. Ambrose was granted the titles Baron Lisle and Earl of Warwick in 1561 with the Lordship of Warwick Castle following in 1562. At the same time, he and his younger brother Robert readopted the bear and ragged staff device.

Dudley, Anne (d. 1663)
Alice and Robin's third daughter, married to Sir Robert Holourne, Solicitor General to Charles I.

Dudley, Arthur (b. 1561?)

In 1587, he claimed to be the illegitimate son of Elizabeth I and the Earl of Leicester when his ship was wrecked in the Bay of Biscay. The Spanish believed him to be an English spy.

Dudley, Edmund (1471/2–1510)

Tudor administrator who served on the Council Learned in the Law with his colleague Sir Richard Empson. They came to represent Henry VII's financial administration which imposed bonds and recognizances upon the nobility. After the accession of King Henry VIII, both men were arrested on charges of treason and executed.

Dudley, Frances, (d. 1663)

Robin's second daughter, married to Sir Gilbert Knyveton of Bradley, Derbyshire.

Dudley, Guildford (d. 1554)

Younger brother of Ambrose and Robert, married to Lady Jane Grey, executed on 12 February 1554.

Dudley, Henry (d. 1557)

Youngest of Northumberland's sons who was killed by a cannonball during the Siege of St Quentin.

Dudley, John, 1st Duke of Northumberland (1504–1553)

Soldier, lord admiral, courtier and politician. He served on the Regency Council of Edward VI having been elevated to the earldom of Warwick in 1547. Following the suppression of Kett's Rebellion in 1549, he toppled the Duke of Somerset from power and ruled in his stead as the Duke of Northumberland. Following the death of Edward VI, he conspired to put Lady Jane Grey on the throne in place of Mary Tudor in 1553 and was executed when his plans failed.

Dudley, John, Earl of Warwick (1530–1554)

Northumberland's oldest surviving son. He married Anne Seymour, the Duke of Somerset's daughter in 1550. Imprisoned with his father and his brothers in the aftermath of Northumberland's attempt to place Lady Jane Grey on the throne, he died shortly after release from the Tower.

Dudley, John, of Stoke Newington (d. 1580)
Part of the extended Dudley family serving both Northumberland and Leicester.

Dudley, Katherine (d. 1673)
Youngest surviving daughter of Robin and Alice Leigh. She married Sir Richard Leveson of Trentham Hall, Staffordshire. She instituted the Lady Katherine Leveson charitable foundation.

Dudley, Katherine, Countess of Huntingdon (d. 1620)
Northumberland married his youngest daughter to Henry Hastings, the heir of the Earl of Huntingdon. The couple were childless but fostered numerous aristocratic children including the younger children of the 1st Earl of Essex.

Dudley, Robert, Earl of Leicester (1532–1588)
Elizabeth I's favourite suspected of the death of his first wife Amy Robsart. He may have married Douglas, Lady Sheffield in a private ceremony in 1573. He married Lettice, Countess of Essex in 1578. In 1585, he led a campaign to the Netherlands and in 1588 was in command of the militia at Tilbury. He died soon afterwards.

Dudley, Robert, Lord Denbigh (1581–1584)
Leicester's legitimate heir who died suddenly when he was three years old. He is buried in the Beauchamp Chapel in St Mary's Church, Warwick with his parents.

Erisa, Avice
Daughter and co-heiress of William Milliton of Pengersey. She married firstly Richard Erisa who died in 1570 followed by Sir Nicholas Parker of Cornwall in 1600.

Ferdinando I de Medici, Grand Duke of Tuscany (1549–1609)
He was made a cardinal in 1562 but was never ordained. When his brother Francesco died in 1587, Ferdinando succeeded as Grand Duke of Tuscany. He married Christina of Lorraine in 1589.

Ferdinando II de Medici, Grand Duke of Tuscany (1610–1670)
He became grand duke in 1621 when he was ten years old. During his minority, Tuscany was ruled by his mother and grandmother. In 1633, he married his cousin Vittoria della Rovere. Tuscany's decline can be dated from Ferdinando's regency.

Francis, Duke of Anjou and Alençon (1555–1584)
The youngest son of King Henri II of France and Catherine Medici. Known to Elizabeth I as her 'Frog'. He was one of her suitors and is regarded as having come closer to attaining Elizabeth's hand than many others.

Guildford, Sir Richard (c. 1450–1506)
Courtier and Master of the Ordnance.

Guildford, Sir Edward (c. 1474–1534)
Soldier, courtier and politician serving Henry VII and Henry VIII. He became the guardian of John Dudley and arranged his ward's marriage to his daughter Jane Guildford.

Hakluyt, Richard (1552–1616)
Best known for his work as a geographer and writer of twenty-five books about travel, exploration and colonisation. His works included the voyages of Drake, Cavendish and Robin's voyage to the West Indies in 1594. His links to Robin's family included service as chaplain and secretary to Sir Edward Stafford, English Ambassador to Paris from 1583–1588. From 1590–1616, he served as rector of Wetheringsett and Brockford.

Hall, Edward (c. 1496–c. 1547)
Lawyer and historian who wrote *Hall's Chronicle*.

Hardwick, Elizabeth, Countess of Shrewsbury (c. 1527–1608)
Better known as Bess of Hardwick she married four times and gained a reputation as a capable business woman. Her marriage to George Talbot, 6th Earl of Shrewsbury ended in estrangement partially because of his role as Mary, Queen of Scots gaoler. One of her granddaughters was Lady Arbella Stuart.

Hastings, Henry, 3rd Earl of Huntingdon (c. 1535–1595)

Puritan nobleman married to Leicester's sister Katherine Dudley. He served as President of the Council of the North from 1572 until his death in 1595.

Hatton, Sir Christopher (1540–1591)

Courtier, privy councillor, Lord Chancellor of England from 1587 until his death and favourite of Elizabeth I.

Howard, Charles, 2nd Baron Howard of Effingham and 1st Earl of Nottingham (1536–1624)

Courtier, diplomat and lord admiral of England who commanded Elizabeth's fleet against the Spanish Armada of 1588 and was joint leader of the Cadiz expedition in 1596.

Howard, Douglas, Lady Sheffield (1542/43–1608)

The eldest daughter of William Howard, 1st Baron Howard of Effingham. She married John Sheffield, 2nd Baron Sheffield in 1560 and after his death started an affair with the Earl of Leicester. She later testified that she secretly married him. Douglas married Sir Edward Stafford in 1579 accompanying him to Paris where he served as English ambassador.

Howard, Frances (d. 1598)

Daughter of William 1st Lord Howard of Effingham and sister of Douglas Howard, Dudley's mother. She became a Gentlewoman of the Privy Chamber in November 1569. In 1573, it was reported that she and her sister Douglas were in love with and competing for the affections of the Earl of Leicester. She married Edward Seymour, Earl of Hertford. In 1595, when the earl was sent for the Tower for two months Elizabeth sent a letter to her 'Good Franke' reassuring her.

Howard, Thomas, 4th Duke of Norfolk (1536–1572)

Son of Henry Howard, Earl of Surrey he was a second cousin to Elizabeth I. He was arrested in 1569 for his involvement in the Northern Rebellion. After his release, he became involved in the Ridolfi Plot to put Mary Queen of Scots on the English throne. He aspired to make her his fourth wife. He was executed in June 1572.

Howard, William, 1st Baron Howard of Efffingham (c. 1510–1573)

Diplomat and soldier who became an ally of Northumberland in his coup against Protector Somerset in October 1549. He was appointed Lord Deputy and Governor of Calais which he held for Queen Mary after the death of King Edward VI in 1553. Mary created him Baron Howard and gave him a patent as Lord Admiral. He supported his great-niece Elizabeth Tudor's claim to the throne when it became clear Mary would have no heirs.

Lee, Sir Henry (1533–1611)

Courtier, politician and Elizabeth I's Champion responsible for the Accession Day tilts held each year. He presented the queen with the so-called Ditchley Portrait during her 1592 visit to his Oxfordshire home. He lived openly with his mistress Ann Vavasour.

Leigh, Alice (1579–1669)

Daughter of Sir Thomas Leigh of Stoneleigh Abbey, Warwickshire. She became the second wife of Sir Robert Dudley but was deserted by him in 1605. She was created Duchess Dudley by Letters Patent issued by Charles I on 23 May 1645.

Leveson, Sir Richard (1598–1661)

Politician who supported the Royalist cause. He married Katherine Dudley.

Lotti, Ottaviano (c. 1575–1634?)

Resident in Paris in 1600 as secretary to Baccio Giovannini before becoming the Grand Duke of Tuscany's agent in London in 1604. He sought to arrange a marriage between Prince Henry and a Tuscan princess. He was recalled to Florence in 1614.

Knollys, Sir Francis (1511/14–1596)

Puritan courtier and politician who served Henry VIII, Edward VI and Elizabeth I. The husband of Catherine Carey who was Elizabeth I's cousin.

Knollys, Lettice, Countess of Essex and Leicester (1543–1634)
Lettice's mother, Catherine Carey, was Elizabeth I's cousin on the Boleyn side. It is generally accepted that they were also half-sisters, making Lettice one of Elizabeth's nearest relations. Lettice married her first husband Walter Devereux, 1st Earl of Essex c. 1562 and had five children. After Essex's death from dysentery in Ireland, Lettice married Robert Dudley, Earl of Leicester in 1578 and was banished from court.

Maria Magdalena of Austria, Grand Duchess of Tuscany (1589–1631)
Wife of Cosimo II. The youngest daughter of Charles II, Archduke of Austria. She acted as Tuscany's regent along with Christina of Lorraine during her son Ferdinando II's minority.

De Mendoza, Bernardino (d. 1604)
Spanish commander and diplomat. He served Philip II as Spanish ambassador in London from 1578 until his expulsion in 1584. He served as ambassador in France for the next six years.

North, Roger, 2nd Baron (1530–1600)
Politician and courtier. Elizabeth I stayed at his house in Kirtling for three days in 1578. North was a personal friend of Leicester and was a witness at his wedding to Lettice, Countess of Essex, in September 1578. He was selected by Leicester to provide a home for Robin before he began his formal education.

Rich, Robert, 1st Earl of Warwick (c. 1559–1619)
Penelope Devereux's first husband who sued for divorce in 1605. He was created Earl of Warwick by James I in 1618.

Robsart, Amy (1532–1560)
The first wife of Robert Dudley, Earl of Leicester. Her unexpected death resulting from a fall down a shallow staircase resulted in the suspicion that she had been murdered by her husband in the hope that he would then be free to marry Elizabeth I. The coroner's report into her death was rediscovered in 2008.

Russell, Lady Anne (1548/9–1604)
Third wife of Ambrose Dudley and one of Elizabeth I's closest companions.

Salvetti, Amerigo (1572–1657)
Born Alessandro Antelminelli of Lucca, he changed his name in 1599 when his family was executed by the state of Lucca and he was sentenced to death. He sought refuge in Florence. A plot by Sir Henry Wotton in 1607 sought to betray him to the authorities in Lucca in exchange for Captain Robert Elliot. Ferdinando I of Tuscany sent Salvetti to London where he remained for the rest of his life. He was appointed Tuscan Resident at the Court of Whitehall by Cosimo II in 1616.

Scheyfve, Jehan (d. 1581)
Imperial Ambassador to England, serving the Holy Roman Emperor Charles V, from 1550 until 1553.

Standen, Sir Anthony (c. 1548?)
Catholic courtier who served Mary Queen of Scots during the 1560s. Worked against Elizabeth's government in Europe during the 1570s before becoming one of Walsingham's double agents during the 1580s and then in the employment of the Earl of Essex. He travelled to Italy at the beginning of James I's reign and was briefly imprisoned in the Tower on Robert Cecil's orders in 1604.

Sheffield, Edmund (1565–1646)
The only son of Douglas, Lady Sheffield and her first husband John, second Baron Sheffield. He inherited his father's title in 1568. Courtier, president of the Council for the North during the reign of James I as well as a soldier and vice-admiral of Yorkshire. He was known for his persecution of Catholics despite being married to one himself. He was an early member of the Virginia Company. Charles I raised him in 1626 to become the first Earl of Mulgrave. He was succeeded by his grandson, also named Edmund.

Shirley, Sir Thomas (1564–1630)
Soldier and privateer who married Frances Vavasour secretly at a time when she was betrothed to Robin.

Sidney, Sir Philip (1554–1586)
Courtier, poet and soldier. Sidney's mother was Lady Mary Dudley. Until his death, he was heir to both Leicester and Warwick. His younger brother Sir Robert Sidney believed that his uncles' titles and estates should have passed to him rather than to Leicester's illegitimate son. Sidney was married to Frances, the daughter of Sir Francis Walsingham. He died of gangrene following injury at the battle of Zutphen.

de Silva, Diego Guzmán (d. 1577)
Venetian Ambassador to England.

de Simier, Jean
Anjou's friend and agent who arrived in England in 1579 to negotiate a marriage between Elizabeth and Anjou.

Stafford, Sir Edward (1552–1605)
English courtier and diplomat. He served as the English ambassador in Paris from 1583–1590.

Stafford, William (d. 1612)
Second son of Lady Dorothy Stafford. He became involved in the so-called Stafford Plot along with Michael Moody, a former servant of Sir Edward Stafford, in 1586 to assassinate Elizabeth I. He was imprisoned for a short time before release. It is thought that he was one of Walsingham's agents.

Stafford, Lady Dorothy (1526–1604)
Descended from the House of York, Dorothy's maternal great grandmother was Margaret Pole, the 8th Countess of Salisbury. She became Elizabeth I's Mistress of the Robes in 1563.

Stuart, Lady Arbella (1575–1615)
The daughter of Charles Stuart and Elizabeth Cavendish. She was the great-granddaughter of Margaret Tudor and in line of succession to the throne. After her mother's death, she was raised by Bess of Hardwick where Arbella felt increasingly alone. She was welcome at the court of James I until in 1610 she secretly married William Seymour, who himself had a claim to the throne. She ended her life in the Tower.

Vavasour, Frances (1568–1606)

She arrived at court in about 1590 when she became a maid of honour to Elizabeth I. By 1591, she and Sir Robert Dudley asked the queen permission to marry. Permission was granted on the proviso that they wait until Sir Robert was older. Later that year Frances secretly married Sir Thomas Shirley. Frances was the younger sister of Ann Vavasour. The pair were part of the Knyvett family on their mother's side which perhaps explains their court appointments.

Vergil, Polydore (1470–1555)

Renaissance scholar who wrote the *Anglica Historia* at the behest of King Henry VII.

Walsingham, Sir Francis (1532–1590)

Politician, diplomat and spymaster. He was English Ambassador to France from 1570 to 1573 during which time he witnessed the St Bartholomew's Day Massacre. He rose to become Principal Secretary to Elizabeth from 1573 until his death.

Wotton, Sir Henry (1568–1639)

Politician and diplomat. He spent most of the last twenty years of his life as the English Ambassador in Venice.

Bibliography

Objects

Gemini, Thomas, *Astrolabe for Queen Elizabeth I, 1559, London*. Museum of the History of Science, Oxford. Collection database inventory number 42223. Accession number 1937–6

Gemini, Thomas, *Quadrant left by Sir Robert Dudley to the Grand Duke of Tuscany in 1649, Museo Galileo*, Florence, Collection database inventory number 2509

Kynvyn, James, *Folding Rule, 1595, London, left by Sir Robert Dudley to the Grand Duke of Tuscany in 1646, Museo Galileo*, Florence, inventory number 2516

Unknown maker, *Windrose left by Sir Robert Dudley to the Grand Duke of Tuscany in 1649, Museo Galileo*, Florence, Collection database inventory number 3372

Whitwell, Charles, *Astrolabe left by Sir Robert Dudley to the Grand Duke of Tuscany in 1649, described as a 'nautical astrolabe,' Museo Galileo*, Florence, Collection database inventory numbers 1123, 1124, 1127

Whitwell, Charles, *Horary quadrant left by Sir Robert Dudley to the Grand Duke of Tuscany in 1649, 1595, London, Museo Galileo*, Florence, Collection database inventory number 2519

Printed Primary Sources

Items indicated with an asterisk* are available online via British History Online: www.british-history.ac.uk

Selected Calendared Papers and abbreviated form

Calendar of the Cecil Papers in Hatfield House: Volume 5, 1594–1595, ed., Roberts, R.A., (HMSO, London, 1894)* (CP)

Calendar of State Papers Colonial, East Indies, China and Japan, 1513–1616, ed., W. Noel Sainsbury (HMSO, London, 1864)* (CSP Colonial)

Calendar of State Papers, Domestic Series, of the Reigns of Edward VI, Mary, Elizabeth and James I 1547–[1625]: 1581–1590: Elizabeth. ed., Green, Mary Anne Everett, and Lemon, Robert. (HMSO, London, 1856–1872)* (CSP Domestic)

Calendar of State Papers, Domestic Series, of the Reign of Elizabeth, 1581–1590, ed., Lemon, Robert, (HMSO, London,1865)* (CSP Domestic, Elizabeth)

Calendar of the State Papers, Domestic Series, of the Reign Elizabeth, Addenda, 1566–1579, ed., Green, Mary Anne Everett, (Longman & Company, London, 1871)* (CSP Domestic, Elizabeth, Addenda)

Calendar of State Papers Foreign: Elizabeth, Volume 19, August 1584–August 1585, ed., Crawford Lomas, Sophie (London, 1916)* (CSP Foreign, Elizabeth)

Calendar of State Papers, Spain (Simancas), 1553–1603, ed., Hume, Martin A S, (HMSO, London, 1892–1899* (CSP Scotland)

Adams, Simon (ed.), *Household Accounts and Disbursement Books of Robert Dudley, Earl of Leicester, 1558–1561, 1584–1586*, (Cambridge University Press, Cambridge, 1995)

Antelminelli, Alessandro, and Skrine, Henry Duncan, *The Manuscripts of Henry Duncan Skrine, Esq: Salvetti Correspondence*, (HMSO, London, 1887)

Ascham, Roger, *The Schoolmaster* (Cassell, London, 1888)

Bacon, Francis and Vickers Brian, ed., *Bacon: The History of the Reign of King Henry VII and Selected Works*, (Cambridge University Press, Cambridge, 1998)

Bruce, John, ed., *Correspondence of Robert Dudley, Earl of Leicester*, (Camden Society, 1844)

Camden, William, *The History of the Most Renowned and Victorious Princess Elizabeth: Selected Chapters*, ed., with an introduction by Wallace T. MacCaffrey (University of Chicago Press, Chicago 1970)

Carey, Robert and Mares, H. ed., *The Memoirs of Robert Carey* (Oxford University Press, Oxford, 1972)

Cunningham, William, *The Cosmographical Glass, Containing the Pleasant Principles of Cosmography, Geography, Hydrography and Navigation (*1559)

Danvers, Frederick Charles, *Report to the Secretary of State for India in Council on the Records of the India Office, Vol. 1, pt. 1*, (Eyre and Spottiswoode, London,1887)*

Dudley, Robert, 'A Voyage of the honourable Gentleman M. Robert Duddeley, now knight, to the isle of Trinidad, and the coast of Paria: with his returne home by the Isles of Granata, Santa Cruz, Sant Juan de Puerto rico, Mona, Zacheo, the shoals called Abreojos, and the isle of Bermuda. In which voyage he and his company tooke and sunke nine Spanish ships, whereof one was an armada of 600 tunnes.'

Written at the request of M. Richard Hakluyt,' in HAKLUYT, R., *The Principal navigations voyages traffiques & discoveries of the English nation. Made by sea or over-land to the remote and farthest distant quarters of the Earth at any time within the compasse of these 1600 yeeres.* (Glasgow, James MacLehose and Sons & New York, The Macmillan Company, 1904)

Dudley, Robert and Vaughan, Thomas, ed., *The Italian biography of sir Robert Dudley. To which are added, some biographical notices of dame Alice Dudley his wife, as also of their four daughters*, (Baxter, Oxford, 1858)

Florio, J. *Second Fruits* (1591)

Gascoigne, G, *The Princely Pleasures at the Court of Kenilworth* (1575)

Hall, Edward, *Hall's Chronicle: containing the history of England, during the reign of Henry Fourth, and the succeeding monarchs, to the end of the reign of Henry the Eighth, in which are particularly described the manners and customs of those periods. Carefully collated with the editions of 1548 and 1550*, (J. Johnson, London, 1809)

Moray, Robert, *Letters of Sir Robert Moray to the Earl of Kincardine, 1657–73.* (Ashgate, Farnham, 2007)

Peck, D.C. ed., *Leicester's Commonwealth: The Copy of a Letter Written by a Master of Art of Cambridge (1584) and Related Documents* (Ohio University Press, Athens, Ohio, 1985)

Quin D.B. ed., *The Last Voyage of Thomas Cavendish 1591–92* (Chicago and London, The University of Chicago Press, 1975)

Raleigh, Walter, *The Discoverie of the Large, Rich and Bewtiful Empire of Guiana* (Cassell, London, 1893)

Skrine, Henry Duncan, *Eleventh Report: Appendix. The manuscripts of Henry Duncan Skrine, Esq. : Salvetti correspondence*, (HMSO, London, 1887)

Vergil, Polydore, *The Anglica Historia of Polydore Vergil*, (ed.), D. Hay, (Camden Society, Third Series, London, 1950)

Warner, Sir George, ed., Kendall, Abram, and Dudley, Robert. *The Voyage of Robert Dudley, Afterwards Styled Earl of Warwick and Leicester and Duke of Northumberland, to the West Indies, 1594–1595*, (Hakluyt Society, London, 1899)

Wright, I.A. ed., *Documents Concerning English Voyages to the Spanish Main, 1569–1580* (Hakluyt Society, London, 1932)

Wright, I. A. ed., *Further English Voyages to Spanish America, 1583–1594* (Hakluyt Society, London, 1951)

Secondary Sources
Oxford Dictionary of National Biography (ODNB) online edition indicated by an obelisk † can be found at www.oxforddnb.com

Adair, Richard, *Courtship, Illegitimacy and Marriage in Early Modern England* (Manchester University Press, Manchester, 1996)

Adams, Simon 'Dudley, Ambrose, earl of Warwick (c1530–1590)', *Oxford Dictionary of National Biography*, online edition (2008) †

Adams, Simon, 'Dudley, Sir Robert (1574–1649),' *Oxford Dictionary of National Biography*, online edition, (2008)†

Adams, Simon. *Leicester and the Court: Essays on Elizabethan Politics*, (Manchester University Press, Manchester, 2002)

Adams, Simon, 'Sheffield (nee Howard), Douglas, Lady Sheffield (1542/3–1608)', *Oxford Dictionary of Biography*, online edition (2008)†

Adlard, George, *Amye Robsart and the Earl of Leycester: a critical inquiry into the authenticity of the various statements in relation to the death of Amye Robsart, and of the libels on the Earl of Leycester, with a vindication of the Earl by his nephew Sir Philip Sydney. And a history of Kenilworth castle, including an account of the splendid entertainment given to Queen Elizabeth by the Earl of Leycester, in 1575, from the works of Robert Lanehom and George Gascoigne; together with memoirs and correspondence of Sir Robert Dudley, son of the Earl of Leycester.* (J.R. Smith, London 1870)

Archer, Jayne Elisabeth, and Elizabeth Goldring, and Sarah Knight, eds, *Progresses, Pageants, and Entertainments of Queen Elizabeth I*, (Oxford University Press, Oxford, 2007)

Blake, Hugo ed., *Gran Bretagna e Italia tra Mediterraneo e Atlantico: Livorno – 'un porto inglese'* / Italy and Britain between Mediterranean and Atlantic worlds: Leghorn – 'an English port' *APM - Archeologia Postmedievale, 19, 2015*

Bellorini, M *'Un medico italiano alla corte di Elisabetta: Giulio Borgarucci'*, *English Miscellany*, 19 (1968)

Bennell, John, 'Borgarucci, Giulio (known as Dr Julio),' *Oxford Dictionary of National Biography*, online edition, (2008)†

Borman, Tracy, *Elizabeth's Women: The Hidden Story of the Virgin Queen*, (Vintage Books, London, 2010)

Capp, Bernard, 'Bigamous Marriage in Early Modern England.' *The Historical Journal*, vol. 52, no. 3, 2009, pp. 537–556.

Carlton, Katherine and Thornton, Tim, 'Illegitimacy and Authority in the North of England, c. 1450–1640,' *Northern History, XLVIII*, 1, March 2011, p. 23–40

Chrimes, S.B., *Henry VII (The English Monarchs Series)* (Yale University Press, Yale and London, 1999)

Collison-Morley, Lacy. *Italy After the Renaissance: Decadence and Display in the Seventeenth Century*, (Routledge, London, 1930)

Cressy, David, *Birth, Marriage and Death: Ritual, Religion, and the Life-Cycle in Tudor and Stuart England*, (Oxford University Press, Oxford, 1997)

Cressy, David, *Education in Tudor and Stuart England*, (Arnold, London, 1974)

Cunningham, Sean, Guildford, Sir Richard (c.1450–1506), *Oxford Dictionary of National Biography*, online edition, (2008) †

Davey, James, ed., *Tudor and Stuart Seafarers: The Emergence of a Maritime Nation, 1485–1707* (Bloomsbury Publishing, London, 2018)

De Divitiis, Gigliola Pagano and Parkin Stephen, translator, *English Merchants in Seventeenth Century Italy (Cambridge Studies in Italian History and Culture)*, (Cambridge, University Press, Cambridge, 1998)

Doran, Susan, *Monarchy and Matrimony: The Courtships of Elizabeth I* (Routledge, London, 1996)

Errico, Clara and Montanelli, Michelle, "*L'architetto navale Roberto Dudley e la sfortunata vicenda del suo vascello Orsa Minore* , *Nuovi Studi Livornesi*, vol. XX 2013. pp 221–248 *Associazione Livornese Di Storia Lettere E Arti*

Enis, C, 'Edward Arden and the Dudley earls of Warwick and Leicester, c. 1572–1583', *British Catholic History*, vol. 33, no. 2, 2016, pp. 170–210

Ferguson, Donald. 'Captain Benjamin Wood's Expedition of 1596.' *The Geographical Journal*, vol. 21, no. 3, 1903, pp. 330–334.

Fraser, Lady Antonia, *The Gunpowder Plot: Terror and Faith in 1605*, (Mandarin, London, 1997)

French, Peter, *John Dee: The World of an Elizabethan Magus* (London, Routledge, 2002)

Folgerpedia Shakespeare Library,'The Elizabethan Court Day by Day' *Folgerpedia*, folgerpedia.folger.edu/The_Elizabethan_Court_Day_by_Day

Gray, Jeffrey Alan, et al, *Trade, Plunder and Settlement: Maritime Enterprise and the Genesis of the British Empire, 1480–1630*, (Cambridge University Press, Cambridge, 1984)

Gristwood, Sarah, *Arbella: England's Lost Queen*, (Bantam Books, London, 2003)

Gristwood, Sarah, *Elizabeth & Leicester*, (Transworld, London, 2007)

Guy, John. *Elizabeth: The Forgotten Years* (Penguin, London, 2016)

Hammer, Paul E. J. 'Myth-Making: Politics, Propaganda and the Capture of Cadiz in 1596.' *The Historical Journal*, vol. 40, no. 3, 1997, pp. 621–642.

Hammer, Paul E. J., 'Sex and the Virgin Queen: Aristocratic Concupiscence and the Court of Elizabeth I.' *The Sixteenth Century Journal*, vol. 31, no. 1, 2000, pp. 77–97.

Hayden, Judy ed., *Travel Narratives, the New Science, and Literary Discourse, 1569–1750* (Ashgate, Farnham, 2012)

Haynes, Alan, *Walsingham: Elizabethan Spymaster & Statesman* (Sutton Publishing, Stroud, 2007)

Horodowich, Elizabeth and Markey, Lia, eds., *The New World in Early Modern Italy, 1492–1750*, (Cambridge, Cambridge University Press, 2017)

Hutchinson, Robert, *The Spanish Armad*a, (Weidenfeld & Nicholson, London, 2014)

Hutchinson, Robert, *Young Henry: The Rise of Henry VIII*, (Orion Books, London, 2011)

Jackson, W, 'The Dudleys of Yanwath,' *Cumberland and Westmorland Antiquarian and Archeological Society Transactions*, vol. 9, (1887) pp.318–332

James, Robert. *Pharmacopœia Universalis: Or, a New Universal English Dispensatory. Containing I. An Account of All the Natural and Artificial Implements and Instruments of Pharmacy ... II. Dissertations on the Various Classes of Simples ... III. Catalogues of the Medicinal Simples ... IV. The Preparations and Combinations of Drugs ... V. A Variety of Extemporaneous Compositions ... With Two Copious Indexes to the Whole. By R. James, M.D. The Third Edition; with Very Large and Useful Additions, and Improvements.* (London, 1764)

John, Lisle C. 'Rowland Whyte, Elizabethan Letter-Writer.' *Studies in the Renaissance*, vol. 8, 1961, pp. 217–235.

Keay, Anna and Watkins, John, eds., *The Elizabethan Garden at Kennilworth Castle*, (Swindon, English Heritage, 2013)

Lacey, Robert, *Robert, Earl of Essex: An Elizabethan Icarus*, (Pheonix Press, London, 2001)

Leader, J. Temple, *The Life of Sir Robert Dudley, Earl of Warwick and Duke of Northumberland*, (Sagwan Press, Oxford, 2018)

Lee, Arthur Stanley Gould, *The Son of Leicester: The Story of Sir Robert Dudley, Titular Earl of Warwick, Earl of Leicester, and Duke of Northumberland, Only Surviving Issue of Queen Elizabeth's Favourite, the Earl of Leicester.* (Gollannz, London, 1964)

Lee, Sidney, *The Autobiography of Edward, Lord Herbert of Cherbury* (Routledge, London, 1906)

Lehmburg, Stanford, 'Guidford, Sir Edward (c.1479–1534)' *Oxford Dictionary of National Biography*, online edition, (2008)†

Leimon, Mitchell and Parker, Geoffrey, 'Treason and Plot in Elizabethan Diplomacy: 'The Fame of Sir Edward Stafford' Reconsidered', *English Historical Review 111* (1996), 1139.

Loomis, Catherine, 'Elizabeth Southwell's Manuscript Account of the Death of Queen Elizabeth [with Text].' *English Literary Renaissance*, vol. 26, no. 3, 1996, pp. 482–509.

de Lisle, Leanda, *After Elizabeth: the Death of Elizabeth and the Coming of King James*, (Harper Collins, London, 2006)

Lorimer, Joyce, ed., *English and Irish Settlement on the River Amazon, 1550–1646*, Second series, vol. 171 (The Hakluyt Society, 1986)

Lovell, Mary S, *Bess of Hardwick: First Lady of Chatsworth*, (Abacus, London, 2012)

McDermott, James, 'Baker, Matthew (1529/30–1631), shipwright' *Oxford Dictionary of National Biography*, online edition, (2004)†

Mabillard, Amanda. *Shakespeare's Education and Childhood. Shakespeare Online*, 12 September 2000 www.shakespeare-online.com

Meyrick, S. Rush. (1829). 'Report of the commissioners appointed to inquire into the amount of booty taken at Cadiz in 1596, with the charges preferred in consequence, by Sir Gelly Meyricke, against Sir Anthony Ashley,' *Archaeologia 22*, Vol 22, pp. 172–189

Moray, Robert, *Letters of Sir Robert Moray to the Earl of Kincardine, 1657–73*, (Ashgate, Farnham, 2007)

Naipaul, V. S., *The Loss of El Dorado: A Colonial History*, (Pan Macmillan, London, 2012)

Napier, Henry Edward, *Florentine History: From the Earliest Authentic Records to the Accession of Ferdinando the Third, Grand Duke of Tuscany*, (E. Moxon, London, 1846)

Nicholl, Charles, *The Reckoning: The Murder of Christopher Marlowe* (Picador, London, 1993)

Nichols, John, *The Progresses and Public Processions of Queen Elizabeth: Among which are Interspersed Other Solemnities, Public Expenditures, and Remarkable Events During the Reign of that Illustrious Princess*, (J. Nichols, United Kingdom, 1823)

Norton, Elizabeth, *The Temptation of Elizabeth Tudor*, (Head of Zeus Ltd, London, 2015)

O Sullivan, Dan, *The Reluctant Ambassador: The life and Times of Sir Thomas Chaloner, Tudor Diplomat*, (Amberley Publishing, Stroud, 2016)

Payne, Anthony, *Richard Hakluyt: London's role in navigation and history* (Gresham College, London, 2009)

Pollen, J.H., ed., 'Lethington's Account of negotiation with Elizabeth in September and October 1565,' *Scottish History*, vol. 43 (1904) pp.38–45

Pope, Alexander, and Ruffhead, Owen. 'Roxana, or the Drawing Room,' *The Works of Alexander Pope, Esq, Poetry and letters-1807*, Volume VI, (London, 1807. p.18)

Robinson, William, *The History and Antiquities of the Parish of Stoke Newington in the County of Middlesex Containing an Account of the Prebendal Manor, the Church, Charities, Schools, Meeting Houses, &c., with Appendices*, (J B Nichols and Son, London, 1842)

Read, Conyers, 'The Fame of Sir Edward Stafford' *The American Historical Review*, vol. 20, no. 2, 1915, pp. 292–313.

Read, Conyers, 'A Letter from Robert, Earl of Leicester, to a Lady,' *Huntingdon Library Quarterly*, April 1936, pp.15–26

Ritchie, Neil, 'Sir Robert Dudley: Expatriate in Tuscan Service,' *History Today*, vol. 26, issue 6, June 1976

Simpson, Sue, *Sir Henry Lee (1533–1611): Elizabethan Courtier*, (Ashgate Publishing, Farnham, 2014)

Skidmore, Chris, *Death and the Virgin: Elizabeth, Dudley and the Mysterious Fate of Amy Robsart*, (Orion, London, 2010)

Speaight, Robert, *Shakespeare: The Man and his Achievement*, (Stein and Day, New York, 1977)

Stater, Victor, 'Sheffield, Edmund, first earl of Mulgrave (1565–1646,)' *Oxford Dictionary of National Biography,* online edition (2004)†

Stedall, Robert. *Elizabeth I's Secret Lover: Robert Dudley, Earl of Leicester,* (Pen & Sword Books, Barnsley, 2020)

Stone, L. *The Family, Sex and Marriage in England 1500–1800,* (Penguin, London, 1977)

Tallis. Nichola, *Elizabeth's Rival. The Tumultuous Tale of Lettice Knollys Countess of Leicester,* (Michael O Mara, London, 2017)

Tazzara, Corey, 'Managing Free Trade in Early Modern Europe: Instituions, Information, and the Free Port of Livorno' *The Journal of Modern History,* vol.86, No 3 (September 2014) pp.493–529

Turner, Gerard L'Estrange, *Elizabethan Instrument Makers: The Origins of the London Trade in Precision Instrument Making.* (Oxford University Press, Oxford, 2000.)

Thornton, Tim and Carlton, Katharine, *The Gentleman's Mistress: Illegitimate Relationships and Children, 1450–1640,* (Manchester University Press, Manchester, 2019)

Warnicke, Retha 'Why Elizabeth I Never Married,' *History Today,* (October 2010)

Whitlock, Anna, *The Queen's Bed: An Intimate History of Elizabeth's Court,* (Picador, London, 2013)

Wilson, Derek, *The Uncrowned Kings of England: The Black Legend of the Dudleys,* (Constable, London, 2005)

Wood, A.C. *Memorials of the Holles Family 1493–1656,* (The Royal Historical Society, London, 1937)

Picture Credits

Sir Robert Dudley (National Museum, Stockholm photo: Erik Cornelius)

The Dudley family crest carved by John Dudley, Earl of Warwick during his imprisonment in the Tower 1554 (Mary Evans Picture Library)

Title page, book six, *Dell'Arcano del Mare* (Skokloster Castle)

Robert Dudley, 1st Earl of Leicester (The Rijksmuseum)

Queen Elizabeth I 'The Ditchley Portrait' (National Portrait Gallery/Bridgeman Images)

Thomas Cavendish (The Rijksmuseum)

Map for the North East coast of South America covering Guiana in *Dell'Arcano del Mare* by Antonio Francesco Lucini (Bridgeman Images)

Battle of Cadiz (The Rijksmuseum)

Astrolabe (Art Institute of Chicago)

Diagram showing the use of an astrolabe (Archives of Pearson Scott Foresman, donated to the Wikimedia Foundation)

Ferdinando I de Medici, Grand Duke of Tuscany (The Rijksmuseum)

Restoring the Aqueduct in Pisa, from the Life of Ferdinand I de' Medici (The Metropolitan Museum of Art)

Cosimo II de Medici, Grand Duke of Tuscany (The Metropolitan Museum of Art)

Chest tomb Lady Frances Kniveton (photo: John Salmon)

Lady Katherine Leveson (The Foundation of Lady Katherine Leveson)

Countess Teresa Dudley de Carpegna (Walters Art Museum, Baltimore)